Claims and Reality of New Museology

Case Studies in Canada, the United States and Mexico

Ficha Técnica

[Título]
Claims and Reality of New Museology: Case Studies in Canada, the United States and Mexico

[Autor]
Andrea Hauenschild

[Editores]
Óscar Navajas Corral & Sofía Sánchez Giménez

[Paginação e Design]
Maria Helena Catarino Fonseca

[ISBN]
9798847031035

[Edição]
Edicões Universitárias Lusófonas
Campo Grande 376, 1700-090 Lisboa
http://loja.ulusofona.pt/

[Capa]
Maria Helena Catarino Fonseca
Ilustração: I Atelier international- Écomusées/nouvelle muséologie. Haute Beauce, 1984

[Revisão]
Giusy Pappalardo

[DOI]
http://doi.org/10.36572/csm.book_07

[Ano de edição]
2022

[Contactos]
Departamento de Museologia / Cátedra UNESCO "Educação, Cidadania e Diversidade Cultural"
Edificio A. sala A.1.1. - Leandro França, Tel: 217 515 500 ext: 714 E-mail: museologia@ulusofona.pt
Universidade Lusófona de Humanidades e Tecnologias. Campo Grande, 376, 1749 - 024 Lisboa

[Todos os direitos desta edição reservados por]
Universidade Lusófona de Humanidades e Tecnologias e Autor

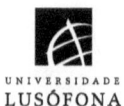 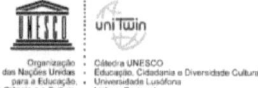 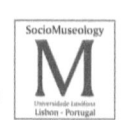 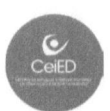 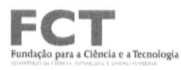

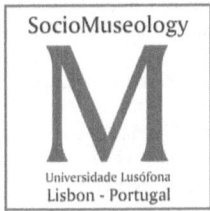

Claims and Reality of New Museology

Case Studies in Canada, the United States and Mexico

Andrea Hauenschild

Editores
Óscar Navajas Corral & Sofía Sánchez Giménez

Departamento de Museologia
Universidade Lusófona de Humanidades e Tecnologias

Lisboa 2022

CLAIMS AND REALITY OF NEW MUSEOLOGY: CASE STUDIES IN CANADA, THE UNITED STATES AND MEXICO
Departamento de Museologia-Universidade Lusófona de Humanidades e Tecnologias, Cátedra UNESCO "Educação Cidadania e Diversidade Cultural".
Centro de Estudos Interdisciplinares em Educação e Desenvolvimento (CeiED)
Autor: Andrea Hauenschild
Editores: Óscar Navajas Corral & Sofía Sánchez Giménez
ISBN: 9798847031035
1. Museology 2. History of Museology 3. Museum 4. Ecomuseum 5. Haute Beauce
CDU: 06

Índice

Foreword to the 2022 edition (Andrea Hauenschield)   13

Foreword (Óscar Navajas Corral & Sofía Sánchez Giménez)   15

Prólogo (Óscar Navajas Corral & Sofía Sánchez Giménez)   41

Acknowledgments   71

1. Introdução   73

2. Elements of New Museology   79

3. Case studies   93

   3.1. The ecomuseum in Quebec, Canada   93

      3.1.1 Ecomusée de la Haute-Beauce, Musée Territoire   93

         3.1.1.1 The Haute-Beauce   93

         3.1.1.2 Origin   97

         3.1.1.3 Conception and objectives   104

         3.1.1.4 Structure and organization   108

         3.1.1.5 Activities and programs   121

3.1.1.6 Evaluation 135

3.1.2 Ecomusée de la Maison du Fier-Monde 141

3.1.2.1 Montréal Centre-Sud 141

3.1.2.2 Origin 143

3.1.2.3 Conception and objectives 146

3.1.2.4 Structure and organization 149

3.1.2.5 Activities and programs 155

3.1.2.6 Evaluation 162

3.2. The neighborhood museum in the United States 165

3.2.1 The Anacostia Neighborhood Museum 165

3.2.1.1 Anacostia 165

3.2.1.2 Origin 167

3.2.1.3 Conception and objectives 172

3.2.1.4 Structure and organization 176

3.2.1.5 Activities and programs 181

3.2.1.6 Evaluation 189

3.3. The integral museum in Mexico 195

3.3.1 Casa del Museo — 195

    3.3.1.1 First project — 195

        3.3.1.1.1 The Zona Observatorio — 194

        3.3.1.1.2 Origin — 196

        3.3.1.1.3 Conception and objectives — 197

        3.3.1.1.4 Structure and organization — 199

        3.3.1.1.5 Activities and programs — 201

        3.3.1.1.6 Evaluation — 204

    3.3.1.2 Second project — 206

        3.3.1.2.1 Pedregal de Santo Domingo de los Reyes — 206

        3.3.1.2.2 Origin — 207

        3.3.1.2.3 Conception and objectives — 208

        3.3.1.2.4 Structure and organization — 209

        3.3.1.2.5 Activities and programs — 211

        3.3.1.2.6 Evaluation — 213

3.3.2 Program for Development of the Educational Function of INAH Museums — 215

3.3.2.1 Origin	215
3.3.2.2 Concept and objectives	217
3.3.2.3 Structure and organization	220
3.3.2.4 Activities and programs	224
3.3.2.5 Evaluation	228
4. Claims and Reality of New Museology: Comparative Analysis of the Case Studies	231
4.1 Objectives	231
4.2 Basic principles	236
4.3 Structure and organization	241
4.4 Approach	255
4.5 Tasks	259
4.6 Critical assessment	268
Bibliography	271

Forewords

FOREWORD TO THE 2022 EDITION

In my work, I like to go back to the source, and I love those moments when we come across historical documents that prefigure, spark or express ideas very similar to those we are developing now, with the sense of breaking new ground... Suddenly we're not alone anymore. In fact, we're in good company.

This doctoral dissertation, originally published in 1988, could almost be considered a historical document today. I reread the opening sentence: a 1985 quote from Hugues de Varine on the museum as a perfect tool for social transformation. Decades have since gone by. New museology has become sociomuseology and various other kinds of community-oriented museologies: participative, collaborative, relational, engaged, even activist... And yet the question of the social role of museums is timelier than ever, discussed and debated at all levels of contemporary museum practice.

This dissertation – a critical assessment of the new museology of the 1980s – went through several stages of translation and transposition. It examines and compares different types of people-oriented museums, developed in very different contexts: an "écomusée" in rural Quebec, another in an industrial sector of Montreal, a neighbourhood museum in an African American area of Washington, D.C., and "Casa del Museo" in impoverished Mexican communities. Since I was doing my doctorate in Germany, my task involved translating all this into German, well aware that in the German-speaking sphere, with its long tradition of local and regional museums, one didn't quite see what was so new about new museology. In the 1990s, the Smithsonian Institution's Office of Museum Programs commissioned the translation and distribution of the dissertation as a reference tool for the creation of museums as instruments of cultural empowerment in First Nations communities.

Now, in 2021, the Lusophone University in Lisbon is reissuing the text, which, despite being somewhat "over-translated", remains almost disconcertingly relevant. Of course, I would say some things differently today. Of greatest interest in my view are still the references to the foundational texts of new museology and the excerpts from interviews with those who put the approach into practice and experienced it first-hand. I was twenty-six years old when I began my doctoral research. I have spent my career in Quebec, working in museums and developing theme-based exhibitions for the general public, all the while keeping track of evolutions in socially engaged museology.

For several years now, new museology has, in its current adaptations, experienced a significant revival. In many countries, museums are exploring and practicing participatory museologies in collaboration with their communities. These approaches are part of a great and ongoing societal transformation: the creation of a true cultural democracy based on the principles of equity, diversity and inclusion. Against the backdrop of shifting cultural and power relations, many museums are developing innovative approaches not only to reflect these new realities, but to become agents of change, involved in the construction of new social imaginaries that engage a plurality of voices.

How can museums do more to contribute to social and cultural justice, economic development, individual and collective well-being and a sustainable future? What real impact can they have on individuals and communities? Can they change the world? The questions that have concerned me for so long are as resonant now as they were four decades ago. I hope this text will be "good company" for today's museum professionals.

With heartfelt thanks to Mario Moutinho, Judith Primo, Sofia Sánchez and Óscar Navajas!

Andrea Hauenschild
Montreal, October 13, 2021

Foreword
Óscar Navajas Corral[1]
Sofía Sánchez Giménez[2]

"Between imaginary beings and forms of life".
(Gruzinski, 2000: 5).

What is a museum? A permanent institution or a polyphonic space? An altruistic, philanthropic or simply for-profit project (economic, cultural and/or social)? An open facility to the public and inclusive, or dedicated to serving the interests of a socio-economic and cultural elite? A place at the service of societies and communities, or spaces for the education of audiences? An enclosure to protect, safeguard the memory and preserve the tangible and intangible heritage of..., a community or of humanity? All these questions - and many others - have been occupying the work of specialists and professionals in the field of museums and museology especially in the last fifty years.

Defining and conceptualising what this entity is and what its raison d'être is in societies and communities has been, and continues to be, one of the challenges of institutions such as the International Council of Museums (ICOM) and its committee for museology, the ICOFOM. Since the founding of the former in the mid-1950s, its task has been to try to reach a consensus on a definition that could bring together the heterogeneity of an institution that has been characterised by the fact that it has been a veritable "battlefield" (Bodei, 1996) for the legitimisation of the identities, symbolic imaginaries, narratives and discourses that are elaborated towards and for it, and which emanate from it.

---
[1] Lecturer at University of Alcalá, oscar.navajas@uah.es
[2] Cultural Heritage Technician at Comarca del Maestrazgo, sofiasanchez77@hotmail.es

The current ICOM definition of a museum is the one adopted in 2007 and states: "A museum is a permanent non-profit institution in the service of society and its development, open to the public, which acquires, conserves, researches, communicates and exhibits the tangible and intangible heritage of humanity and its environment for the purpose of education, study and enjoyment"[3]. In September 2019, the 25th General Conference of ICOM took place in Kyoto. One of the challenges of this meeting was to establish and renew the definition of a museum[4]. Due to various circumstances, there was no consensus for the nearly 3000 museum professionals who gathered in the Japanese city. The proposal that was:

> Museums are democratising, inclusive and polyphonic spaces for critical dialogue about pasts and futures. Acknowledging and addressing the conflicts and challenges of the present, they are custodians of artefacts and specimens for society, safeguard diverse memories for future generations, and ensure equal rights and equal access to heritage for all peoples.
>
> Museums are not-for-profit. They are participatory and transparent, and work in active collaboration with and for diverse communities to collect, preserve, research, interpret, exhibit, and expand understandings of the world, with the purpose of contributing to human dignity and social justice, global equality and planetary well-being[5].

This proposition was really a declaration of intent, that is, more a way of stating the mission and vision of the museological entity than a

---

[3] Definition adopted at the 2007 Austria meeting. See: https://icom.museum/es/ressource/icoms-statutes/ [Accessed: 20/02/2022].

[4] The start for the development of a new definition of museums began in 2016 at the ICOFOM meeting in Paris, and following the adoption of the 2015 UNESCO Recommendation on the Protection and Promotion of Museums and Collections, their Diversity and their Role in Society. In 2017, the Standing Committee on Museum Definition, Prospects and Potential (MDPP) was established. This committee established the parameters and methodology with which to propose the precepts of the future museum definition to be voted on at the ICOM Kyoto meeting in 2019.

[5] See the working documents at the official ICOM headquarters and a synthesis at: https://icom.museum/es/news/el-icom-anuncia-la-definicion-alternativa-del-museo-que-se-sometera-a-votacion/ [accessed: 20/02/2022].

syncretic definition. It succinctly summarised the evolution of these social and cultural spaces/institutions, both since their "legendary" creation in Hellenistic Greece and since the birth of the contemporary museum after the liberal revolutions of the late 18th and early 19th centuries.

New imaginary "beings", such as: democracy, inclusion, participation, social justice, equality, social innovation, etc., have been coming to life and gaining prominence over those that referred to the conservation and contemplation of collections.

The path of this conceptual evolution and the transformation of the entity has been a long one. The first official definitions of ICOM appeared as soon as it was created, to designate these spaces as entities dedicated to the research, conservation and dissemination of a diverse heritage. Since then, the debates on what museums are and how to define them have not ceased. The first contributions came from the French-speaking world. George Henri Rivière, in the 1960s, linked the definition to the ICOM statutes, understanding museums as places that safeguard heritage collections, but whose functions are linked to social welfare.

The qualitative leap in the museological debates on the conceptualisation of the museum - and of the museum - came in the 1970s and 1980s. At the 9th General Conference of ICOM in 1971, held in Paris and Grenoble, and a year later, at the Round Table in Santiago de Chile, organised by ICOM and UNESCO, under the theme "The role of museums in relation to the social and economic needs of Latin America", the new challenges facing museums in the last third of the 20th century were reflected: participation, development and communication. Echoes of these meetings can be seen in ICOM's 1974 definition:

> A museum is a permanent, non-profit institution at the service of society and its development, open to the public, which acquires, conserves, researches, communicates and exhibits, for the purpose of study, education and enjoyment, material evidence of man and his environment.

We will dwell for a moment on perhaps the most relevant concept in this definition: "at the service of society and its development". This consideration is possibly the one that has marked the evolution of museums, and is where the text we are presenting is framed. The *counter-power* that questioned the legitimised and imposed hierarchisation of the institution, the gaps in symbolic and cultural capital that predominated in their discourses, and the paradox of being entities open to the whole of society (Andrade, Mellado, Rueda and Villar, 2018: 11), but closed to a majority was the New Museology.

Andrea's text was one of the first scientific documents to analyse the "new" museum and the "new museology" at the very moment it was being forged. As we shall see, Andrea was able to make evident the essence of something that, although it had roots in previous decades, was actually under construction and was to become the current future of contemporary museums.

Building a museum for democracy

Most modern museums have mutated, there is no doubt: from entities focused on safeguarding heritage, to educational spaces, to immersive experiences generated by the Cultural, Tourist and Creative Industries. However, along the way, a generation of experiences will emerge that will understand the institution as a practical instrument for the active investigation of the identities of groups - especially marginalised groups - in communities.

The second half of the 20th century will mark these two evolutionary lines. On the one hand, that of leisure and training (and education) that will eventually consolidate into a system that "educates for income" (Nussbaum, 2012), i.e., one that is capable of turning everything into consumer products, even the most basic values that make us human beings. On the other hand, the social one that tries to foster an "education for democracy" (Nussbaum, 2012), i.e., one that is capable of generating egalitarian and caring societies, skilled and innovative professionals, and ethical and socially responsible people.

The distinction, from our point of view and the one that Andrea's research will reflect, is that the museum is not just about satisfying needs, but its raison d'être is to create them. It is not there to answer questions, but to create them. It is not an institution - solely - destined to fulfil the missionary role of the Enlightenment, as Bauman mentioned, but it must take the reins of its strategic importance in the construction of democratic societies. Its challenges, therefore, lie in the citizenship of the post-globalisation era, in human beings wandering aimlessly in a mestizo time (Andrade, Mellado, Rueda and Villar, 2018: 19). This is the legacy of the New Museology. The museum was conceived by the project of modernity as a temple of knowledge; the New Museology wanted to turn it into a modern agora.

Let us not forget that the content of museums has been formed through an unnatural process of social construction and legitimation (Prats, 1998, 63; y 2004), that is, "(…) it is an institution that presents material residues that, in turn, represent an absent image" (Andrade, Mellado, Rueda and Villar, 2018: 36). The museum is a cultural and social process circumscribed to an economic system in a world that García Canclini has broken down as heterogeneous, mobile and (desterritorialización) de-territorialised (2001: 155-156). This leads us to believe that this institution is - or has to be - a space that is diverse, democratic and inclusive of different histories, memories and voices. In fact, the last definition of the museum we quoted above proposed by ICOM was along these lines.

However, delegitimising and decolonising the museum in order to achieve this is not a question of eradicating certain narratives, but an idea of including those silenced and silenced voices that, on the other hand, have managed to resist over time. It is not, therefore, a matter of annulling one to replace it with another, but of including, recognising, assuming and empathising. For Hugues de Varine "(…) the museum, for us, is or should be one of the most highly perfected tools available to society to prepare and accompany its own transformation" (1985: 4). This idea reflects the phase through which museums and their disciplinary field, museology, had been passing since the 1960s. The museum as a nineteenth-century institution was being transformed into an entity at the service of society.

Andrea analyses in his text four experiences that marked this current vision of museums that educate for democracy, and a new museological revolution (Mensch, 1992). Her research work focused on the analysis of the *Écomusée de la Haute Beauce*, the Écomusée *de la Maison du Fier Monde*, both in Canada; the *Anacostia Neighborhood Museum*, in the USA; and *La Casa del Museo*, in Mexico. These case studies are a sample of the background to the museological thinking that marked the New Museology and the influence of the birth and expansion of French ecomuseums. He conducted 35 interviews, a total of 63 hours of recording that generated 800 pages of transcripts.

Methodical and scientific work. The experiences

The first "stepping stone" in the gestation of the Anacostia Quarter Museum project took place in 1966 when Smithsonian Institution Secretary Dillon Ripley considered starting a neighbourhood museum in some modest Washington neighbourhood. The Anacostia community[6] was chosen for this experimental neighbourhood museum by the *Greater Anacostia Peoples* (GAP), an association that was rooted in the community and worked to lift the community out of marginality and social, cultural and economic problems (Kinard, 1985 [1971]: 219). On 15 September 1967, a newly refurbished cinema opened its doors, this time as the Museo de Barrio de Anacostia. Crucial to its development and to the mobilisation of the community would be the figure of John Kinard,

---

[6] The Anacostia neighbourhood is a community of modest origins, with a population of around 200,000 in the 1960s, located in the southeastern corner of Washington, DC. The possibility of creating a museum to help solve the neighbourhood's problems prompted the population to mobilise the Smithsonian to carry out the project. In addition, the Smithsonian's collections contained references to Anacostia's history with which to begin work on the construction of the neighbourhood's memory (Alexander, 1997: 148).

a Smithsonian professional, who for Seale (1997) would open America's eyes to the social responsibility of museums.

The second experience, the Casa del Museo, had its genesis in the cultural policies emanating from the National Museum of Anthropology and the National Institute of Anthropology and History (INAH) and the cultural democratisation supported by intellectual movements associated with a critical Mexican anthropology (Iniesta, 1999: 116). In the 1960s, the National Museum of Anthropology, dependent on INAH[7], was one of the most important projects of its time. Apart from its innovative architecture and its museographic programme presenting the great civilisations of Mexican territory, the museum was created with the maxim of serving the country's schoolchildren and fostering their sense of identity and dignity. However, shortly after its creation, its director, Mario Vázquez, stated:

> The National Museum of Anthropology has not been able to function as we had envisaged... It is not made for the real Mexicans, nor for the people of the countryside and even less for schoolchildren. The wealthy and the well-educated of the city like it very much. Moreover, the museum has become the most popular tourist attraction in Mexico. It was necessary to surrender to the evidence that it had been built for a purpose it could not serve. We had forgotten that marble floors are too cold for little bare feet (Cameron, 1992 [1968]: 43).

INAH initiated a community project called "La Casa del Museo", directed by Mario Vázquez himself, with the aim of integrating the museum into the community through social participation and organisation, and where the themes addressed responded to the interests and needs of the

---

[7] The National Institute of Anthropology and History had the particularity of being born at the end of the 1930s as a multidisciplinary institution in which architects, curators, anthropologists, educators, etc. shared space to plan research, education and communication of the nation's heritage in response to Mexican idiosyncrasy (Herreman et al, 1980: 96). The way to achieve this was not based on the simple selection and assembly of museums, but on the approach to communities (rural and urban) in order to make them aware of the importance of discovering their heritage, of revaluing their culture, of managing it, and of seeing in this process a mechanism of global pedagogy.

community itself (Méndez, 2008: 7). La Casa del Museo was extended to several popular neighbourhoods in Mexico City for eight years. The work methodology revolved around the conception of the museum as a support for the solution of the problems of the most disadvantaged communities. The aim was to create a more active and participatory museum, more in tune with the reality of marginalised communities. In short, a museum in which they would see themselves reflected and which would serve as a place of critical reflection on themselves and their future development.

The scope of the Casa del Museo and of the philosophy perceived in Mexican museum, heritage and educational policies can be seen in other projects. In 1972, the School Museum Programme was launched, coordinated by the museographer Iker Larrauri, with the intention of creating a museum in every school in the country. In 1983, INAH brought together this experience and the Casa del Museo in the Programme for the Development of the Educational Function of Museums (PRODEFEM), formed by a multidisciplinary team (anthropologists, historians, psychologists, architects, pedagogues, biologists, etc.) coordinated by Miriam Arroyo. The legacy of both experiences gave rise to the methodological basis that led to the Mexican community museums and their national network, defined in 1993 in the National Programme of Community Museums (PNMC), in collaboration with the National Institute of Anthropology and History and the General Directorate of Popular Cultures (Méndez, 2008: 7-8).

The last two experiences that Andrea will analyse correspond to the typology of ecomuseums. The French-speaking part of Canada was one of the places where ecomuseums first took root. From 1974, bilateral communications were established between the ecomuseums of the French Regional Parks and some young Quebec museologists. Georges Henri Rivière was one of the intermediaries in some of these meetings, which resulted in documents, courses and even the proposal to *Parcs Canada* to adopt the ecomuseum formula. It was from this formative beginning that the ecomuseum experience of Haute-Beauce, which officially became an ecomuseum in 1983, began.

Haute-Beauce encompassed thirteen rural parishes belonging to different federal districts in southeastern Quebec, at a geographically comparable distance from the point of view of communications, and with a historical and socio-economic concordance (as in Hauenschild's Dissertation, 1988). The trigger for the experience was the collection of ethnographic and historical objects belonging to Napoleon Bolduc. In 1978, Bolduc put the collection up for sale, but there was little interest from the administration and minimal public awareness. Between 1978 and 1979, Pierre Mayrand sought support with the idea of creating a team with which to formulate a museological project linking the collection and the territory. In 1979, the *Centre d'Interpretation de la Région de l'Haute-Beauce* (CRIHB) was founded, giving the initiative a legal entity.

With the creation of the museum and interpretation centre, a five-year development plan (1979-1983) was adopted for the formation of an ecomuseum based on the triangularisation model (Mayrand, 1983: 25). In addition, a users' committee was created, made up of the thirteen villages that made up the region. Until then, Pierre Mayrand had not mentioned the concept of an ecomuseum, but the idea was underway. In 1982, the change came about. There was a fear that the museum would become a static entity, a traditional museum, which led Mayrand to convene an assembly to promote the idea of creating an ecomuseum. The initial Museum and Regional Interpretation Centre was renamed the *Ecomuseum de la Haute-Beauce.*

Fier-Monde, on the other hand, were the two oldest working-class districts located in the south-central part of Montreal. An important industrial and transportation location in the 1930s and 1940s, but after World War II they began to close and move their location. Between 1960 and 1980 the population declined by about 50%. Of the resident population, 20% were unemployed, 26% were on low incomes and 20% were pensioners. Unemployment and social conditions demanded alternative ways out of the situation.

In June 1980, the citizen-initiated *Maison de Fier-Monde* was inaugurated to house residential co-operatives. Although it was an overall popular project, the initiative was confined to a small group who occupied a special position in the community as a result of their expertise. A committee was formed for the future museum, and in 1982 the name was changed to the *Ecomuseum de la Maison du Fier-Monde*. The aim of the project was to improve the quality of life and self-esteem of the population. The ecomuseum was intended to be a reference point for job creation, promoting industrial reconversion and cooperative initiatives and calling for improvements in the urban environment and in the quality of life of the inhabitants.

New Museology

Andrea began research into these experiences in June 1984 and completed it in 1988, when he published the manuscript presented here. These dates coincide with the formation and creation of the International Movement for a New Museology (MINOM). It is the time when the idea of ecomuseums and community museums (and neighbourhood museums) is spreading, and the time when the maelstrom of action of community museological experiences will begin to be made visible in the specialised literature; in short, her research and her text will arrive at the moment of epistemological reflection on what will later become a new disciplinary field. Andrea will be a "witness" to a process of a discipline under construction. She herself asked herself what the New Museology is.

As happens in Art History with every innovative moment in artistic manifestations, the only thing that the New Museology did was to break the "canon". On the one hand, Andrea noted how the New Museology traced a discourse from the social, the cultural and the political, establishing practical models in different communities and territories with socio-economic - sometimes unfavourable - and identity needs (Hauenschild, 1988: 3). On the other hand, the rupture or revolution of the New Museology was not so much about a conceptual change of the institution, but of its use and destiny for people (Hauenschild, 1988: 3).

To understand this transformation, Andrea identified the pillars of what would become the New Museology, which are presented below.

Generating a useful tool

The crucial distinction between the traditional museum and the "new" museum lies in the perception and formulation of a social task aimed at societal development (Hauenschild, 1988: 113).

The museums of the New Museology are to be understood and constituted as practical instruments in an active search for identity by mainly marginalised population groups. A form of cooperation with the community to determine their historical, present and possible future relationship with other socio-cultural groups, which helps to generate identity. This characteristic of working with disadvantaged and marginalised social groups enables the inclusion of identities and narratives that differ from the "official", elite and minority but dominant classes (Hauenschild, 1988: 114). The Museo del Barrio de Anacostia, for example, was the first museum in the US to focus on the history, culture and current issues of that particular African American community, making it visible through actions such as exhibitions and museum media[8].

The "new" museum therefore aimed to deal with everyday life by specifying problems and possible solutions. These museums become a popular university. This conceptualisation of Andrea is still valid today in the field of Social Museology and Sociomuselogy. In the Bogota Declaration of MINOM 2018 the motto was: "The museum that is not useful for life is not useful at all"[9].

---

[8] The main tool of this museum was the exhibition. Among the exhibitions that were organised, the one that caused the greatest impact due to its social repercussions was *The Rat, Man's Unwanted Guest*, which dealt with a real problem in the neighbourhood and the community. With this exhibition, the concept and usefulness of the museum was turned upside down. It became a way of reflecting the problems of the community and, at the same time, of proposing solutions to them.

[9] *Declaration of Bogotá (2018). XIX Minom International Conference, II Latin American Chair of Museology and Cultural Heritage Management, I Latin American Conference on Social Museology.* Accessible at: http://www.minom-icom.net/files/declaracion_de_bogota_minom_2018.pdf.

Institutionalisation and awareness-raising spaces

New museology claims that museums should be "grass-rooted," that is, that they should be founded through community effort (Hauenschild, 1988: 117).

The experiences analysed and, ultimately, the experiences of the New Museology environment were not born through a technical, administrative and/or exogenous decision to the community. The implementation process will differ from traditional museums. Specialists (museologists, historians, educators, etc.), appointed by members of the community or local authorities, or intervening on their own initiative, will have as their main task to identify the prevailing community needs and problems (Hauenschild, 1988: 118).

To preserve this inclusive character with a focus on people's lives, these entities strive to maintain a low degree of institutionalisation. They will aim to influence marginalised social groups so that they structure their present and future according to their specific cultural characteristics. This allows Andrea to conceptualise these entities beyond the objectives of cultural educational institutions: The communication of identity and history, of knowledge and skills is considered by all the museums studied as a step towards the realisation of the highest goal of social development, to change the social reality of a community.

Self-management and autarchy

How the museum is financed affects the degree of influence and control. To be active sponsors of the "new" museum, the community must shoulder some or all of its financial support (Hauenschild, 1988: 121).

Institutionalisation implies economic independence, which in turn fosters the processes of autarky and self-management. In his analysis, Andrea noted that in order to preserve independence, the different experiences will focus on strengthening the region's resources, the contributions of local businesses and economic activities, and the contributions of citizens. However, beyond this claim, Andrea is aware that these projects will need a strong governmental impetus to sustain themselves. He notes: "Comparative analysis of the case studies reveals great differences in methods of financing. The demand for self-financing, particularly regarding the scope and professional standard of projects, is generally proving to be extremely unrealistic, since we are dealing with financially weak and underprivileged groups. Consideration of the case studies reveals that "new" museums-apart from isolated contributions in kind or money from the community-are largely government financed" (Hauenschild, 1988: 121).

Territory and decentralisation

"Spatial decentralization of "new" museums is a strategy to ensure affinity with the population and to open up opportunities for identification and influence" (Hauenschild, 1988: 123).

In contrast to the traditional museum, where activities are generally confined to the "four walls" of the institution's building, the cases analysed argue for a decentralised spatial structure. The marking of its boundaries will not be an administrative delimitation, but the result of the evolution of the interactions of individuals in the community with it (Mayrand, 2004: 25). In Andrea's analysis, this marking will materialise in spaces of identity identification for the community with its heritage and its territory, which for Andrea means a "museum made of fragments" (Hauenschild, 1988: 125). An element that offers the population an active role in forming and participating in the museum.

In this sense, the museum became a space without defined limits if not for the community itself. The goods that it "accumulates", therefore, were not destined to be housed in a building, but the traditional concept of collection was now transferred and was made up of everything that was found in the territory and belonged to the community. This turned heritage and culture into a living heritage, in constant creation and evolution.

Community participation and inclusion.

Representatives of new museology reject institutional ordering in the "new" museum. I believe that this is based on a misconception. What one wants to prevent are strictly formulated structures that impede dynamic action. But it cannot be ignored that a museum is basically an institution, that is, a social entity characterized by certain patterns of order and rules and performing specific functions (cf. Hartfiel, 1976: 307) (quoted in Hauenschild, 1988: 120).

Participation will be a key issue. Andrea was both critical and realistic in this aspect. Citizen participation in the experiences analysed will take a qualitative leap with respect to traditional museums. The "new" museums will be based on citizen organisations in which anyone can participate, where each member is a main actor. This requires a specific participatory structure that gives the population the necessary competence to actively intervene in the museum.

In his detailed analysis of each of the museums, these processes are detailed. For example, while in the first *Museum House* the community had no role in decision-making, in the second, more informal and unstructured project, self-governance structures that already existed in the community were implemented to allow residents, along with museum staff, to have control and determine what activities would take place. For Andrea, *Museum House II* was a perfect form of participation and self-governance for what was intended as New Museology.

In the case of the *Museo del Barrio de Anacostia*, it began with an informal founding committee. Any interested citizen could participate, make proposals, give their opinion on the projects, etc., i.e., be part of the decision-making process. Later, this founding committee was transformed into a museum advisory committee, composed of representatives of socially relevant groups and citizens. The problem for Andrea is that this skewed participation to a delegation of a reduced representation of the population, as citizens did not always have access to and competence over these representative groups, and the proposals and advice of this committee were not binding for the museum's management, nor for the museum itself.

In the other two cases, the *Ecomuseum de la Maison du Fier-Monde* and the *Ecomuseum de la Haute-Beauce*, both were structured through a board of directors, as well as committees of users, executives, etc. A more complex structure, although it followed the precepts of the first community ecomuseum in which Hugues de Varine was involved. The executive committee of the *Ecomuseum de la Haute-Beauce* originally served as a link between the museum and the population of Haute-Beauce and functioned as such in the early days of the ecomuseum. When its initial vigour evaporated, the activities of the users' committee gradually came to a halt.

This brings us to another of the variables: the professionals, the remaining element to forge what Rivard (1987) will call a Critical Culture in this type of project. The role transferred to the new professional in the community projects analysed by Andrea is that of an advisor, consultant, and trainer who, in time, will be dispensable. The role of catalyst and advisor should be underlined by the decision not to occupy official museum positions, such as director or president.

Importance of intangible heritage, the collective memory

The value of heritage is generated in community use and in the understanding of this as the transmitter of a heritage universe (Smith, 2006): The conception of a heritage for life, a lived heritage (Varine, 2017). Andrea noted that the work on "collective memory" by authors such as Maurice Halbwachs (2004 [1968]) was fundamental. The identification of heritage is not the work of technicians alone but is an act of responsibility and public awareness. The appropriation of heritage must be an act that emanates from working with the population, which will allow the development of feelings of identity and relevance, as well as turning it into a testimony of the past, an element to understand the present and where to look for innovation and transformation towards the future.

Weaknesses of counter-power

What really was this New Museology? A question which, as we have seen, will be pursued in this paper and which we will try to unravel through the analysis of experiences and the approach to the characteristics and "pillars" of the New Museology.

Throughout her research and reflections on the material collected, Andrea realised that for the "new museologists" conceptualisation, systematisation and definition were a symptom of losing their dynamism and the possibility of innovation. It was based on methods of action and learning by doing. If anything is really crucial in this document, it is Andrea's critical, scientific vision.

Andrea noted in the case studies that all of them have positioned themselves as the antithesis, metamorphosis and evolution of traditional museums, but that their theories and approaches were still to be developed (Hauenschild, 1988: 138-148). This can be seen in some accurate reflections on the weaknesses of those pillars of the New Museology that she herself identified.

One of the examples is the decentralisation of the territory and the creation of antennae, which in some cases produced resistance from citizens, and did not become spaces for identification and community marking.

> The Ecomusée de la Maison du Fier-Monde also encountered community resistance in establishing antennas. [...] On the whole, spatial decentralization may work in some cases but cannot be an end in itself. In my view, antennas should not be set up in the initial phase of a museum merely to give the impression, as quickly as possible, of outwardly satisfying

a certain museum concept. Antennas appear to be unsuitable as initiators of community sensitization. "New" museums should begin by creating lasting contacts with citizen groups, a move which holds greater promise of sensitization and ensures antennas will be geared to local needs and interests. If antennas are to be more than reminders that a museum exists in the region or neighbourhood, they must express the declared will and reflect the identity of the community (Hauenschild, 1988: 123-124).

Something similar happens with citizen participation. In all the projects, this has been decreasing until it has become practically non-existent in some cases. The problem for Andrea lies in maintaining social mobilisation and not falling into what she calls "citizen passivity". For Andrea, having a participatory democratic structure with broad decision-making power at the disposal of the population is no guarantee that citizens will effectively assume the positions to which they are entitled and their possibilities (Hauenschild, 1988: 125). And he asks: Why is this the case, what is the problem, what must happen for the population to exercise its decision-making power, as the new museology claims (Hauenschild, 1988: 125). In his opinion, these experiences and this museology have failed to prove their validity or have failed to understand communities. One of the solutions he proposes is to create structures and spaces that ensure participatory environments led and managed by the citizens themselves.

In addition to this problem, Andrea detected a problem with relations between specialists and members of the community, even though in some of these museums there was a participatory and democratic structure.

Specialists continued to control daily actions and decision-making processes. Most projects are developed by professionals and submitted for approval to the bodies representing the population. For Andrea, the specialists have not fulfilled their promise to cooperate on equal terms with the representatives of the population (an exception is the Museum House II). In practice, cooperation between specialists and residents creates inequalities and hierarchies. This indicates that the New Museology had not yet been assimilated.

For Andrea, a transformation of the professional is necessary: "only a change in the behaviour and self-esteem of the museum professional can remedy this problem", which he calls an act of individual will[10]. For Andrea, the museologist must: (1) try, first of all, to share his or her knowledge and skills with the population; (2) must get to know the knowledge and skills of the population through a learning process based on reciprocity and include them as a constitutive element of the museum's work; (3) and must be aware of the constellation of values and interests of the community, and must constantly orient his or her work towards them, respecting the population and entrusting it with full responsibility and freedom of decision, the new museum professional should be destined to boost the community's self-awareness and confidence.

These are some of the elements that lead Andrea to argue that the New Museology was still traditional because it was based on the nineteenth-century conception of the museum as an educational institution at the service of society (Haueschild, 1988: 1 and 53). However, it was necessary to change this very register: the museum was no longer to be an educational institution, but a social entity.

Building science...and a new language

Andrea's text is a magnificent document for knowing what the experiences of the New Museology were and where they failed. She was able to identify the essence and spirit of the incipient New Museology: "The "new" museum wants to make a concrete contribution to coping with everyday life by pointing out problems and possible solutions"

---

[10] In this sense, the new museology shows interesting parallels with the "anthropology of action", which is mainly based on new respectful relationships between an anthropologist and a given population, placing the anthropologist radically at the service of the population in question (Seithel 1986, quoted by Hauenschild, 1988).

(Hauenschild, 1988: 6). She even confronted the complexity of the utopian meaning of the experiences of the New Museology:

> A question that is frequently heard from all sides is whether the "new"; museum, with its high ideals, is unrealistic and utopian. de Varine writes (no year: 5): "On the one hand, I believe that such a radical rethinking is the only possible salvation for the museum as a useful factor in the life of Society in the modem world. Utopia is no danger as long as it is aware of itself and inspires positive action with concrete efforts. On the other hand, old and recent experience proves that the above museological principles are practicable and effective". One of the tasks of my research is to investigate, using case studies, how the "new" museum has been realised in various social contexts and how these realisations relate to the claims of new museology, that is, to what extent we are dealing with "concrete utopias" (Hauenschild, 1988: 14).

In a succinct and indirect way, Andrea's document establishes a series of concepts for the language of the new museological panorama: inclusion, innovation, awareness-raising, identity, democracy, etc. Although one of its great difficulties is how to bring together the different experiences it analyses under the same common denominator. The concept of ecomuseum was born in France and spread to French-speaking Canada; neighbourhood museums developed in the USA, and the Museum House was the beginning of community museums; what will be the most appropriate nomenclature? Andrea settles it with the term *"new" museum*. A term as lax as it is accurate, because the importance of the New Museology and the experiences it analyses are not the *label*, but the spirit, process and methodology. This is what she states at the beginning of her text:

> Basically, I consider the changes in museum practice demanded by new museology, particularly with respect to local and regional museums, to be desirable and, through a scientific study of the relationship of theory to

practice, I intend to produce a more precise definition of and solid basis for new museology. This work aims to make new museology accessible and comprehensible, clarify its problem areas and stimulate its practice in order to advance the museum as an educational institution and agent of social change (Hauenschild, 1988: 3).

In this sense, one of the importance of Andrea's paper is that it can be considered the first scientific text for the New Museology. As she herself points out:

It cannot be denied that relatively much of the available literature, which consists predominantly of short articles, has-with a few exceptions-a certain propagandistic nature. A body of research, properly speaking, is next to non-existent. At best, one can speak of a "body of thought," a "collection of ideas." The single longer work on new museology by René Rivard (1984) makes no scientific claims and should be viewed as a general compendium of ideas on the subject. With the exception of the case studies of Gariépy (1986), Céré (1985) and Antúñez et al. (1976), there has been no comprehensive analysis of new museology according to systematic, empirical criteria (Hauenschild, 1988: 10).

What is certain is that the New Museology emerged at a time of radical social change through a far-reaching democratisation of culture. Both the bid to open up this democratisation and the frustration of what it was becaming is where the "new" museum and the counter-power claims of the New Museology practitioners found their grounding. It is based on the assumption that culture can be both the subject and the instrument of an emancipatory educational process directed towards democratic social change. The new museology's innovative approach to modern museum work complements and extends that of traditional museums (Hauenschild, 1988: 113).

For Andrea, although the new museology originated in the examination of the practical experiences of museums, it was not strictly speaking a scientific theory derived from systematic empirical research; its validity depended on the existing conditions of communities and territories. It lacks a dogmatic schema, to make the new museology a useful discipline and methodology for those beyond the circle of its supporters.

> New museologists worry that when one defines what new museology is, it will lose its dynamic and the scope for innovation. This is, in my view, incomprehensible and unjustified. By refusing to be pinned down, new museologists risk manoeuvring new museology into a dead end and depriving it of criticism and assessment, that is, in the end, preventing change (Hauenschild, 1988: 114).

What Andrea detected is that for many of its representatives, the new museology is a dynamic process of creating innovative forms of museum work. It is less directed towards the development of definitions and theories than strongly oriented towards action. Concrete actions are grounded intuitively rather than rationally.

Vision for the future

From Andrea's research we have inherited a museum that must have its meaning in the communal relations that allow the survival of heritage "and be directed towards the achievement of lives that deserve to be lived" (Barcenilla, 2019: 42). The museum, what she called the "new museum", that we build "(…) must speak to us of different temporalities. It must stop prioritising the fracturing of its chronogram through exhibitions' (Barcenilla, 2019: 42).

The experiences analysed by Andrea in separate social contexts: neighbourhood museums in the United States, community museums in Latin America, particularly in Mexico, and ecomuseums in Quebec; and the creation of an association during the 1980s, MINOM, shaped cultural and political rather than scientific approaches (Hausenchild, 1988).

However, like any other social innovation, the museum that was being forged had to overcome enormous obstacles. Andrea's prophetic words leave us with a future in a loop:

> Since then, in countless museum conferences, academic lectures and articles, critics have lamented the obsolete character of museums and have questioned the conception museums have of themselves and their right to exist. But, in fact, museums appear to be surviving the crisis. Instead of the feared closing of museums, headlines announce new openings. Here the question inevitably arises: Have museums changed so that they enjoy increasing popularity? One thing is sure: museum people, under the pressure of events and in reaction to vehement criticism, have awakened from their torpor and are trying hard to make changes. Yet, even today many museums still consider their primary role to be that of "preservation institutions". This view is reflected in the museological literature, which is largely devoted to conservation, restoration and security (Hauenschild, 1988: 2).

Time has been giving answers to Andrea's text, constructing a theoretical, conceptual and scientific account of the New Museology. The trajectory of the approaches and philosophy of the New Museology have been coining new names: community museology, sociomuseology, alter-museology, ecomuseology, etc., in what ended up being the unofficial denomination of "new museology" (Díaz Balerdi, 2010).

Today, the New Museology is still alive. In Portugal, the Lusófona University of Lisbon has a department specialising in training in sociomuseology[11], which not only supports Portuguese museums with the practice of social museology, but has also implemented training (bachelor's, master's and doctoral degrees) and research in this field. In Italy, the anthropic idea of landscape (human and/or cultural) has been promoted, but also the legislative aspects, creating specific regulations to

---

[11] See: https://www.ulusofona.pt/doutoramento/museologia [Accessed 14/01/2022].

regulate and promote ecomuseums[12]. On the Asian continent, ecomuseums are expanding and are beginning to develop a network of associations, as well as research and reflection[13]. In Latin American countries, the development of community museology has been consolidated with the creation of networks, such as the *Associação Brasileira de Ecomuseus e Museus Communitários* (ABREMC)[14], the *Unión Nacional de Museos Comunitarios y Ecomuseos de México*[15] or *the Red Museos Comunitarios de América Latina y El Caribe*[16]. And at the international level, apart from MINOM, the network that acts as an "observatory" of community experiences is the *International Network of Community Ecomuseums and Museums DROPS*[17].

Our society continues to manifest social inequalities (gender, migration, human rights, (post)colonialism, etc.) and economic inequalities (unequal distribution of resources), in a system that hierarchises social rights according to economic and symbolic parameters. A neoliberal system that promotes a society educated for consumption and income. However, the living panorama of the New Museology (Social Museology and Sociomuseology) is making it a reality to develop actions - both theoretical and practical - to generate dialogue and critical perspectives that make museums capable of facing the challenges of the 21st century[18]. The ultimate goal is to ensure that these entities contribute to making a better world, with human beings who are aware and educated for democracy.

We should look at and read Andrea's text as the beginning of a path that would have no return. Her research opened a door to build a social discipline of museums, and to be able to learn and improve the

---

[12] It is recommended to consult the *Mondi Locali - Local Worlds* network: http://www.ecomusei.eu/mondilocali/ [Accessed 14/01/2022].
[13] An example can be found at the *Japan Ecomuseological Society* (JECOMS): http://www.jecoms.jp/ [Accessed 14/01/2022].
[14] See: http://www.abremc.com.br/ [Accessed 14/01/2022].
[15] See: https://www.gob.mx/cultura [Accessed 14/01/2022].
[16] See: https://www.museoscomunitarios.org/ [Accessed 14/01/2022].
[17] See: https://sites.google.com/view/drops-platform/home [Accessed 14/01/2022].
[18] These challenges were set out in the *Lugo-Lisbon Declaration* of the 20th Minom International Workshop: http://www.minom-icom.net/files/declaracion_lugo-lisboa_gal_es_pt.pdf.

weaknesses that had innovative experiences of those convulsive, fertile and utopian years for heritage, culture and museums.

References

ALEXANDER, E. (1997). *The Museum in America. Innovators and pioneers*. London, New Delhi: Altamira Press, Wolnut Creek, published in Cooperation with The American Association for State and Local History.

ANDRADE, P., MELLADO, L., RUEDA, H., & VILLAR, G. (2018). *El Museo Mestizo. Fundamentación museológica y disciplinar para el cambio de guion*. Santiago: Museo Histórico Nacional de Chile.

BARCENILLA, H. (2019). Rethinking the museum from life. In *Diferents. Revista de museus* núm. 4, 2019, pp. 28-43.

BODEI, R. (1996). Tumult of frozen creatures, or on the logic of museums. In *Revista de Occidente* nº 177/1996, pp. 21-35.

CAMERON, D. (1992 [1968]). Un point de vue : le musée considéré comme système de communication et les implications de ce système dans les programmes éducatifs muséaux. In DESVALLÉES, A. (org.). BARY, M. and WASSERMAN, F. (eds.). *Vagues: une anthologie de la nouvelle muséologie*. Mâcon: Editions W. vol. 1, pp. 77-98.

DÍAZ BALERDI, I. (2010). *Imaginary archipelagos. Museums of the Autonomous Community of the Basque Country*. Urduliz (Biscay): Editorial Nerea, Servicio Central de Publicaciones del Gobierno Vasco, Administración de la Comunidad Autónoma del País Vasco.

CANCLINI, N. G. (1990). La sociología de la cultura de Pierre Bourdieu. *Sociología y cultura*, n° 76, pp. 75-97

GRUZINSKI, S (2000). *El pensamiento mestizo*. Barcelona: Paidós.

HALBWACHS, M. (2004 [1968]). La memoria colectiva. Zaragoza: Prensa Universitaria de Zaragoza.

HAUENSCHILD, A. (1988). Claims and Reality of New Museology: Case Studies in Canada, the United States and Mexico, Dissertation for the Degree of Doctor of Philosophy of the University of Hamburg

HERREMAN, Y.; GÓNZALEZ DE LA MORA, S.; and SCHMIDHUBER, G. (1980). Mexico: Museums 1972-1980. In *Museum*, vol. XXXII, n° 3, pp. 92-107.

ICOM (2019). The museum definition. The backbone of museums. In *Museum International*, vol. 71, n. 281-282.

INIESTA GONZÁLEZ, M. (1999). Museos locales, patrimonios globales. in VV. AA. *Patrimonio Etnológico. New perspectives of study*. Granada, Cuadernos del Instituto Andaluz del Patrimonio Histórico, Consejería de Cultura de la Junta de Andalucía, pp. 110-127.

KINARD, J. (1985 [1971]). The neighbourhood museum, catalyst for social change. in *Museum*, n°. 4, pp. 217-223.

MAYRAND, P. (1983). Les défis d'écomusée : un cas. celui de la Haute-Beauce. In *Symposium International for Museology. Museum - Territory - Society. New tendencies / New Practices. Addenda*, ICOFOM-ICOM, pp. 23-27.

MAYRAND, P. (2004). *Haute-Beauce. Psycholosociologie d'un écomusée*. Cadernos de Sociomuseologia, n° 22, Lisbon: Centro de Estudos de Sociologia, Universidade Lusófona de Humanidades e Tecnologias.

MÉNDEZ LUGO, A. (2008). *Map of the situation of community museums in Mexico. Report for UNESCO*. Unpublished document.

MENSCH, P. V. (1992). *Towards a Methodology of Museology*. University of Zagreb, Faculty of Philosophy, doctoral thesis.

NUSSBAUM, M. (2012). *Non-profit. Why democracy needs the humanities*. Buenos Aires: Katz editores.

PRATS, Ll. (1998). El concepto de patrimonio cultural. *Política y sociedad*, 27(1), pp.63-76.

PRATS, Ll. (2004). *Antropología y Patrimonio*. Barcelona: Ariel.

RIVARD, R. (1987). Muséologie et cultures. In *Actas del IV Taller Internacional del Movimiento para la Nueva Museología (MINOM)*, Molinos (Spain), document SIGNUD, cota, doc. 1987-005-03. Lusophone University.

SEALE, W. (1997). Foreword. In ALEXANDER, E. (ed.). *The Museum in America. Innovators and pioneers.* London, New Delhi: Altamira Press, Wolnut Creek, published in Cooperation with The American Association for State and Local History, pp. 9-12.

SMITH, L. (2006). *Uses of heritage*. New York: Routledge.

VARINE, H. de (1985). Notes en forme d'avant-propos. In NICOLAS, A. (ed.). *Nouvelles Muséologies. Muséologie Nouvelle et experimentation sociale.* Marseille: M.N.E.S. pp.3-4.

VARINE, H. de (2017). *L'écomusée singulier et pluriel. Un témoignage sur cinquante ans de muséologie communautaire dans le monde.* Paris: L'Harmattan.

Prólogo

Óscar Navajas Corral[1]
Sofía Sánchez Giménez[2]

«Entre seres imaginarios y formas de vida».
(Gruzinski, 2000: 5).

¿Qué es un museo? ¿Una institución permanente o un espacio polifónico? ¿Un proyecto altruista, filantrópico o simplemente con fines de lucro (económico, cultural y/o social)? ¿Un equipamiento abierto al público e inclusivo, o dedicado a servir a los intereses de una élite socioeconómica y cultural? ¿Un lugar al servicio de las sociedades y de las comunidades, o espacios para la educación de las audiencias? ¿Un recinto para proteger, salvaguardar la memoria y preservar el patrimonio material e inmaterial de..., una comunidad o de la humanidad? Todas estas cuestiones –y muchas otras– han estado ocupando el trabajo de especialistas y profesionales del campo de los museos y de la museología sobre todo en los último cincuenta años.

Definir y conceptualizar qué es esta entidad y cuál es su razón de ser en las sociedades y comunidades ha sido, y es, uno de los retos de instituciones como el Consejo Internacional de Museos (ICOM) y de su comité para la museología, el ICOFOM. Desde la fundación del primero de ellos a mediados de los años cincuenta del siglo XX, su cometido ha sido intentar consensuar una definición que pudiese aglutinar la heterogeneidad de una institución que se ha caracterizado por transitar por un auténtico «campo de batalla» (Bodei, 1996) para la legitimización de las identidades, los imaginarios simbólicos, las narraciones y los discursos que se elaboran hacia y para él y que emanan de él.

---

[1] Profesor en la Universidad de Alcalá, oscar.navajas@uah.es
[2] Técnica de Patrimonio Cultural en la Comarca del Maestrazo, sofiasanchez77@hotmail.es

La actual definición de museo del ICOM es la que se aprobó en 2007 y reza: «Un museo es una institución permanente sin fines de lucro al servicio de la sociedad y su desarrollo, abierta al público, que adquiere, conserva, investiga, comunica y exhibe el patrimonio tangible e intangible de la humanidad y su entorno con fines de educación, estudio y deleite»[3]. En septiembre de 2019 tuvo lugar en Kioto la XXV Conferencia General del ICOM. Uno de los retos de este encuentro fue establecer y renovar la definición de museo[4]. Por diversas circunstancias no hubo consenso para los cerca de 3000 profesionales de la museología que se dieron cita en la ciudad nipona. La propuesta que fue:

> Los museos son espacios democratizadores, inclusivos y polifónicos para el diálogo crítico sobre los pasados y los futuros. Reconociendo y abordando los conflictos y desafíos del presente, custodian artefactos y especímenes para la sociedad, salvaguardan memorias diversas para las generaciones futuras, y garantizan la igualdad de derechos y la igualdad de acceso al patrimonio para todos los pueblos.
>
> Los museos no tienen ánimo de lucro. Son participativos y transparentes, y trabajan en colaboración activa con y para diversas comunidades a fin de coleccionar, preservar, investigar, interpretar, exponer, y ampliar las comprensiones del mundo, con el propósito de contribuir a la dignidad humana y a la justicia social, a la igualdad mundial y al bienestar planetario[5].

---

[3] Definición aprobada en la reunión de Austria de 2007. Véase: https://icom.museum/es/ressource/icoms-statutes/ [Consultado: 20/02/2022].

[4] El inicio para el desarrollo de una nueva definición de museos comenzó en el año 2016 en la reunión del ICOFOM de París, y tras la adopción de la Recomendación de la UNESCO de 2015 sobre la protección y promoción de los museos y las colecciones, su diversidad y su función en la sociedad. En 2017 se creó el Comité Permanente de Definición, Perspectivas y Potencial de Museo (MDPP). Este comité estableció los parámetros y la metodología con los que proponer los preceptos de la futura definición de museo que sería votada en la reunión del ICOM de Kioto de 2019.

[5] Véase los documentos de trabajo en la sede oficial del ICOM y una síntesis en: https://icom.museum/es/news/el-icom-anuncia-la-definicion-alternativa-del-museo-que-se-sometera-a-votacion/ [consultado: 20/02/2022].

Esta proposición se configuraba en realidad como una declaración de intenciones, es decir, más como una forma de constatar la misión y la visión de la entidad museológica que como una definición sincrética. Recogía de una forma sucinta la evolución de estos espacios/instituciones sociales y culturales, tanto desde su creación «legendaria» en la Grecia helenística como desde el nacimiento del museo contemporáneo tras las revoluciones liberales de finales del siglo XVIII y principios del XIX.

Nuevos «seres» imaginarios, como: democracia, inclusión, participación, justicia social, igualdad, innovación social, etc., han ido cobrando vida y protagonismo frente a los que hacían referencia a la conservación y la contemplación de las colecciones.

El camino de esta evolución conceptual y de la transformación de la entidad ha sido largo. Las primeras definiciones oficiales del ICOM aparecieron nada más crearse este, para designar a estos espacios como entidades dedicadas a la investigación, la conservación y la difusión de un patrimonio diverso. Desde ese momento los debates sobre qué son los museos y cómo definirlos no ha cesado. Las primeras aportaciones provinieron de la influencia francófona. George Henri Rivière, en los años sesenta, vincularía la definición a los estatutos del ICOM, entendiendo los museos como lugares que salvaguardan colecciones patrimoniales, pero cuyas funciones se enlazan con el bienestar social.

El salto cualitativo en los debates museológicos sobre la conceptualización del museo –y de lo museal– llegaría en los años setenta y ochenta. En la IX Conferencia General del ICOM de 1971, celebrada en París y Grenoble, y un año después, en la Mesa Redonda de Santiago de Chile, bajo el lema de «El papel de los museos en relación con las necesidades sociales y económicas de Latino América», organizada por el ICOM y la UNESCO, se reflejaron los nuevos desafíos a los que se enfrentaban los museos del último tercio del siglo XX: participación, desarrollo y comunicación. Los ecos de estos encuentros se pueden constatar en la definición del ICOM de 1974:

Un museo es una institución permanente sin fines de lucro, al servicio de la sociedad y su desarrollo, abierta al público, que adquiere, conserva, investiga, comunica y exhibe, con fines de estudio, educación y deleite, evidencias materiales del hombre y su entorno.

Nos detendremos un instante en el concepto quizás más relevante de esta definición: «al servicio de la sociedad y su desarrollo». Esta consideración es posiblemente la que ha marcado el devenir de los museos, y es donde enmarcamos el texto que presentamos. El *contra-poder* que cuestionó la jerarquización legitimada e impuesta de la institución, las brechas del capital simbólico y cultural que predominaban en sus discursos, y la paradoja de ser entidades abiertas a toda la sociedad, pero vedada a una mayoría (Andrade, Mellado, Rueda y Villar, 2018: 11) fue la Nueva Museología.

El texto de Andrea fue uno de los primeros documentos científicos en analizar el «nuevo» museo y la «nueva museología» en el mismo momento que se estaba fraguando. Como veremos, Andrea fue capaz de evidenciar la esencia de algo que, aunque tenía raíces en décadas anteriores, en realidad estaba en construcción y se iba a convertir en el futuro actual de los museos contemporáneos.

La construcción de un museo para la democracia

La mayoría de los museos modernos han mutado, no cabe duda: de entidades enfocadas en salvaguardar el patrimonio, a espacios educativos, hasta experiencias inmersivas generadas por las Industrias Culturales, Turísticas y Creativas. Sin embargo, en ese camino irá surgiendo una generación de experiencias que entenderán la institución como un instrumento práctico para la investigación activa de las identidades de los grupos –sobre todo marginales– de las comunidades.

La segunda mitad del siglo XX marcará esas dos líneas evolutivas. Por un lado, la del ocio y el entrenamiento (y la educación) que con el tiempo se consolidará en un sistema que «educa para la renta» (Nussbaum, 2012), es decir, aquel que se capaz de convertir todo en productos de consumo, incluso los valores más básicos que nos hacen ser seres humanos. Por otro lado, la de lo social que intenta fomentar una «educación para la democracia» (Nussbaum, 2012), es decir, aquella que es capaz de generar sociedades igualitarias y solidarias, profesionales cualificados/as e innovadores/as, y personas éticas y socialmente responsables.

La distinción, desde nuestro punto de vista y del que reflejará la investigación de Andrea, es que el museo no tiene solo el cometido de satisfacer necesidades, sino su razón de ser está en crearlas. No está para responder preguntas, sino para crearlas. No es una institución –únicamente– destinada a cumplir el papel misionero de la Ilustración, que mencionaba Bauman, sino que debe tomar las riendas de su importancia estratégica en la construcción de sociedades democráticas. Sus retos, por tanto, se encuentran en la ciudadanía de la era de la posglobalización, en los seres humanos que vagan sin rumbo en un tiempo mestizo (Andrade, Mellado, Rueda y Villar, 2018: 19). Esta es la herencia de la Nueva Museología. El museo fue concebido por el proyecto de la modernidad como un templo del saber; la Nueva Museología lo quiso convertir en un ágora moderna.

No olvidemos que el contenido de los museos se ha formado por medio de un proceso no natural de construcción y legitimación social (Prats, 1998, 63; y 2004), es decir, «(…) es una institución que presenta residuos materiales que, a su vez, representa una imagen ausente» (Andrade, Mellado, Rueda y Villar, 2018: 36). El museo es un proceso cultural y social circunscrito a un sistema económico en un mundo que García Canclini desmenuzaba como heterogéneo, móvil y desterritorializado (2001: 155-156). Esto nos conduce a que esta institución sea –o tenga que ser– un espacio diverso, democrático e inclusivo con las diferentes historias, memorias y voces. De hecho, la última definición que hemos citado anteriormente del museo propuesta por el ICOM se encaminaba en estos términos.

Si bien, deslegitimizar y descolonizar el museo para llegar a esto no es una cuestión de erradicar unas narrativas, sino una idea de incluir aquellas voces acalladas y silenciadas que, por otro lado, han conseguido resistir en el tiempo. No es, por tanto, anular una para sustituirla por otra, sino de incluir, reconocer, asumir y empatizar. Para Hugues de Varine «(...) el museo, para nosotros, es o algo debe ser una de las herramientas lo más altamente posible perfeccionadas que la sociedad tiene disponible para preparar y para acompañar su propia transformación» (1985: 4). Esta idea es la que refleja la fase por la que estaban transitando los museos y su campo disciplinar, la museología, desde la década de los sesenta del siglo XX. El museo como institución decimonónica se transformaba hacia una entidad al servicio de la sociedad.

Andrea analiza en su texto cuatro experiencias que marcaron esta visión actual sobre los museos que educan para la democracia, y una nueva revolución museológica (Mensch, 1992). Su trabajo de investigación se enfocó en el análisis del *Écomusée de la Haute Beauce*, el *Écomusée de la Maison du Fier Monde*, ambos en Canadá; el *Anacostia Neighborhood Museum*, en EE.UU.; y *La Casa del Museo*, en México. Estos casos de estudio son una muestra de los antecedentes del pensamiento museológico que marcó la Nueva Museología y la influencia del nacimiento y expansión de los ecomuseos franceses. Realizó 35 entrevistas, un total de 63 horas de grabación que generaron 800 páginas de transcripciones.

Un trabajo metódico y científico. Las experiencias

La primera «piedra» en la gestación del proyecto del Museo del Barrio de Anacostia tuvo lugar en 1966 cuando el secretario de la Smithsonian Institution, Dillon Ripley consideró poner en funcionamiento un museo vecinal en algún barrio modesto de Washington. La comunidad de Anacostia[6] fue elegida para instalar este museo experimental de barrio

---

[6] El barrio de Anacostia es una comunidad de origen modesto, con una población que oscilaba los doscientos mil habitantes en los años sesenta, ubicado en el extremo sur oriental de Washington D.C. La posibilidad de crear un museo destinado a ayudar a solventar los problemas del vecindario, hizo

por la *Greater Anacostia Peoples* (GAP), una asociación que estaba arraigada en la comunidad y trabajaba para sacar a la comunidad de la marginalidad y de los problemas sociales, culturales y económicos (Kinard, 1985 [1071]: 219). El día 15 de septiembre de 1967, un cine recién reformado abrió sus puertas, esta vez, como el Museo de Barrio de Anacostia. Para su desarrollo y para la movilización de la comunidad será crucial la figura de John Kinard, un profesional de la Smithsonian, que para Seale (1997) abriría los ojos de América a la responsabilidad social de los museos.

La segunda experiencia, la Casa del Museo, tuvo su génesis en las políticas culturales que emanaron del Museo Nacional de Antropología y del Instituto Nacional de Antropología e Historia (INAH) y de la democratización cultural apoyada por movimientos intelectuales asociados a una antropología mexicana crítica (Iniesta, 1999: 116). En los años sesenta el Museo Nacional de Antropología, dependiente del INAH[7], fue uno de los proyectos más importantes de su tiempo. Aparte de su innovadora arquitectura y de su programa museográfico que presentaba las grandes civilizaciones del territorio mexicano, el museo fue creado con la máxima de servir a los escolares del país y favorecer sus sentidos identitarios y sus dignidades. Sin embargo, poco tiempo después de su creación, su director, Mario Vázquez afirmaría:

> El Museo Nacional de Antropología no ha sabido funcionar como habíamos previsto... No está hecho para los verdaderos mexicanos, ni para las gentes del campo y menos para los escolares. A los adinerados y los bien

---

que la población se movilizase para que la Smithsonian realizara el proyecto. Además, esta institución poseía en sus colecciones referencias de la historia de Anacostia con la que empezar a trabajar sobre la construcción de la memoria del barrio (Alexander, 1997: 148).

[7] El Instituto Nacional de Antropología e Historia tenía la particularidad de nacer a finales de los años treinta como una institución pluridisciplinar en la que arquitectos, conservadores, antropólogos, educadores, etc. compartían espacio para planificar las acciones de investigación, educación y comunicación del patrimonio de la nación dando respuesta a la idiosincrasia mexicana (Herreman et al, 1980: 96). La forma de conseguirlo no partía de la simple selección y montaje museográfico sino que se fundamentaba en el acercamiento a las comunidades (rurales y urbanas) con el fin de concienciarlas de la importancia de descubrir su patrimonio, de revalorizar su cultura, de gestionarla, y de ver en este proceso un mecanismo de pedagogía global.

educados de la ciudad les gusta mucho. Más aún el museo se ha convertido en la atracción turística más popular de México. Era necesario rendirse a la evidencia que había sido construido para una finalidad que no podía atender. Habíamos olvidado que los suelos de mármol son demasiado fríos para los pequeños pies desnudos (Cameron, 1992 [1968]: 43).

El INAH iniciaba un proyecto comunitario denominado «La Casa del Museo», dirigido por el propio Mario Vázquez, con el objetivo de integrar el museo en la comunidad por medio de la participación y organización social, y donde las temáticas abordadas respondieran a los intereses y necesidades de la propia comunidad (Méndez, 2008: 7). La Casa del Museo se extendió a varias colonias populares de la Ciudad de México durante ocho años. La metodología de trabajo giraba en torno a la concepción del museo como un apoyo a la solución de los problemas de las comunidades más desfavorecidas. Se pretendía un museo más activo y participativo, más afín a la realidad de las comunidades marginales. En definitiva, un museo en el que se viesen reflejados y les sirviese como un lugar de reflexión crítica sobre ellos mismos y sobre su futuro desarrollo.

El alcance de la Casa del Museo y de la filosofía que se percibía en las políticas museísticas, patrimoniales y educativas mexicanas podemos verlo reflejado en otros proyectos. En 1972 se ponía en marcha el Programa de Museos Escolares, coordinado por el museógrafo Iker Larrauri, con la intención de crear un museo en cada escuela del país.). En 1983, el INAH aglutinó esta experiencia y la Casa del Museo en el Programa para el Desarrollo de la Función Educativa de los Museos (PRODEFEM), formado por un equipo multidisciplinar (antropólogos, historiadores, psicólogos, arquitectos, pedagogos, biólogos, etc.) coordinado por Miriam Arroyo. La herencia de ambas experiencias dio lugar a la base metodológica que desembocó en los museos comunitarios mexicanos y su red nacional, definida en 1993 en el Programa Nacional de Museos Comunitarios (PNMC), en colaboración con el Instituto Nacional de

Antropología e Historia y la Dirección General de Culturas Populares (Méndez, 2008: 7-8).

Las últimas dos experiencias que analizará Andrea corresponden con la tipología de los ecomuseos. La parte francófona de Canadá fue uno de los lugares donde primero calaron los ecomuseos. Desde 1974 se establecieron comunicaciones bilaterales entre los ecomuseos de los Parques Regionales franceses y algunos jóvenes museólogos de Quebec. Georges Henri Rivière fue uno de los intermediarios en algunos de estos encuentros, cuyo resultado fueron documentos, cursos e incluso la propuesta a *Parcs Canada* de adopción de la fórmula del ecomuseo. De este inicio formativo es de donde comenzó la experiencia ecomuseal de Haute-Beauce, convertido oficialmente en ecomuseo en 1983.

Haute-Beauce abarcaba trece parroquias rurales pertenecientes a diferentes distritos federales al sudeste de Quebec, ~~a una distancia geográfica asimilable desde el punto de vista de las comunicaciones, y con una concordancia histórica y socioeconómica (Hauenschild, 1988)~~. El detonante de la experiencia estaba en la colección de objetos etnográficos e históricos pertenecientes a Napoleón Bolduc. En 1978 Bolduc ponía en venta la colección, pero el interés de la administración sería escaso y el conocimiento por parte de la población mínimo. Entre 1978 y 1979 Pierre Mayrand fue buscando apoyos con la idea de crear un equipo con el que formular un proyecto museológico que vinculase la colección y el territorio. En 1979 se funda el *Centro de Interpretación de la Región del Haute-Beauce* (CRIHB), lo que le otorgaba una entidad jurídica a la iniciativa.

Con la creación del museo y centro de interpretación se adoptó un plan de desarrollo quinquenal (1979-1983) para la formación de un ecomuseo basado en el modelo de triangularización (Mayrand, 1983: 25). Se creó, además, un comité de usuarios formado por las trece poblaciones que formaban la región. Hasta ese momento, Pierre Mayrand no había mencionado el concepto de ecomuseo, pero la idea estaba en marcha. En 1982 se produjo el cambio. Existía el miedo de que el museo se convirtiera en una entidad estática, en un museo tradicional, lo que llevó Mayrand a convocar una asamblea para promover la idea de crear un ecomuseo. El Museo y Centro de Interpretación Regional inicial pasó a denominarse *Ecomuseo de la Haute-Beauce*.

Fier-Monde, por su parte, eran los dos distritos más viejos de los de clase obrera situado en el centro sur de Montreal. Un lugar industrial y de transporte importante en los años treinta y cuarenta, pero que tras la II Guerra Mundial comenzaron a cerrar y a mover su ubicación. Entre 1960 y 1980 la población disminuyó cerca de un 50%. De la residente, un 20% se encontraba en paro, un 26% con bajos ingresos y un 20% eran pensionistas. El desempleo y las condiciones sociales demandaban alternativas para salir de dicha situación.

En junio de 1980 se inauguró la *Maison de Fier-Monde* de iniciativa ciudadana prevista para albergar cooperativas residenciales. Aunque fue un proyecto popular global, la iniciativa se ciñó a un grupo pequeño que ocupó una posición especial en la comunidad como resultado de sus conocimientos técnicos. Se formó un Comité para el futuro museo, y en 1982 se cambió el nombre por el de *Ecomuseo de la Maison du Fier-Monde*. El objetivo del proyecto era mejorar la calidad de vida y la autoestima de la población. El ecomuseo intentaba ser un referente para la creación de empleo, potenciando la reconversión industrial y las iniciativas cooperativistas y reclamando mejoras en el entorno urbano y en la calidad de vida de sus habitantes.

Nueva Museología

Andrea inició la investigación de estas experiencias en junio de 1984 y la finalizó en 1988, cuando publicó el manuscrito que presentamos. Estas fechas coinciden justo con la formación y creación del Movimiento Internacional para una Nueva Museología (MINOM). Es el momento en el que se está expandiendo la idea de los ecomuseos y museos comunitarios (y museo de barrio), y el momento en el que la vorágine de acción de experiencias museológicas comunitarias empezará a ser visibilizadas en la literatura especializada, es resumen, su investigación y su texto llegarán en el momento de la reflexión epistemológica de lo que será posteriormente un nuevo campo disciplinar. Andrea será «testigo» de un proceso de una disciplina en construcción. Ella misma se preguntó qué es la Nueva Museología.

Como sucede en la Historia del Arte con cada uno de los momentos innovadores en las manifestaciones artísticas, lo único que hizo la Nueva Museología fue romper el «canon». Por un lado, Andrea constató cómo la Nueva Museología trazaba un discurso desde lo social, lo cultural y lo político, estableciendo modelos prácticos en diferentes comunidades y territorios con unas necesidades socioeconómicas –en ocasiones desfavorables– e identitarias (Hauenschild, 1988: 3). Por otro lado, la ruptura o revolución de la Nueva Museología no era tanto sobre un cambio conceptual de la institución, sino del uso y destino que tenía para las personas (Hauenschild, 1988: 3).

Para comprender esta transformación, Andrea identificó los pilares de lo que sería la Nueva Museología, que se presentan a continuación.

Generar una herramienta útil

> The crucial distinction between the traditional museum and the "new" museum lies in the perception and formulation of a social task aimed at societal development (Hauenschild, 1988: 113).

Los museos de la Nueva Museología se van a entender y constituir como instrumentos prácticos en una búsqueda activa de identidad por parte de grupos poblacionales principalmente marginales. Una forma de cooperación con la comunidad para determinar su relación histórica, presente y posible futura con otros grupos socioculturales, lo que ayuda a generar identidad. Esta característica de trabajar con grupos sociales desfavorecidos y marginados, que posibilita la inclusión de identidades y relatos, difiere de la «oficial», de las élites y de las clases minoritarias pero dominantes (Hauenschild, 1988: 114). El Museo del Barrio de Anacostia, por ejemplo, fue el primer museo en los EE.UU. que se dedicó a la historia, la cultura y los problemas actuales de esa comunidad afroamericana en particular, visibilizándolo por medio de acciones como las exposiciones y los medios museográficos[8].

El «nuevo» museo tenía, por tanto, como objetivo hacer frente a vida diaria precisando problemas y soluciones posibles. Estos museos se convierten en una universidad popular. Esta conceptualización de Andrea aun hoy sigue vigente en el campo de la Museología Social y de la Sociomuseología. En la Declaración de Bogotá del MINOM de 2018 el lema fue: «El museo que no sirve para la vida no sirve para nada»[9].

Institucionalización y espacios de concienciación

> New museology claims that museums should be "grass-rooted," that is, that they should be founded through community effort (Hauenschild, 1988: 117).

Las experiencias analizadas y, en definitiva, las experiencias del entorno de la Nueva Museología no nacieron mediante una decisión técnica, administrativa y/o exógena a la comunidad. El proceso de implementación diferirá de los museos tradicionales. Los especialistas (museólogos, historiadores, educadores, etc.), designados por miembros de la comunidad o por las autoridades locales, o que intervienen por iniciativa propia, tendrán como principal cometido identificar las necesidades y problemáticas comunitarias imperantes (Hauenschild, 1988: 118).

Para preservar este carácter inclusivo enfocado en las vidas de la gente estas entidades se esfuerzan mantener un grado bajo de institucionalización. Pretenderán influenciar a grupos sociales marginales

---

[8] La herramienta principal de este museo fue la exposición. Entre las exposiciones que se organizaron, la que causó mayor impacto por su repercusión social fue La rata, indeseada convidada del hombre, que trataba un problema real del barrio y de la comunidad. Con esta exposición se daba un giro a la concepción y utilidad el museo. Se convertía en la forma de reflejar los problemas de la comunidad y, al mismo tiempo, de proponerles soluciones.

[9] *Declaración de Bogotá* (2018). XIX Conferencia Internacional del Minom, *II Cátedra Latinoamericana de Museología y Gestión del Patrimonio Cultural, I Jornada Latinoamericana de Museología Social.* Accesible en: http://www.minom-icom.net/files/declaracion_de_bogota_minom_2018.pdf.

de modo que estructuren su presente y futuro conforme a sus características culturales específicas. Esto le permite a Andrea conceptualizar estas entidades más allá de los objetivos de instituciones educativas culturales: La comunicación de la identidad y la historia, del conocimiento y de las habilidades es considerada por todos los museos estudiados como paso hacia la realización de la meta más alta del desarrollo social, de cambiar la realidad social de una comunidad.

Autogestión y autarquía

> How the museum is financed affects the degree of influence and control. To be active sponsors of the "new" museum, the community must shoulder some or all of its financial support (Hauenschild, 1988: 121).

La institucionalización lleva implícita una independencia económica que, a su vez, fomente los procesos de autarquía y autogestión. En su análisis Andrea constató que para preservar la independencia las diferentes experiencias se volcarán en potenciar los recursos de la región, las contribuciones de los negocios y actividades económicas locales y las aportaciones de los ciudadanos. Si bien, más allá de esta pretensión, Andrea es consciente de que estos proyectos van a necesitar un impulso gubernamental fuerte para sostenerse. Apuntará: «Comparative analysis of the case studies reveals great differences in methods of financing. The demand for self-financing, particularly in regard to the scope and professional standard of projects, is generally proving to be extremely unrealistic, since we are dealing with financially weak and underprivileged groups. Consideration of the case studies reveals that "new" museums-apart from isolated contributions in kind or money from the community- are largely government financed» (Hauenschild, 1988: 121).

Territorio y descentralización

«Spatial decentralization of «new» museums is a strategy to ensure affinity with the population and to open up opportunities for identification and influence» (Hauenschild, 1988: 123).

En contraste con el museo tradicional, en donde las actividades se circunscriben por norma general a las «cuatro paredes» del edificio de la institución, en los casos analizados se aboga por una estructura espacial descentralizada. El «marcaje» de sus límites no será una delimitación administrativa, sino el resultado de la evolución de las interacciones de los individuos de la comunidad con este marcaje (Mayrand, 2004: 25). En el análisis de Andrea este marcaje se materializará en espacios de identificación identitaria para la comunidad con su patrimonio y su territorio, lo que para Andrea supone un «museo hecho a fragmentos» (Hauenschild, 1988: 125). Un elemento que ofrece a la población un papel activo de formar y participar en el museo.

En este sentido el museo se convertía en un espacio sin límites definidos si no es por la propia comunidad. Los bienes que «acumula», por tanto, no estaban destinados a ser albergados en un edificio, sino que el concepto tradicional de colección ahora se trasladaba y la componía todo aquello que se encontraba en el territorio y pertenecía a la comunidad. Esto convertía el patrimonio y la cultura en una herencia viva, en constante creación y evolución.

Participación e inclusión de la comunidad.

Representatives of new museology reject institutional ordering in the "new" museum. I believe that this is based on a misconception. What one wants to prevent are strictly formulated structures that impede dynamic action. But it cannot be ignored that a museum is basically an institution, that is, a social entity characterized by certain patterns of order and rules and performing specific functions (cf. Hartfiel 1976: 307) (citado en Hauenschild, 1988: 120).

La participación será un punto clave. Andrea fue tan crítica como realista en este aspecto. La participación ciudadana en las experiencias analizadas va a dar un salto cualitativo con respecto a los museos tradicionales. Los «nuevos» museos se sustentarán en organizaciones ciudadanas en las que cualquier persona puede participar, donde cada miembro es un actor principal. Esto requiere una estructura participativa específica que confiera a la población la competencia necesaria para intervenir activamente en el museo.

En el análisis pormenorizado que hace de cada uno de los museos se detallan estos procesos. Por ejemplo, mientras que en la primera *Casa del Museo* la comunidad no tuvo relevancia en la toma de decisiones, en el segundo proyecto, más informal y sin estructura, se implementaron estructura de autogobierno que ya existían en la comunidad para permitir a los residentes, junto con el personal del museo, tener control y determinar qué actividades que se iban a desarrollar. Para Andrea la *Casa del Museo II* fue una forma perfecta de participación y autogobierno para lo que eran las pretensiones de la Nueva Museología.

En el caso del *Museo del Barrio de Anacostia*, este comenzó con un comité fundador informal. Todo ciudadano interesado podía participar, hacer propuestas, opinar sobre los proyectos, etc., es decir, ser parte de la toma de decisiones. Posteriormente, este comité fundador se transformó en un comité asesor del museo, compuesto por representantes de grupos socialmente relevantes y ciudadanos. La problemática para Andrea es que esto sesgaba la participación a una delegación en una representación reducida de la población, pues la ciudadanía no tenía siempre una accesibilidad y competencia sobre estos grupos representantes; así como las propuestas y asesoramientos de este comité no eran vinculantes para la dirección del museo, ni para el propio museo en sí.

En los otros dos casos, el *Ecomuseo de la Maison du Fier-Monde* y el *Ecomuseo de la Haute-Beauce*, ambos se estructuraron mediante una junta directiva, así como comités de usuarios, ejecutivos, etc. Una estructura más compleja, que si bien seguía los preceptos del primer ecomuseo comunitario en el que participó Hugues de Varine. El comité ejecutivo del *Ecomuseo de la Haute-Beauce* originalmente sirvió como enlace entre el museo y la población de Haute-Beauce, y funcionó como tal en los primeros días del ecomuseo. Cuando su vigor inicial se evaporó, las actividades del comité de usuarios se paralizaron gradualmente.

Con esto entramos en otra de las variables: los profesionales, el elemento que restaba para forjar lo que Rivard (1987) denominará una Cultura Crítica en este tipo de proyectos. El papel del que se le transfiere a nuevo profesional de los proyectos comunitarios analizados por Andrea es el de un asesor, consultor y formador que, con el tiempo, será prescindible. La función es la de catalizador y asesor debe ser subrayada por la decisión de no ocupar puestos oficiales del museo, como director o presidente.

Importancia del patrimonio inmaterial, la memoria colectiva

El valor del patrimonio se genera en el uso comunitario y en la comprensión de este como el transmisor de un universo patrimonial (Smith, 2006). La concepción de un patrimonio para la vida, un patrimonio vivido (Varine, 2017). Andrea constató que los trabajo sobre la «memoria colectiva» de autores como Maurice Halbwachs (2004 [1968]) fueron fundamentales. La identificación del patrimonio no es un trabajo únicamente de los técnicos, sino que es un acto de responsabilidad y de concienciación ciudadana. La apropiación patrimonial debe ser un acto que emana del trabajo con la población, lo que permitirá desarrollar sentimientos identitarios y de pertinencia, así como convertirlo en un testimonio del pasado, un elemento para comprender el presente y donde buscar la innovación y transformación hacia el futuro.

Debilidades del contra-poder

¿Qué era realmente esa Nueva Museología? Una pregunta que como hemos visto perseguirá este escrito y que se intenté desgranar con el análisis de las experiencias y el planteamiento de las características y «pilares» de la Nueva Museología.

A lo largo de su investigación y de las reflexiones del material recopilado, Andrea, se dio cuenta de que para los «nuevos museólogos» la conceptualización, sistematización y definición eran un síntoma para que ésta perdiera su dinamismo y la posibilidad de la innovación. Se fundamentaba en métodos de acción y aprendizaje desde la práctica. Si algo es realmente crucial en este documento es la visión crítica, científica, de Andrea.

Andrea constató en los estudios de casos que todos ellos se han posicionado como la antítesis, metamorfosis y evolución de los museos tradicionales, pero que sus teorías y planteamientos estaban aún por desarrollar (Hauenschild, 1988: 138-148). Esto se puede constatar en algunas reflexiones certeras de las debilidades que mostraban esos pilares de la Nueva Museología que ella misma identificó.

Uno de los ejemplos es la descentralización del territorio y la creación de antenas que produjeron en algunos casos resistencia por parte de la ciudadanía, no llegando a ser esos espacios de identificación y marcaje comunitario.

> The Ecomusée de la Maison du Fier-Monde also encountered community resistance in establishing antennas. [...] On the whole, spatial decentralization may work in some cases but cannot be an end in itself. In my view, antennas should not be set up in the initial phase of a museum merely to give the impression, as quickly as possible, of outwardly satisfying a certain museum concept. Antennas appear to be unsuitable as initiators of community sensitization. "New" museums should begin by creating lasting contacts with citizen groups, a move which holds greater promise of sensitization and ensures antennas will be geared to local needs and interests. If antennas are to be more than reminders that a museum exists in the region or neighborhood, they must express the declared will and reflect the identity of the community (Hauenschild, 1988: 123-124).

Algo similar ocurre con la participación ciudadana. En todos los proyectos esta fue disminuyendo hasta ser prácticamente inexistente en algunos casos. El problema para Andrea se encuentra en mantener la movilización social y no caer en lo que denomina «pasividad ciudadana». Para Andrea disponer de una estructura democrática participativa con amplio poder de decisión a disposición de la población no es garantía de que los ciudadanos asuman efectivamente los cargos a los que tienen derecho y sus posibilidades (Hauenschild, 1988: 125). Y se pregunta: ¿Por qué es eso? ¿Cuál es el problema? ¿Qué debe suceder para que la población ejerza su poder de decisión, como pretende la nueva museología? (Hauenschild, 1988: 125). En su opinión, estas experiencias y esta museología no han logrado demostrar su validez o han errado a la hora de comprender a las comunidades. Una de las soluciones que propone es la crear estructuras y espacios que aseguren entornos de participación liderados y gestionados por la propia ciudadanía.

Añadido a esta problemática, Andrea detectó un problema con las relaciones entre especialistas y miembros de la comunidad, aunque en algunos de estos museos hubiera una estructura participativa y democrática

Los especialistas continuaban controlando las acciones diarias y los procesos de toma de decisiones. La mayoría de los proyectos son desarrollados por profesionales y presentados para su aprobación a los órganos que representan a la población. Para Andrea los especialistas no han cumplido su promesa de cooperar en igualdad de condiciones con los representantes de la población (una excepción es la Casa del Museo II). En la práctica, la cooperación entre especialistas y residentes crea desigualdades y jerarquías. Lo que nos indica que la Nueva Museología aún no había sido asimilada.

Para Andrea es necesaria una transformación del profesional: «solo un cambio en el comportamiento y la autoestima del profesional del museo puede remediar este problema», lo que llama un acto de voluntad individual[10]. Para Andrea el museólogo debe: (1) intentar, en primer lugar, compartir sus conocimientos y habilidades con la población; (2) debe conocer los conocimientos y habilidades de la población a través de un proceso de aprendizaje basado en la reciprocidad e incluirlos como un elemento constitutivo de la labor del museo; (3) y debe ser consciente de la constelación de valores e intereses de la comunidad, y debe orientar constantemente su trabajo hacia ellos, respetando a la población y confiándole plena responsabilidad y libertad de decisión, el nuevo profesional de la museología debería estar destinado a impulsar la autoconciencia y la confianza de la comunidad.

Estos son algunos elementos que lleva a Andrea a plantear que la Nueva Museología seguía siendo tradicional pues partía de la concepción decimonónica de considerar al museo como una institución educativa al servicio de la sociedad (Haueschild, 1988: 1 y 53). Sin embargo, fue necesaria para cambiar este mismo registro: el museo ya no debía ser una institución educativa, sino una entidad social.

Construyendo ciencia...y un nuevo lenguaje

El texto de Andrea es un magnífico documento para saber qué fueron las experiencias de la Nueva Museología y en qué fallaron. Supo identificar la esencia y el espíritu de la incipiente Nueva Museología: «The "new" museum wants to make a concrete contribution to coping with everyday life by pointing out problems and possible solutions» (Hauenschild, 1988: 6). Incluso afrontó la complejidad del significado de la utopía de las experiencias de la Nueva Museología: «A question that is frequently heard from all sides is whether the "new"; museum, with its high ideals, is unrealistic and utopian. de Varine writes (no year:5): "On the one hand, I believe that such a radical rethinking is the only

---

[10] En este sentido, la nueva museología muestra interesantes paralelos con la «antropología de la acción», que se basa principalmente en nuevas relaciones respetuosas entre un antropólogo y una población determinada, que colocan al antropólogo radicalmente al servicio de la población en cuestión (Seithel 1986, citado por Hauenschild, 1988).

possible salvation for the museum as a useful factor in the life of Society in the modem world. Utopia is no danger as long as it is aware of itself and inspires positive action with concrete efforts. On the other hand, old and recent experience proves that the above museological principles are practicable and effective". One of the tasks of my research is to investigate, using case studies, how the "new" museum has been realized in various social contexts and how these realizations relate to the claims of new museology, that is, to what extent we are dealing with "concrete utopias"» (Hauenschild, 1988: 14).

De una forma sucinta e indirecta el documento que elaboró Andrea irá fijando una serie de conceptos para el lenguaje del nuevo panorama museológico: inclusión, innovación, concienciación, identidad, democracia, etc. Aunque una de sus grandes dificultades es como aglutinar bajo un mismo denominador común las diferentes experiencias que analiza. El concepto de ecomuseo nació en Francia y se extendió al Canadá francófono; los museos de barrio se desarrollaron en EE.UU., y la Casa del Museo fue el inicio de museos comunitarios; ¿cuál será la nomenclatura más acertada? Andrea lo zanja con el vocablo de «*nuevo*» *museo*. Un vocablo tan laxo como acertado, pues la importancia de la Nueva Museología y de las experiencias que analiza no son el *rótulo*, sino el espíritu, proceso y metodología. Así lo sentencia en el inicio de su texto:

> Basically, I consider the changes in museum practice demanded by new museology, particularly with respect to local and regional museums, to be desirable and, through a scientific study of the relationship of theory to practice, I intend to produce a more precise definition of and solid basis for new museology. This work aims to make new museology accessible and comprehensible, clarify its problem areas and stimulate its practice in order to advance the museum as an educational institution and agent of social change (Hauenschild, 1988: 3).

En este sentido, una de las importancias del documento de Andrea es que se puede considerar el primer texto científico para la Nueva Museología. Como ella misma apunta:

> It cannot be denied that relatively much of the available literature, which consists predominantly of short articles, has–with a few exceptions–a certain propagandistic nature. A body of research, properly speaking, is next to nonexistent. At best, one can speak of a "body of thought," a "collection of ideas." The single longer work on new museology by René Rivard (1984) makes no scientific claims and should be viewed as a general compendium of ideas on the subject. With the exception of the case studies of Gariépy (1986), Céré (1985) and Antúñez et al. (1976), there has been no comprehensive analysis of new museology according to systematic, empirical criteria (Hauenschild, 1988: 10).

Lo cierto es que la Nueva Museología surgió en un momento de cambio social radical por una democratización de la cultura de gran alcance. Tanto por la apuesta por abrir esta democratización como por la frustración de en lo que se iba a convertir es donde encontró su abono el «nuevo» museo y las reivindicaciones del contra-poder de los profesionales de la Nueva Museología. Se basa en el supuesto de que la cultura puede ser tanto el sujeto como el instrumento de un proceso educativo emancipador dirigido hacia el cambio social democrático. El enfoque innovador de la nueva museología para el trabajo de los museos modernos complementa y amplía el de los museos tradicionales (Hauenschild, 1988: 113).

Para Andrea, aunque la nueva museología se originó en el examen de las experiencias prácticas de los museos, no era en sentido estricto una teoría científica derivada de la investigación empírica sistemática; su validez dependía de las condiciones existentes de las comunidades y los territorios. Echa en falta de un esquema dogmático, para hacer que la nueva museología se convierta en una disciplina y metodología útil para quienes están más allá del círculo de sus partidarios.

New museologists worry that when one defines what new museology is, it will lose its dynamic and the scope for innovation. This is, in my view, incomprehensible and unjustified. By refusing to be pinned down, new museologists risk manoeuvring new museology into a dead end and depriving it of criticism and assessment, that is, in the end, preventing change (Hauenschild, 1988: 114).

Lo que detectó Andrea es que para muchos de sus representantes, la nueva museología es un proceso dinámico de creación de formas innovadoras de trabajo museístico. Está menos dirigido al desarrollo de definiciones y teorías que fuertemente orientado a la acción. Las acciones concretas se fundamentan intuitivamente más que racionalmente.

Visión de futuro

De la investigación de Andrea hemos heredado un museo que debe tener su sentido en las relaciones comunales que permitan la pervivencia del patrimonio «y dirigirse hacia la consecución de vidas que merecen ser vividas» (Barcenilla, 2019: 42). El museo, el que ella denominaba «nuevo museo», que construyamos «(…) debe hablarnos de diferentes temporalidades. Debe dejar de dar prioridad a la fracturación de su cronograma a través de exposiciones» (Barcenilla, 2019: 42).

Las experiencias analizadas por Andrea en contextos sociales separados: museos de barrio en los Estados Unidos, museos comunitarios en América latina, particularmente en México, y ecomuseos en Quebec; y la creación de una asociación durante los años 80, el MINOM, configuraban unos planteamientos culturales y políticos más que científicos (Hausenchild, 1988). No obstante, como cualquier otra innovación social el museo que se estaba fraguando debía superar enormes obstáculos. Las palabras proféticas de Andrea nos dejan un futuro en bucle:

Since then, in countless museum conferences, academic lectures and articles, critics have lamented the obsolete character of museums and have questioned the conception museums have of themselves and their right to exist. But, in fact, museums appear to be surviving the crisis. Instead of the feared closing of museums, headlines announce new openings. Here the question inevitably arises: Have museums changed so that they enjoy increasing popularity? One thing is sure: museum people, under the pressure of events and in reaction to vehement criticism, have awakened from their torpor and are trying hard to make changes. Yet, even today many museums still consider their primary role to be that of "preservation institutions." This view is reflected in the museological literature, which is largely devoted to conservation, restoration and security (Hauenschild, 1988: 2).

El tiempo ha ido dando respuestas al texto de Andrea, construyendo un relato teórico, conceptual y científico de la Nueva Museología. La trayectoria de los planteamientos y la filosofía de la Nueva Museología han ido acuñando nuevos apelativos: museología comunitaria, sociomuseología, altermuseología, ecomuseología, etc.; en lo que acabo siendo la denominación no oficial de «nuevas museología» (Díaz Balerdi, 2010).

En la actualidad, la Nueva Museología sigue viva. En Portugal, la Universidad Lusófona de Lisboa posee un departamento especializado en formación en sociomuseología[11], donde no solo se apoya con la práctica de una museología social a los museos portugueses, sino que se ha implementado formación (grado, máster y doctorado) e investigación en este campo. En Italia se han potenciado la idea antrópica del paisaje (humano y/o cultural), pero también los aspectos legislativos, creando normativas específicas para regular y potenciar los ecomuseo[12]. En el continente asiático los ecomuseos están en expansión y comienzan un tejido asociativo, así como de investigación y reflexión[13]. En países latinoamericanos el desarrollo de la museología comunitaria se ha ido afianzando con la creación de redes, como la *Associação Brasileira de Ecomuseus e Museus*

---

[11] Véase: https://www.ulusofona.pt/doutoramento/museologia [Consultado el 14/01/2022].
[12] Se recomienda consultar la red Mondi Locali – Local Worlds: http://www.ecomusei.eu/mondilocali/ [Consultado el 14/01/2022].
[13] Un ejemplo lo encontramos en la *Japan Ecomuseological Society (JECOMS)*: http://www.jecoms.jp/ [Consultado el 14/01/2022].

Communitãrios (ABREMC)[14], la *Unión Nacional de Museos Comunitarios y Ecomuseos de México*[15] o *la Red Museos Comunitarios de América Latina y El Caribe*[16]. Y a nivel internacional, aparte del MINOM, la red que actúa como «observatorio» de experiencias comunitarias la *Red Internacional de Ecomuseos y Museos Comunitarios DROPS*[17].

Nuestra sociedad continúa manifestando desigualdades sociales (género, migración, derechos humanos, (post)colonialismo, etc.) y económicas (distribución desigual de los recursos), en un sistema que jerarquiza los derechos sociales en función de parámetros economicistas y simbólicos. Un sistema neoliberal que potencia una sociedad educada para el consumo y la renta. No obstante, el panorama vivo que hemos reflejado de la Nueva Museología (la Museología Social y la Sociomuseología) está haciendo que sea una realidad el desarrollo de acciones –teóricas y prácticas– para generar diálogos y miradas críticas que hagan que los museos sean capaces de afrontar los retos del siglo XXI[18]. El objetivo final es conseguir que estas entidades contribuyan a hacer un mundo mejor, con seres humanos concienciados y educados para la democracia.

Debemos mirar y leer el texto de Andrea como el inicio de un camino que no tendría retorno. Su investigación abrió una puerta para construir una disciplina social de los museos, y poder aprender y mejorar las debilidades que tuvieron experiencias innovadoras de aquellos años convulsos, fecundos y utópicos para el patrimonio, la cultura y los museos.

Referencias

ALEXANDER, E. (1997). *The Museum in America. Innovators and pioneers.* London, New Delhi: Altamira Press, Wolnut Creek, published in Cooperation with The American Association for State and Local History.

---

[14] Véase: http://www.abremc.com.br/ [Consultado el 14/01/2022].
[15] Véase: https://www.gob.mx/cultura [Consultado el 14/01/2022].
[16] Véase: https://www.museoscomunitarios.org/ [Consultado el 14/01/2022].
[17] Véase: https://sites.google.com/view/drops-platform/home [Consultado el 14/01/2022].
[18] Estos retos quedaron fijados en la *Declaración Lugo-Lisboa* emanada del XX Taller Internacional del Minom: http://www.minom-icom.net/files/declaracion_lugo-lisboa_gal_es_pt.pdf.

ANDRADE P., MELLADO L., RUEDA H., y VILLAR G. 2018. *El Museo Mestizo. Fundamentación Museológica para cambio de guion*. Santiago de Chile: Éd. Museo Histórico Nacional.

BARCENILLA, H. (2019). Rethinking the museum from life. In *Diferents. Revista de museus* núm. 4, 2019, pp. 28-43.

BODEI, R. (1996). Tumult of frozen creatures, or on the logic of museums. In *Revista de Occidente* n° 177/1996, pp. 21-35.

Delated because not quoted in the text:

CAMERON, D. (1992 [1968]). Un point de vue : le musée considéré comme système de communication et les implications de ce système dans les programmes éducatifs muséaux. In DESVALLÉES, A. (org.). BARY, M. and WASSERMAN, F. (eds.). *Vagues: une anthologie de la nouvelle muséologie*. Mâcon: Editions W. vol. 1, pp. 77-98. DÍAZ BALERDI, I. (2010). *Imaginary archipelagos. Museums of the Autonomous Community of the Basque Country*. Urduliz (Biscay): Editorial Nerea, Servicio Central de Publicaciones del Gobierno Vasco, Administración de la Comunidad Autónoma del País Vasco.

GARCÍA CANCLINI, N. (2001). *Culturas híbridas: estrategias para entrar y salir de la modernidad*. Buenos Aires: Paidós.

GRUZINSKI, S (2000). *El pensamiento mestizo*. Barcelona: Paidós.

HALBWACHS, M. (2004 [1968]). La memoria colectiva. Zaragoza: Prensa Universitaria de Zaragoza.

HAUENSCHILD, A. (1988). Claims and Reality of New Museology: Case Studies in Canada, the United States and Mexico, Dissertation for the Degree of Doctor of Philosophy of the University of Hamburg

HERREMAN, Y.; GÓNZALEZ DE LA MORA, S.; and SCHMIDHUBER, G. (1980). Mexico: Museums 1972-1980. In *Museum*, vol. XXXII, n° 3, pp. 92-107.

ICOM (2019). The museum definition. The backbone of museums. In *Museum International*, vol. 71, n. 281-282.

INIESTA GONZÁLEZ, M. (1999). Museos locales, patrimonios globales. in VV. AA. *Patrimonio Etnológico. New perspectives of study*. Granada, Cuadernos del Instituto Andaluz del Patrimonio Histórico, Consejería de Cultura de la Junta de Andalucía, pp. 110-127.

KINARD, J. (1985 [1971]). The neighbourhood museum, catalyst for social change. in *Museum*, n°. 4, pp. 217-223.

MAYRAND, P. (1983). Les défis d'écomusée : un cas. celui de la Haute-Beauce. In *Symposium International for Museology. Museum - Territory - Society. New tendencies / New Practices. Addenda*, ICOFOM-ICOM, pp. 23-27.

MAYRAND, P. (2004). *Haute-Beauce. Psycholosociologie d'un écomusée*. Cadernos de Sociomuseologia, n° 22, Lisbon: Centro de Estudos de Sociologia, Universidade Lusófona de Humanidades e Tecnologias.

MÉNDEZ LUGO, A. (2008). *Map of the situation of community museums in Mexico. Report for UNESCO*. Unpublished document.

MENSCH, P. V. (1992). *Towards a Methodology of Museology*. University of Zagreb, Faculty of Philosophy, doctoral thesis.

NUSSBAUM, M. (2012). *Non-profit. Why democracy needs the humanities*. Buenos Aires: Katz editores.

PRATS, Ll. (1998). El concepto de patrimonio cultural. *Política y sociedad, 27*(1), pp.63-76.

PRATS, Ll. (2004). *Antropología y Patrimonio*. Barcelona: Ariel.

RIVARD, R. (1987). Muséologie et cultures. In *Actas del IV Taller Internacional del Movimiento para la Nueva Museología (MINOM)*, Molinos (Spain), document SIGNUD, cota, doc. 1987-005-03. Lusophone University.

SEALE, W. (1997). Foreword. In ALEXANDER, E. (ed.). *The Museum in America. Innovators and pioneers.* London, New Delhi: Altamira Press, Wolnut Creek, published in Cooperation with The American Association for State and Local History, pp. 9-12.

SMITH, L. (2006). *Uses of heritage.* New York: Routledge.

VARINE, H. de (1985). Notes en forme d'avant-propos. In NICOLAS, A. (ed.). *Nouvelles Muséologies. Muséologie Nouvelle et experimentation sociale.* Marseille: M.N.E.S. pp.3-4.

VARINE, H. de (2017). *L'écomusée singulier et pluriel. Un témoignage sur cinquante ans de muséologie communautaire dans le monde.* Paris: L'Harmattan.

In memoriam

Dr. Herbert Ganslmayr 1937-1991

Acknowledgments

In connection with my work as a museum ethnologist at the Übersee Museum in Bremen I asked myself the question – prompted by Dr. Herbert Ganslmayr, Director of the Übersee. Museum – whether and how local and regional museums as adult educational institutions could contribute to societal development, that is, to coping with everyday life and to improving the conditions of life. In my exploratory research on this subject, which I carried out at the ICOM/UNESCO documentation center in Paris, I "discovered" new museology, a trend in modern museology in which the concept of the museum appeared to hold an answer to my question and which I have therefore made the subject of a detailed study within the framework of my doctoral work in the field of ethnology.

The new conception of the Übersee Museum and my practical work for the Übersee Museum form the basis of my museological background, which, together with systematic ethnology as a basic science for the study of culture, has determined the genesis and orientation of this work. My particular thanks go to Dr. Herbert Ganslmayr, who has had a decisive influence on my professional career, introduced me to museum work and finally stimulated and supported the present work. I wish to thank Dr. Ganslmayr for exposing me to new ways and new possibilities for working independently and gathering experience in the field of museology.

My very special thanks also go to Prof. Jürgen Jensen of Hamburg University, who was my supervisor until the time of my master's examination and who in this way has had a crucial influence on my studies as an ethnologist. I wish to thank Prof. Jensen for his interest in the present work and for his untiring support and constant readiness to advise me.

This work would not have been possible without my colleagues and interviewees in Quebec (Canada), the United States and Mexico. I wish to thank them for their interest, their extraordinary readiness to cooperate, their remarkable hospitality and the support they bestowed on my research work. My particular thanks go to René Rivard for arranging numerous contacts.

I wish to thank my friends and colleagues Dr. Sibylle Benninghoff-Lühl, Dr. Thomas Labahn, Johannes Sommerfeld (M.A.) and Dr. Andreas Köchert for their readiness to talk with me, their critical spirit and the important suggestions concerning the present work.

Special thanks go to Madame Anne Rafin, director of the UNESCO-ICOM Documentation Center in Paris, for her friendly and tireless help in obtaining literature. Moreover, I wish to thank Monique Bonneau and Clara Valverte for help with transcription and for proof reading the parts of the work not in German. I wish to thank my former teacher, Mr. Klaus Papies, and Dr. Thomas Labahn for their willingness to proof read the German manuscript.

From the beginning of this work in June 1984 until its completion I received a grant from the Konrad Adenauer Foundation (Institute for Educational Excellence, Division of Graduate Support). I wish to thank the Konrad Adenauer Foundation for supporting my work, and especially Mr. Konrad S. Krieger.

Finally, I wish to thank with all my heart my parents, my sister and my friends and colleagues, who stood beside me in word and deed in the course of this work and, in particular, found words of support time and again.

My particularly heartfelt thanks go to my companion in life, Jean-François Mercier, who has supported me in my endeavors in every respect and whose kind and critical sympathy has contributed to the successful outcome of this work.

While I wish to thank all the people named for the various forms of stimulus they gave to the present work, I wish to state explicitly that I alone am responsible for any errors and omissions.

Hamburg, January 11, 1988 Andrea Hauenschild

1. INTRODUCTION

New museology[1] is an idea of the museum as an educational tool in the service of societal development (de Varine, 1985, p. 4): "[...] the museum, for us, is, or rather should be, one of the most highly perfected tools that society has available to prepare and accompany its own transformation."

At the center of this idea of a museum lie not things, but people (cf. de Varine, 1976b, p. 127). Although it is described as "new"[2] and must be considered a phenomenon of the seventies and eighties, new museology actually follows the tradition among museum people dating back to the nineteenth century of considering the museum as an educational institution in the service of society.

In 1971, at the Ninth General Conference of the International Council of Museums, Stanislas Adovéti, a philosopher and author from the People's Republic of Benin, with the approval of the Mexican Mario Vásquez, pointed out the precarious situation of the museum (cf. Adovéti, 1972; de Varine, 1978b, p. 29). He believed that the museum as an institution would either have to change radically or lose its right to exist and sooner or later disappear.

Since then, in countless museum conferences, academic lectures and articles, critics have lamented the obsolete character of museums and have questioned the conception museums have of themselves and their right to exist. But, in fact, museums appear to be surviving the crisis. Instead of the feared closing of museums, headlines announce new openings. Here the question inevitably arises: Have museums changed so that they

---

[1] The term "new museology" used here is a translation of the commonly used French and Spanish terms "nouvelle muséologie" and "nueva museologia."
[2] In this regard, it should be noted that this idea was developed definitively by French museologists and is, in fact, relatively "new" in the context of centralized French museum work.

enjoy increasing popularity? One thing is sure: museum people, under the pressure of events and in reaction to vehement criticism, have awakened from their torpor and are trying hard to make changes[3]. Yet, even today many museums still consider their primary role to be that of "preservation institutions." This view is reflected in the museological literature, which is largely devoted to conservation, restoration and security.

Characteristic of the current controversies on museum work are the contrasting comments on the meaning and purpose of a museum in a recent issue of the journal Muse, published by the Canadian Museums Association (vol. 5./ 1987 (1)). White Graham-Bell (1987, p. 5) emphasizes "that the care of collections is the primary duty" (cf. Edwards, 1987), Sheila Stevenson (1987, p. 30) states that the museum is in the first place a social institution and that the opinion "that the object is sacred and that treasure houses, shrines and other such beautified places are the only true museums, is an approach that simply doesn't work for many museum workers or the public" (cf. Weil, 1986, p. 25-27).

In his remarks on the "prehistory" of new museology, de Varine (1978b, p. 29), Secretary General of the International Council of Museums (ICOM) from 1965 to 1974, noted the discouragement of museologists in the course of their attempts to change the museum, since all efforts to modernize the museum and achieve cultural relevance had failed to catch on: "[...] the most enterprising and innovative museologists throughout the world had lost their illusions: the museum as an institution devoted to tradition was in the course of dying, despite the efforts being made on all sides to invent a future for it."

Varine (1978b, p. 29) argued further in this regard that the modernization of museum architecture, display technology and research on target groups led to a tremendous increase in costs and

---

[3] These changes are expressed, among other features, in the modified definition of the museum put out by the International Council of Museums in 1974 (ICOM, 1974, p.1): "The museum is a permanent non-profit institution, open to the public, *in the service of society and its development*, which does research on the material evidence of man and his environment, acquires such evidence, preserves it, communicates it and, in particular, displays it for the purpose of study, education and enjoyment." [Emphasis added]

commercialization, without changing the quality of the museum visit and motivating city residents – with the exception of captive public-school classes – to increase museum visitation (cf. de Varine, 1987b, pp. 1-2).

Dissatisfied with attempts to reform traditional museums, museologists in various countries looked for possibilities to change radically the working methods, content and structure of an institution that some thought outmoded. The purpose was to help museums achieve social meaning, less in the sense of recognition and increased attendance, but more in regard to the museum's concrete contributions to everyday life. These considerations finally led to the creation and testing of new forms of the museum. Three parallel developments occurred, independent of one another and in separate social contexts: neighborhood museums in the United States, integral museums in Latin America, particularly in Mexico, and ecomuseums in France and Quebec (cf. chap. 2).

A consequence of the protest against and attempt to change established, stagnating, museum practice was the formation during the 1980s of an association of museum workers called the International Movement for New Museology (MINOM). The group consists of museologists who came together to explore ideas of the "new" museum as a democratic, educational institution in the service of social development (particularly at the local and regional levels).

Baron (1987, p. 1) specifies the thrust of new museology as follows: "[...], this new active or community museology resolutely challenges the museum as an institution, the omnipotence and omniscience of the curators, the domination of the fine arts over all other disciplines, aesthetic pleasure as the essential criterion of an object's value, the absolute precedence of objects over life and the abiding nature of the history and values of an elite that turns to its profit the resources of the planet, the creativity of its inhabitants and taxes of its fellow citizens."

Of course, distinctions must be made, in particular, that the "new" museum does not see itself as an alternative to the established museum but as a supplement opening up new dimensions. Although a systematic and detailed comparison is not possible here, in fact, new museology shares much with traditional museology. Many modem museums–particularly local and regional museums, folk-art museums and natural history museums–follow ideas similar to those of new museology[4]. What is new about the "new" museum lies less in its individual elements than in its overall concept.

The discourse of new museology is essentially cultural and political, not scientific. de Varine (1983b: no page no.) admits to the difficulty of defining the essential features of new museology: "There are no established rules or models, just theories that have been immediately belied by practice." Correspondingly, questions related to the nature and theory of new museology have been avoided, as Michel Roy (1987, p. 8) emphasizes: "These practices are characterized by a refusal to develop a precise museological model, a practice based on a precise theory. Exploration and experimentation are still underway."

It cannot be denied that relatively much of the available literature, which consists predominantly of short articles, has–with a few exceptions–a certain propagandistic nature. A body of research, properly speaking, is next to non-existent. At best, one can speak of a "body of thought," a "collection of ideas." The single longer work on new museology by René Rivard (1984a) makes no scientific claims and should be viewed as a general compendium of ideas on the subject. With the exception of the case studies of Gariépy (1986), Céré (1985) and Antúñez et al. (1976), there has been no comprehensive analysis of new museology according to systematic, empirical criteria.

A first attempt to relate the claims and reality of new museology to each other and to subject them to a comprehensive, critical analysis will be undertaken in the present research work. Basically, I consider the changes in museum practice demanded by new museology, particularly with respect to local and regional museums, to be desirable and, through

---

[4] The wide spectrum of discussions of so-called traditional museology is clear, for example, in the publications of the International Commission for Museology (ICOFOM) (cf. ICOFOM, 1980, 1983, 1987; cf. also Sola, 1987).

a scientific study of the relationship of theory to practice, I intend to produce a more precise definition of and solid basis for new museology. This work aims to make new museology accessible and comprehensible, clarify its problem areas and stimulate its practice in order to advance the museum as an educational institution and agent of social change.

The plan of the "new" museum in chapter 2 is a theoretical construct, an ideal type, in which the claims of new museology are put to the test. The hypothesis that the "new" museum is feasible leads to testing these claims against the reality of museums generally classified as examples of new museology. For this purpose, I carried out a series of empirical case studies (cf. Aleman and Ortlieb, 1975), which form the central element of the present work and are dealt with in detail in chapter 3.

The following museum projects were selected as case studies: the Ecomusée de la Haute Beauce, musée territoire, Haute-Beauce, Quebec, Canada; the Ecomusée de la Maison du Fier Monde, Montreal, Quebec, Canada; the Anacostia Neighborhood Museum, Washington, D.C., the Casa del Museo project, Mexico; the Program for the Development of the Educational Function of the INAH Museums, Mexico.

These examples represent varied applications of new museology. Each project shows peculiarities that distinguish it from the others.

The main emphasis was intentionally placed on a qualitative investigation of the individual aspects of new museology. Data derived from intensive structured, non-standardized interviews and research of the literature and documents.

In total I interviewed 35 individuals for a total of 63 hours, recorded on tape cassettes. Transcribed word for word, the interviews produced 800 pages of written text. The questions addressed the development of the museum project, each country's system of museum practice and the personal experiences, assessments, views and judgments of the respondents. A wealth of material on new museology emerged from the interviews that differs considerably from the "official" discourse of publications and conferences.

Of course, the bulk of the data reflects the specific conditions of each museum during the period of investigation. However, an effort was made to clarify the course of the museum's development over a longer period of time. Current data were produced through interview questions related to the previous conditions of the museum being studied and by maintaining personal contact with the informants throughout the two-and-a-half-year evaluation phase.

2. ELEMENTS OF NEW MUSEOLOGY

The representatives of new museology have made only limited attempts to systematize their prior experiences and develop definitions[5]. Since 1986, however, a working group of MINOM members (Jean-Claude Duelos, Eulalia Janer, Mário Moutinho, Girard Colling, Marc Maure) has published a paper outlining the principles of new museology. In it, Duelos et al. (1986) distinguish the objectives and means of new museology from its missions and functions (Duelos et al., 1987). As a first attempt (Duelos et al., 1986), the authors classified as objectives the following elements of new museology: a global view of reality; research that satisfies social requirements; action that is continually adapted to a population and its territory; and an approach, research and actions that contribute to individual and social development. The same work (Duelos et al., 1986) also identified the means of new museology as follows: collection, conservation, research (interdisciplinarity), exhibition and museum education (participation).

I will, therefore, attempt (of course, with no claim to "final truth") to specify the ideal type of the "new" museum, relying on the statements of practitioners of new museology.

With regard to the general definition of the museum as an institution, I consider that the following constituent elements should be distinguished: objectives ("objectifs" or "missions" in Duelos et al. 1986; 1987), basic principles, and structure and organization, approach, and tasks ("moyens" or "fonctions" in Duelos et al. 1986; 1987).

According to new museology, the "new" museum is defined by its socially relevant objectives and basic principles. Its work as an educational

---

[5] However, Rivard (1984a) gives a good overview; some broad outlines also appear in the Document de travail (1984) and in the Groupe de Recherche en Patrimoine (1983). Stevenson (1987, p. 31) and Lacouture (1987, p. 21) compare traditional and new museology.

institution is directed toward making a population aware of its identity, strengthening that identity, and instilling confidence in a population's potential for development. In this regard, Maure (1985a, p. 17) writes: "A museum is a means, a tool available to a society to find, give form to, mark, demarcate its identity, i.e., its territory and its frontiers in time and space, with respect to other societies and other social and cultural groups."

Rivard (1984a, p. 13f) and Taborsky (1978, p. 22f; 1982:1-9, cf. Taborsky, 1985) speak of this connection of identity as the totality of images that a group has of itself, its past, present and future. The role of the museum is, first and foremost, to put a population in a position that will enable it to visualize, be aware of and name these images, which are manifested at the material and non-material levels in everyday life. Taborsky (1978, p. 23) speaks in this regard of the important role of the museum in the process of "positive imagizing." The business of museums must be to realize a population's right "[...] to imagize, to name, to define what objects are, as locally perceived; to define what the local needs are, and the objects which meet those needs."[6]

By identifying and naming the material and non-material elements that constitute their environment, people realize their right to their own local and regional identity, they take possession of their world and gain a certain control over it (cf. Maure 1985a:21). Museums consciously take up the search for identity. However, the objective of the "new" museum goes beyond the formation of identity. The "new" museum wants to make a concrete contribution to coping with everyday life by pointing out problems and possible solutions. Museums as educational institutions can contribute to a population's consciousness of its neighborhood or region

---

[6] In his feasibility study for the museum of the Inuit in Inukjuak, Quebec, Rivard (1985a, p. 17) wrote: "A museum can play a vital role in helping a society to define its present reality, collecting the images that it readily has and exhibiting/communicating these images to the people. When the museum is actively engaged in presenting and discussing the present and local images-as some do-it is a prime method for helping a people to gain control over their activities, to clarify the issues of actuality, to discuss concerns, and to gather vitality and self-identity. With the help of an active museum/cultural centre, Inuit society can readily deal with its social and economic conditions. But the first step is to imagize them. And the museum is able to involve people with imagizing not only the past but also the present and the future, with imagizing not only what is beautiful and traditional, but also social concerns, current existence, economic situations, society in general."

(cf. chapter 2) and act upon it in a formative way. Putting the theoretical model into words, de Varine (no year, p. 4) described the "new" museum as a kind of people's university: "[...]: the place which can and must mirror the questions which individuals and social groups are asking themselves-not to supply answers, but to state the problems, point to alternatives, and offer materials and information to assist them to realize and decide what attitudes to take up."

By attaining the immediate goals of forming identity and coping with everyday life, the "new" museum strives to influence the integrated development of a region and its population (Document de travail, 1984, p. 4).

The radical expansion and application of the principles of public orientation and territoriality, as the fundamental principles of the "new" museum, follow from the goal of service to society (cf. de Varine, no year, p. 4)[7]. If a museum really wants to initiate identity-forming and development-relevant work within the context of a given population, it must orient itself to the local conditions and to the specific interests and needs of that population. The "new" museum may not isolate itself from society in a self-sufficient manner, but rather must open itself outward to society, in order to have an effect on the public.

The far-reaching orientation to the public for which the "new" museum strives, requires that its potential public be identified. Here the basic principle of territoriality comes into play. The "new" museum relates to a clearly demarcated territory and its population. These are defined by cultural and natural boundaries (for example, a city, a neighborhood, a cultural and geographical region), rather than tied to given administrative divisions (Rivard 1984a, p. 50). The function of strongly defining the museum's relationship to its locality provides meaning to the public (Bellaigue-Scalbert, 1983, p. 35)[8].

---

[7] Particularly the works of Rivard (1981, 1983b, 1984a, 1984b).
[8] So that the "new" museum may avoid reactionary nostalgia for homeland and self admiration, an additional element must be added to its sense of locality: openness to the outside, i.e., expansion of local and regional horizons through correlations and dependencies linking homeland to the outer world on the national and international levels. The representatives of new museology have specifically referred to the danger of idealization (cf. Hubert, 1985, p. 189).

Based on the objectives and basic principles of the "new" museum, representatives of new museology have developed a view as to what a museum – its structure, approach and tasks – should be, and this view will be examined below.

In order to preserve its experimental character and maintain the greatest possible openness to the constantly changing reality of people's lives, the "new" museum strives to maintain a low degree of institutionalization. Neither the spatial nor the organizational structure is fixed. Employees are engaged on the basis of time-limited contracts so that the staff may be continually renewed (cf. de Varine, 1978b, p. 37). Rivard (1984a, p. 38) understands the "new" museum as a dynamic movement rather than a fixed institution: "A fortiori, movement and institutionalization are opposed to each other, since movement itself will be threatened by death if it is 'put in a box', as in the long run this will remove its dynamism, its popularity, its centrifugal force."

In order to preserve independence, the "new" museum' s budget depends, as much as possible, on the resources of the region. That includes museum funds generated through contributions from local businesses and citizens. State subsidies make up the difference in the required budget (cf. de Varine, 1978b, p. 37; Rivard 1985b, p. 204).

In contrast to the traditional museum, where activities are limited as a rule to the "four walls" of the museum building, the "new" museum advocates a decentralized spatial structure. It marks its territory by creating so-called identification markers. The Document de travail (1984, p. 4) states: "New museology proposes to remove barriers in different ways: to go into environments not favorable to museums, to extend the museum throughout an area, to make sporadic excursions into non-museum environments, to give shows before neglected publics, to distribute the museum throughout homes, families and other social and productive cells (hospitals, factories, people's houses)." Because of this spatial branching and splitting, the "new" museum is often referred to as "fragmented museum."

A crucial element in the structure and organization of the "new" museum is that it offers the population an active role in shaping and participating in the museum (cf. Rivard, 1984a, pp. 48- 50). The work of the "new" museum is based on the knowledge and energy of the "living forces" of the population and thus includes the public in its various activities. Ideally the museum will be supported by the public itself and the population will at the same time be the actor and object of the museum's work (Rivard 1984a, p. 16).

This form of museum work, which is distinguished by public participation, is described by representatives of new museology as "people's museography."[9] As to the position of the visitor, the Document de travail states (1984, p. 5): "Collective memory, social subjects and creative movement completely change the concept of the museum visitor. Contemplation and intellectual pleasure are supplanted by the participation and involvement of the visitor, who in this way becomes an integral part of the new museum in place of being merely a guest: Through his knowledge and his living forces he is called upon either to participate in the museum adventure itself or to involve himself in the sociocultural and even economic development of his territory. He is no longer a visitor; he becomes a decision-maker, an actor, a museographer and an agent of multiplication."

The "new" museum has an organizational structure geared to the greatest possible inclusion and participation of the community. The museum is linked and accountable to an association of citizens who meet in a general assembly to approve the museum's annual programming. There residents choose representatives for the board of directors. The board advises the museum personnel between general meetings. The population is offered further possibilities for active participation by joining various working groups.

---

[9] Rivard (1984a, p. 84) defines "people's museography" as ". . . a body of techniques and practices applied by a population to the conservation and enhancement, in a museum or otherwise, of the collective heritage of the community and its territory."

The team of museum employees (both salaried and volunteer) consists in so far as possible of citizens of the neighborhood or region. They acquire the necessary skills through practical museum work, through participation in special courses in people's museology and through periods of practical training in other "new" museums. Scientific and technical personnel and the active public cooperate as equals in the areas of conception, programming, production and evaluation. There is no hierarchical decision-making structure within the museum.

Beyond the specific elements of structure and organization, the "new" museum – in contrast to the usually specialized traditional museum – is distinguished by an integrated and integral approach to reality. French-speaking scholars frequently refer to this element as the "system approach" (Maure, 1977/78, p. 33). Human activity is dealt with as part of a complex whole.

This "new" view of reality (cf. for example de Rosnay, 1975; Morin, 1977; 1980; Terradas, 1983) requires an interdisciplinary approach to museum work. Maure (1985a, p. 21) comments: "Another central aspect of these "new museums" is the importance accorded to the ecological perspective. The traditional specialization between different disciplines, such as art, ethnology, history, natural sciences etc., is replaced by an interdisciplinary approach that puts the accent on the relationships between man and his environment."

The work of the "new" museum is theme-centered, in distinction to predominantly object oriented, traditional museum work. The themes to be addressed arise from the "collective memory" and from contemporary needs.

The approach followed by the "new" museum also includes not only recording, documenting, conserving, and investigating the past, i.e., the cultural and natural heritage, but also making the museum usable for coping with the present. This is done by giving the past value and viewing it with critical awareness. Conservation and development are not treated as antithetical, but as integral components of an evolutionary process (cf. Collin, 1985, p. 1).

In order to enhance its outward-directed effectiveness, the "new" museum actively engages and cooperates with a region's already existing institutions (cf. Rivard, 1984a, pp. 58-61).

The tasks ("means" or "functions" in Duelos, et al. 1986; 1987) that the "new" museum performs are set by themselves to achieve the desired objectives. The descriptions of these tasks – collection, documentation, research, conservation, public programs – correspond to a great extent with those of traditional museums. But in the "new" museum, "continuing education" and "evaluation" are added to the list of tasks. However, fundamental differences exist in the interpretation of the tasks. Two of the primary functions of a museum are generally the collection and conservation of a given heritage. In the case of the traditional museum, these activities are directed to recording as completely as possible the available inventory of artifacts. In the "new" museum, the stress of collection and conservation activities is placed on the non-material cultural heritage. In this regard, the Document de travail (1984, p. 3) states: "All knowledge, all historical and social perceptions, all testimony become subjects and objects of conservation."

Practitioners of new museology use the expression "collective memory" to define the totality of a group's non-material heritage. "Collective memory" comes from the work of Maurice Halbwachs (1950). In the "new" museum, only the material goods that possess information and communication value relative to the collective memory are collected and conserved (Document de travail, 1984, p. 3): "[...] material goods become part of the heritage only as a function of the needs of this collective memory, either to illustrate, or to keep a representation that is real rather than imaginary, or to seize the future."

Objects without meaning for the "collective memory" are not treated as part of the heritage. This means that identifying an area's cultural heritage is not determined in the first place by scholars, as is the case in traditional museums, but rather it is the collective memory of the population of a given region that determines the heritage to be preserved.

That which is alive today in human memory, significant and useful in the present determines heritage (cf. Rivard 1984a, pp. 46-48).

The "new" museum does not conserve for conservation's sake, but proceeds from the requirements of the present (Bellaigue-Scalbert, 1983, p. 38). Thus, the job of the "new" museum is first of all to collect, keep and study the elements of this collective memory, which is manifested in individual testimony. The "new" museum forms collections in the sense of placing objects in museums only to a limited degree. The emphasis of collection activity is placed rather on forming an extensive data-bank that records the natural and cultural inventory or heritage of a community and its territory (cf. de Varine no year, p. 2f; Querrien, 1985, p. 199). Everything that exists is interpreted as part of a system of interactions that humans form with their natural and cultural environments. The inventoried heritage is available to everyone. If possible, it is left in situ and kept in its original context. In this regard, de Varine (no year:3) states the following: "this means that the museum as bank of things must burst its bounds to include-in spatial terms-the whole of its community; and the real things which it accumulates must not be in effect laid aside in a building dedicated to this purpose, but must count as virtually and scientifically belonging to the museum collection, though without having to give up their physical location or their usefulness."

Only a limited number of objects, which, in some way, are deemed representative, significant, aesthetically interesting, rare or delicate, are acquired and conserved. This assures that they are preserved and remain accessible as part of the public heritage (cf. de Varine, no year, p. 3)[10]. Elsewhere (1979, p. 83) de Varine describes the significance of the collection for the "new" museum: "The *collection* is composed of everything this territory has and everything that belongs to its inhabitants, both real and personal property, material or non-material goods. This is a living heritage, constantly changing and constantly being created, belonging essentially to individuals, families, small collectives, which a

---

[10] Regarding collection policy, cf. Veillard (1985).

motivation and research team can use as needed for all kinds of actions. The acquisition of fragments of this heritage is not programmed and takes place in effect only in the case of abandonment, risk of alienation prejudicial to the community, voluntary gift or definitive use for another purpose. It is only a last resort and the collection proper of the museum, in the institutional sense, cannot be an end in itself." [emphasis added]

Just as collection and conservation refer to the needs of a given population, so too is research into the inventoried and conserved heritage not conducted as an end in itself. Research problems stem from social reality with solutions geared to coping with everyday life and shaping community. The starting point of research is the concrete social conditions and requirements upon which the research results finally act (cf. de Varine, 1983a).

In contrast to presentation formats that focus on aesthetics, a notion prevalent in traditional museums[11], "new" museums employ theme-oriented presentation means. Through the use of audio-visual materials as well as real or reconstructed "environments," objects are represented in context and make social references. They convey the meanings as interpreted from the standpoint of the population.

For citizens to be actors in the various spheres of museum work, the "new" museum uses museum-specific continuing education to prepare the population to perform museum tasks to which they are entitled and to do them independently.

Another task the "new" museum explicitly assumes for itself is evaluation: the continuing process of calling itself into question and scrutinizing its work. This is done to ensure that the museum will constantly adapt itself to the changing conditions and needs of the population. Rivard (1984a, p. 10) speaks about evaluation as opening the museum to criticism.

---

[11] Lacouture (1983, p. 3ff) ascribed the main reason for the elitist nature of museums to the aestheticized forms of presentation adopted by traditional museums.

In summary, the model of the "new" museum as it emerges from the discourse on new museology can be represented as follows:

Schematic representation of the ideal "new" museum

1. Objectives:
Build identity
Coping with everyday life
Foster social development

2. Basic principles:
Extensive, radical public orientation
Territoriality

3. Structure and organization:
Little institutionalization
Financing through local resources
Decentralization
Participation
Teamwork based on equal rights

4. Approach:
Subject: complex reality
Interdisciplinarity
Theme orientation
Linking the past to the present and future
Cooperation with local/regional organizations

5. Tasks:
Collection
Conservation
Mediation
Continuing education
Evaluation

The "new" museum is avowedly opposed to (while thoroughly acknowledging the progress made by modernized traditional museums) those traditional museums that remain untouched by a general reorientation and still consciously adhere to an elitist concept of the museum that neglects social relationships (cf. Baron, 1987, p. 1).

The "new" museum, then, is the counterpart of the elitist, traditional museum. According to de Varine (1978b, p. 35) the latter has the following "sacrosanct" characteristics: ". high priority respect for the imperatives of conservation, the notion of the masterpiece and the preeminence of the acquisition function, absolute obeisance to the classifications of the sciences and disciplines, particularly with respect to the human sciences, subordination of the public and its needs to the precondition of the performance of the museum's other functions, imperatives of security, notions of safety, good taste, scientific rigor, etc."

The traditional museum, which constitutes the point of departure for the criticisms of new museology, may be represented as follows[12]:

Schematic representation of the traditional museum

1. Objective:
Preserve and protect a given material heritage[13]

2. Basic principle:
Protection of the objects

3. Structure and organization:
Institutionalization

---

[12] The attempt is made here to depict an "opposing model" to the ideal type of the "new" museum, but without setting out more fully the details of the traditional museum. This would go too far in terms of the subject and framework of the present study. The outline is a typification, clearly emphasizing characteristic features. They are referred to
for purposes of comparison in the evaluation for the case studies (cf. chapter 4). It should be stressed that this outline does not refer to the "modernized" traditional museum.

[13] In the case of local and regional museums within an easily defined territory. However, territoriality is not a basic principle for traditional museums.

Government financing
Central museum building
Professional staff
Hierarchical structure

4. Approach:
Subject: extracted from reality (objects placed in museums)
Discipline-oriented restrictiveness
Orientation to the object
Orientation to the past

5. Tasks:
Collection
Documentation
Research
Conservation
Mediation

A comparison of the two outlines shows that the "new" museum, like the modernized traditional museum, has thoroughly incorporated elements of the traditional museum, but, as stated above, interprets them differently. Fundamental differences, moreover, are found in the areas of objectives, basic principles, structure and approach (cf. chapter 4). Beyond the differences in individual aspects, what is new in this museum theory lies in the whole, that is, in the overall conception of the museum. The point of departure of this concept-and this is an innovation-lies not only in the recognition of the educational potential of museums, but more so in the recognition of their potential to bring about social change. Representatives of new museology believe that this desired social relevance can be achieved only through a radical opening of the museum.

Varine (1983c, p. 4ff; cf. Rivard, 1984a, p. 44ff) explains this innovative concept as follows: the conventional kind of museum consists of the following three elements: a *collection* in a *building* for a *public*. Many authors (cf. Rivard 1984a, p.44f) add a fourth element to this list: the *specialists,* who carry on the museum's work. New museology redefines these constituent elements (cf. de Varine, 1983c, p. 4ff; Nicolas, 1984, pp. 1-2):

1. The collection is the totality of the heritage.
2. The building is the totality of the territory.
3. The public is the totality of the population.

Using Rivard's terminology (1984a, p. 7), the "new" museum is ideally "without architectural barriers, without disciplinary barriers and without barriers to public access"-and is therefore an "open" museum in the most extreme sense (cf. Sola, 1987, p. 48).

A question that is frequently heard from all sides is whether the "new"; museum, with its high ideals, is unrealistic and utopian. de Varine writes (no year, p. 5)[14]: "On the one hand, I believe that such a radical rethinking is the only possible salvation for the museum as a useful factor in the life of Society in the modem world. Utopia is no danger as long as it is aware of itself and inspires positive action with concrete efforts. On the other hand, old and recent experience proves that the above museological principles are practicable and effective."

One of the tasks of my research is to investigate, using case studies, how the "new" museum has been realized in various social contexts and how these realizations relate to the claims of new museology, that is, to what extent we are dealing with "concrete utopias."

---

[14] For the criticism of new museology, cf. chapter 4.

3. CASE STUDIES

3.1 The ecomuseum in Quebec, Canada

3.1.1 Ecomusée de la Haute-Beauce, Musée Territoire
3.1.1.1 The Haute-Beauce[1]

Haute-Beauce is a rural area in the southeastern part of Quebec. It is located in the southwestern hinterland of the Beauce region proper, which consists of flourishing small towns such as St. Joseph, Ste. Marie, Beauceville and St. Georges along the Chaudière River.

The Haute-Beauce region is physically separated from this center of small towns principally by its position on an Appalachian high plateau that reaches as much as 873 meters in elevation. Besides the traditional region of Beauce in the northwest, Thetford-Mines in the west, Lac Mégantic in the south and Sherbrooke in the southwest form the important zones of influence. The southern boundary is only a few kilometers from the U.S. border. Haute-Beauce comprises a total of 13 rural parishes[2]: La Guadeloupe, St. Evariste, Ste. Clothilde, St. Hilaire, St. Benoit, Çourcelles, St. Sébastien, St. Victor, Lac Drolet, Lambton, St. Romain, St. Honoré and St. Ephrem. In connection with the establishment of a mill street as a tourist attraction, there have been attempts made in the Haute-Beauce since 1986 to include the East Broughton parish in the area of the Haute-Beauce (cf. Des liens se tissent avec East Broughton, 1987).

---

[1] When the origin of statements is not specified more precisely in the following text, these are summaries I made of the available material. When I refer to certain persons by name, without providing further details, these are statements made in interviews by my respective respondents: Pierre Mayrand (1-18-85), Maude Céré (1-25-85), Denis Hovanec/Johanne Badeau (1-25-85), Luc Lafontaine/Lorraine Charest (1-24-85), Jacinthe Roy (1-31-85), Guy Baron/Paul Bolduc (2-1-85), Lucille Létoumeau (1-31-85), Candide Dubord (1-31-85), Ginette Fortin (1-31-85), Monique Pomerleau (2-1-85). To be distinguished from the usual citations, all of the cited portions of interviews appear in **bold face**.
[2] The 13 parishes belong to 16 separate "municipalités."

The 13 parishes named above belong to various administrative units: the federal districts ("comtés fédéraux") of Beauce and Frontenac, the provincial administrative regions of Quebec and Estrie and the four MRCs ("municipalités régionales de comté") of Beauce-Sartigan, Robert Cliche, l'Amiante and Du Granit.

A description of the region beyond this basic information is complicated by the fact that the creation of this territorial unity of Haute-Beauce is inextricably linked to the Ecomusée de la Haute-Beauce. This is why the genesis and peculiarities of the Haute-Beauce region need to precede the activities of the ecomuseum.

The Haute-Beauce region, which properly speaking does not have its own center and has to be defined essentially by its location "between [...]" and "on the bank of [...]" (Fortin), did not exist before the establishment of the Ecomusée de la Haute-Beauce or its predecessor, the Musée et centre régional d'interprétation de la Haute-Beauce. "Haute-Beauce" as a regional unit was created in the late 1970s and early 1980s in connection with the founding of the Ecomusée de la Haute-Beauce. Because territoriality is a cornerstone of the ecomuseum and no predefined territory existed, the initiators of the Ecomusée de la Haute-Beauce gradually delimited and determined such a territory. The name "Haute-Beauce," which was little used until then, was given to a geographical and cultural unit that in their opinion-rather, according to their intuition-was identifiable. It was first used in 1957 by a geographer to indicate the area that nestles like a horseshoe in the curve of the Chaudiere River (cf. Céré 1985:13). Although the name "Haute-Beauce" had not been widely used by the region's inhabitants, it does reflect a tradition in the area to distinguish between the "upper Beauce" and the "lower Beauce."

But the recent association of the 13 villages in a territorial unit may be attributed in a very limited degree to the initiative of the population. Its association with a museum project was advanced by people who were more or less outsiders. Céré described the complex process as follows:

When the project was started in 1978, it was Pierre Mayrand who [...] began to do motivation work in the three nearby villages, St. Evariste, St. Hilaire de Dorset and La Guadeloupe, three very nearby villages. And he slowly created a more inclusive concept of the villages around there and at a given time he would go as far as St. Martin, St. Méthode. With experience and usage, it was realized that 13 was the maximum it was possible to go to, because geographically this began costing too much, transportation, moving, telephone, long distances. [...]. So, it was seen that this was the high plateau [. . .]. So, the part between the old Beauce and L'Estrie was included in the limits and it was decided not to touch the Chaudiére region or the L'Amiante region. It was really those 13 villages that are jammed together inside that geographic area.

Céré later referred to the problems of this kind of delimitation and the criteria underlying it. One selection criterion was the economy and efficiency of the museum's work. A second was the geographical location of the 13 villages on the high plateau. Furthermore, a crucial factor for the territorialization (cf. Rivard, 1984a, p. 50) of the Haute-Beauce region was its commonality in historical and socio-economic terms. Despite the artificiality of combining the 13 villages (split among various administrative zones), the Haute-Beauce region is relatively homogeneous.

What unites the Haute-Beauce population is their common historical origin and traditions. White people only settled the high plateau around the middle of the nineteenth century. Traditionally, residents earned their living in agriculture, forestry and granite quarrying. Sheep breeding and wool processing also formed important industries. Even today the Haute Beauce is predominantly rural-around 16,000 people live in the 13 communes (cf. Céré, 1985, p. 13).

In addition to agriculture, wood processing and the textile industry constitute important sources of employment (cf. Gariépy, 1986, p. 34-42 for the current economic structure). Family businesses are widespread. A total of 82.9 percent of the inhabitants earn their living in the region itself

(Gariépy, 1986, p. 49). For a rural area, the unemployment rate, when compared to the rest of Quebec, is astonishingly low. On the one hand, this may be explained by the existence of a large number of middle-class industrial businesses, but, on the other hand, also by the emigration of part of the working population, particularly those between the ages of 25 and 45, to the urban centers of Quebec and Montreal (Gariépy, 1986, p. 33 ff). The real structural weakness of the area and the consequences of the economic crisis, particularly in the textile industry, were thus concealed. Urban emigration due to the absence of suitable education and work opportunities represents one of the greatest problems facing the Haute-Beauce region. Moreover, respondents complained of an inadequate road system, relative isolation and neglect on the part of the provincial government (cf. the detailed account of the region's economic condition and infrastructure by Baron, 1985).

Overall, however, this is a relatively prosperous region-far removed from poverty and squalor-in which life takes its usual course, free of disruptions. Gariépy shares this conclusion (1986, p. 42), when she speaks of a "rural environment not faced with acute social and economic problems." She goes on: "The plateau of the Beauce back country, despite its relative isolation, appears to enjoy a certain prosperity."

How did the population react to the creation of an Haute-Beauce region? Did the amalgamation correspond to current consciousness and existing community needs? The awareness of a common heritage among the various villages appears part to have been awakened by the Ecomusée de la Haute-Beauce (beyond border and family ties that are common to all the parishes).

On the whole, however, Haute-Beauce is treated as an autonomous and meaningful unit, independent of the traditional Beauce region, with which the population identifies more and more. Céré noted that:

> When the ecomuseum of the Haute Beauce was named, this had an extraordinary dynamic effect [...]. At first this word 'haut' flattered people's ego; then they immediately told us that there was an impression of being

born, or coming into the world, and this was really important to people. The name was a very important triggering element.

Rivard (1984a, p. 86), following Edwina Taborsky, speaks of the "power to name." Yet it was outside motivators who exercised the "power to name," in order to offer the population a name and a concept. Céré expressly noted: "It was we who defended the position of the Haute-Beauce and in the end the people are connecting with it quite well." Gariépy (1986, p. 52) also criticized the lack of community involvement in the process of territorialization and "naming."

Thus, Haute-Beauce as a regional unit reflects less the reality of the citizen's everyday life than represents a new element that only gradually is winning social acceptance through various promotional techniques.

In the end, however, it should be emphasized that all the respondents- all individuals who had already undergone a certain sensitization process- agreed without reservations that the merging of the 13 parishes made sense and offered the population previously unexplored possibilities for identification and action. The role the Ecomusée de la Haute-Beauce played will be addressed in the following sections.

3.1.1.2 Origin
The Musée et centre regional d'interpretation de la Haute-Beauce

The origin of the Ecomusée de la Haute-Beauce is completely "un-ecomuseological": an extensive collection of objects by and large placed in a museum. This collection of 1,600 ethnographic and historical objects documenting the popular culture of the high plateau belonged to a private person- cabinet-maker and antique dealer Napoléon Bolduc, who lived in the village of La Guadeloupe. Displayed in private rooms, it had been accessible to visitors since 1970.

In 1978 Bolduc put the collection up for sale. Rather than sell individual pieces to American antique dealers who were passing through, he preferred to dispose of the complete collection locally. The collection represents a unique testimony of the Haute-Beauce's cultural heritage and Boldúc ascribed great importance to its remaining within the region.

Thus, he repeatedly tried to get the Quebec Ministry of Culture to erect a history center, but unfortunately without success (cf. Le Comité Culturel de la Guadeloupe, no year). Bolduc received little support from his fellow citizens. With some exceptions, the residents of La Guadeloupe and surrounding villages were unaware of the collection's existence (Luc Lafontaine).

Therefore, Bolduc contacted an outsider, Pierre Mayrand, an art historian and museologist at the University of Quebec at Montreal (UQAM), who owned a second home in St. Hilaire de Dorset and had visited the small private museum several times (cf. Céré 1982a). Mayrand declared himself prepared to take on the development of a project that combined keeping the collection in the region and erecting a museum or interpretation center. He described the basis for his decision:

> There was a general context conferred on it, a political context as well, from the fact that there were now in Quebec people who were very up to date on ecomuseology and who wanted to experiment with it on the ground. Because what is ecomuseology actually? It's experimentation for the purpose of stepping in and experimenting. And, second, there was the fact that I was available and circumstances were such that I was able to take a concrete interest in that region.

Mayrand took the first steps in 1978 as a solo effort. From the first, he strived to create a cultural institution that would be of benefit not only to a single place - La Guadeloupe - but to an entire region yet to be defined. In the initial phase, Mayrand scouted around and found recruits for his project through newspaper articles and contacts with municipal officials. He formed a small committee with interested locals and outsiders.

In 1979, after a year of promotion, Mayrand and the committee officially founded the CRIHB (Centre régional d'interprétation de la

Haute-Beauce) Corporation, in order to provide a legal basis for further action (cf. Musée et centre régional d'interprétation de la Haute-Beauce, 1979). The corporation decided to establish a museum and interpretation center[3] with a regional orientation and in this connection to keep the name "Haute-Beauce," which Mayrand had introduced, **because this was something that could create a dynamic in the region and permit us to achieve our goal** (Mayrand).

Through an intensive house-to-house public-relations campaign, CRIHB sought to gain the support of the population for the acquisition of Bolduc's collection and for the establishment of a museum. In accordance with the concept as developed by Mayrand, "the museum would be an organization concerned with the present and future as well as the past; its role would be to reveal the identity of that particular part of Quebec" (Stevenson, 1982, p. 7).

By the end of 1979 some partial successes could already be counted (cf. Report of the Musée et centre régional d'interprétation de la Haute-Beauce, 1982a): the Haute-Beauce museum and interpretation center was created as a "focus for the identification and promotion of the region," (Stevenson 1982, p. 8). For a token rent of one Canadian dollar per year, the parish allowed the corporation to use a hystoric presbytery in St. Evariste, the geographic center of the Haute-Beauce. An agreement was reached with Bolduc to purchase the collection for a price of $60,000 (Can.) payable over a period of five years. According to Mayrand:

> This was an extremely serious, extremely important agreement, it was the main test of a certain kind of credibility in the area, to see if the organization was capable of keeping on in the area.

And the museum did receive the expected and necessary support of the population during this initial phase. In a large-scale door-to-door

---

[3] Up to this time, there had been no talk of an ecomuseum. For Mayrand, however, the following was clear from the beginning: **It was the ecomuseum that we wanted to get to at the end of the line.**

promotional campaign, $27,000 (Can.) were raised within the region for the museum and interpretation center. For Mayrand (1980, 15) this money was "the symbol of success, of a collective effort," and it covered the first installment to purchase the Bolduc collection and pay for the renovations and furnishing of the museum building. The project also received a government subsidy (Mayrand). In this way the population made a considerable contribution to the establishment of the museum, which was considered by many to be an indication of an existing need and active approval.

With the exception of the prominent people who served as representatives of the population during the initial phase, the potential general public did not play a part in the conception and creation of the institution. The population's only activity (or passivity) was limited to "sensitization" or "motivation" and subsequently to the donation of $27,000 (Can.). The great majority of citizens knew nothing of the formation phase, most of them becoming aware of the Museé et centre régional d'interprétation de la Haute-Beauce only over a period of time when it became an accomplished fact. All respondents agreed the museum and interpretation center did not arise from a citizen initiative. Lucille Létourneau, the current vice president of the Ecomusée de la Haute-Beauce, commented:

> [...] it was not the whole population [...], one must not say that. This came from a small part of the population, because there were people involved at the beginning who were also part of the population, but always under the direction of Pierre Mayrand and Maude Céré. [...]. Maude Céré and Pierre Mayrand were really the masters of the work, 1 believe, at least the conceivers of it.

Although the idea of a museum had already been conceived and implemented in a preliminary way by a citizen of the Haute-Beauce, the Musée et centre régional d'interprétation de la Haute-Beauce goes back to an idea of Mayrand's, who played a key role in bringing it about. Ginette

Fortin confirms this: if there had been no Pierre Mayrand, [...] it wouldn't be there, there would be no story to tell.

Here is an interesting paradox. Although the museum did not stem from a citizen initiative, the question of whether it was imposed is categorically denied. Lucille Létourneau stated:

> No, oh no, not at all, because there was a group of people who joined onto their idea right at the first, [...], the surrounding parishes were quickly won over to this idea. No, this was not imposed. Of course, not everyone was sensitized on the same day [...].

Basically, the respondents did not question the leading roles of Mayrand and Céré, who were the ones who had the necessary knowledge, experience, awareness and relevant contacts to drive the project forward. Létourneau:

> As with anything else, someone has to take the lead. For my part, I think that the population follows rather than innovates.

I will return to the problems of this position in connection with the subject of "participation." First, however, the organizational development of the Musée et centre régional d'interprétation de la Haute-Beauce will be pursued further.

Ecomusée de la Haute-Beauce, musée territoire

After five years of building awareness in the Haute-Beauce, Mayrand and Céré succeeded in officially founding the Ecomusée de la Haute-Beauce. For them this had been the aim from the beginning. But, at first, it was not discussed openly and, in the end, it met with resistance. It was not possible to consummate the founding of the ecomuseum without some losses: it was preceded by the resignation of the museum's advisory board, which held a more traditional concept of a museum and distanced itself from the attempts to set up an ecomuseum.

The museum founders first introduced the term ecomuseum in 1982. This was done to ensure the museum was dynamic and would not go-like many traditional museums-into a state of static self-satisfaction. After a long debate, the resistance of the advisory board manifested itself more and more strongly. Mayrand decided to organize a counter-initiative for the purpose of founding the ecomuseum. He recalls:

> I stepped in and proposed to all the groups that had been sensitized in the other villages that a parallel body be created. Thus, in my own body I created a parallel body so as to be able to change the power relationships and, if necessary, reverse the other bodies and create the ecomuseum and the regrouping associated with the ecomuseum.

By October 1983, Mayrand had mobilized the ecomuseum supporters to such an extent that it was possible to call an extraordinary meeting of the members of the corporation of the museum. During the meetings, the articles of incorporation were changed and the Ecomusée de la Haute-Beauce was founded (Mayrand; cf. Musée et centre régional d'interprétation de la Haute-Beauce 1983a; 1983b).

Despite the best intentions not to let the museum and interpretation center degenerate into a lifeless place for storing objects, doubts do arise regarding the practices described above. Certainly, those present at the extraordinary meeting had the right to express themselves and vote; and, in fact, the majority approved of the ecomuseum. Democratic appearances were thus observed, but it should not be forgotten that this required intensive efforts of mobilization and persuasion. The people, by themselves, would not have thought of the idea of the ecomuseum, never mind take a stand against the board. This conclusion is also indicated by the two following statements:

This did not arise from the needs of the local people nor from an idea of the local people. (Guy Baron),

and, in Paul Bolduc's view:

This did not arise from a need, but it happened at just the right moment.

The concept of the ecomuseum is an approach that is alien to the general public. Even Céré noted that most people did not know what it meant. Although the initiators knew the problem very well, they made no effort to explain the nature of an ecomuseum to the affected community. They should have gradually familiarized citizens with the concept of the ecomuseum through participation in the museum's programs. Céré on this subject:

You don't spend your time making the theory with other people, you do concrete and specific actions.

René Rivard expressed himself similarly:

They should not get involved in the definition… It is preferable, in my opinion, with regard to motivation, to get organized for doing concrete things. And this is the whole thing, the dynamism of what makes people understand in action.

"Learning and knowing through experience" is not a method that should be rejected on principle, but here it is accompanied by the fact that the residents of the Haute-Beauce practically started out by buying a "pig in a poke," when they agreed to the founding of the ecomuseum. The question arises here as to whether it is possible to come to a responsible decision within the framework of a democratic decision-making process when the concept to be discussed and approved is not understood. I believe that this is not possible, which means that this decision was a sham democratic one. Agreement was reached on a matter that indeed seemed attractive to its supporters, but which was not widely understood by those affected by it.

Until 1983 supporters acted to popularize the new museological concept among the citizens. However, the people directly involved only had a vague and fragmentary understanding of the workings of an ecomuseum. What the Ecomusée de la Haute-Beauce really is-leaving aside the problematic establishment phase-and how it is to be classified, can best be judged from its objectives, structure and operations.

3.1.1.3 Conception and objectives

As stated by its bylaws (Ecomusée de la Haute-Beauce, 1983a, p. 2), the museum is intended to contribute to the "better conditions and better life of the region corresponding to territory of the Haute-Beauce." In this regard Denis Hovanec clarified:

> The objectives were to sensitize the people, make them aware of themselves, their environment, their territory, their problems, their needs, and finally to attempt to work together collectively to respond to these needs in order to bring about better development.

The Ecomusée de la Haute-Beauce views itself as a people's university, which can engender a learning process and bring about social change through citizen involvement in a variety of educational activities. First of all, it should be stressed that the objectives of the Ecomusée de la Haute-Beauce and the way it views itself were shaped decisively by two key individuals, Céré (educator, museologist and art historian) and Mayrand (museologist and art historian). The two borrowed its elaborate educational concept from the "pedagogy of liberation" put forward by Paolo Freire and his followers.

Consistent with the ecomuseological approach, the Ecomusée of the Haute-Beauce does not wish to be a fixed, static educational institution, but sees itself as evolutionary and part of a dynamic process. Céré (1985, p. 1) refers to a "laboratory of didactic experimentation in a rural environment" that strives for social change while continually changing and adapting to changed conditions (cf. the functional model "triangle of creativity" in chapter 3.1.1.4).

The educational process that the Ecomusée de la Haute-Beauce strives for is directed less to the unilateral communication of a given content than to "learning through participation," "learning through experience," "learning through action"-synonyms for the central point of view that Céré (1985, p. 62), citing Edgar Faure, summarized as follows:

> Henceforward, education will no longer be defined with respect to a determined content that is to assimilated, but will be conceived of as it really is, as a process of being which, through the diversity of its experiences, teaches one to express oneself, to communicate, to question the world and always to improve.

The implication of this was summarized by Céré (1985, p. 61) as follows:

> The ecomuseum has taken the side of self-teaching rather than that of education in the unique sense used by specialized museums, which are anxious to democratize Knowledge, to spread the good word of Culture. We have opted rather for the demanding challenge of working in osmosis with a population so as to enhance its·knowledge and its cultures with a view to regional development.

The overall educational activity of the Ecomusée de la Haute-Beauce is carried out ideally on two levels: first, to generate on the individual level self-respect, self-confidence and the aptitude for self-determined action, and second to affect the development of the region. According to Céré:

There is individual development, where each person can find his place and develop, can use the museum as a personal springboard, but this is also a tool for regional development. I believe that for me these are the two great objectives of the ecomuseum.

The Ecomusée de la Haute-Beauce basically strives to educate the population through its active participation in the museum so that it can answer the questions: "Where do we come from?", "Who are we?", and "Where do we want to go?". The first two questions refer to the objectives of identification-to create a sense of territorial identity by considering a community's history, its cultural and natural heritage and by linking its past and present. The third question, however, raises the issue of future prospects or goals and their corresponding strategies for action. Both elements-identification and future-oriented thought and action-make up a comprehensive development process.

During the identification phase, the cornerstone should be laid for the next stage. Identity building should include the acquisition of certain work skills. Through active participation in the ecomuseum, the population is supposed to learn **to reflect, to work collegially, to plan, to draw up a schedule of what is due and what is owed, to act on the basis of this schedule as a function of the planning that has been done** (Céré) and finally to take responsibility. In this way the population can use the ecomuseum as a tool, so that identification can lead to initiative and self-determined action directed to shaping the future (Mayrand):

> It seems to me that development is very closely linked to people's autonomy, to their basic capacity to make these decisions and not wait for others to impose them, to be capable of taking their own matters into hand and not having them imposed or fabricated, rather than saying "let's wait for the government to give us something before starting".

What does development mean for the Ecomusée de la Haute-Beauce? Céré:

> It is when one departs from everyday life to make an improvement in the quality of life on the individual level and then on the level of the region.

An important element here is contact with the outside world, which imparts security and an impulse to innovate. (Céré):

> It is important to develop oneself, to find other people, to exchange, to see how things work elsewhere, to look for new ideas, and to act so as to evolve in society for oneself and for the region.

On the subject of development, Mayrand observed:

> For me development is expressed in terms of initiative... These are not isolated attempts at development, these are attempts that are interconnected and that basically make it possible to achieve a certain number of objectives so that a region is able basically, for example, to improve the quality of its life.

Despite a certain vagueness, development is generally equated with an improvement in living conditions. The quality of these improvements and changes is to be defined-in accordance with the approach presented here-by the population itself! In sum, one can state that in the Ecomusée de la Haute-Beauce the concept of the "ecomuseum of discovery" (borrowed from Georges Henri Riviere) and the concept of the "ecomuseum of development" (borrowed from Hugues de Varine) are combined. The Ecomusée de la Haute-Beauce understands its role to be not only the mirror of the population, but a tool of self-determination and development for the inhabitants of the Haute-Beauce.

The following section will show whether and how the Ecomusée de la Haute-Beauce can realize its ambitious objectives. The determining question to which particular attention should be given is: Can this institution, created in the Haute-Beauce by outside specialists, become an instrument of collective action accepted by the population as its own? Or does the structural weakness noted in the museum's origins run through the entire project?

3.1.1.4 Structure and organization

The administrative headquarters and service center of the Ecomusée de la Haute Beauce is located in a former presbytery designated a historic monument since 1983-in St. Evariste, the geographic center of the Haute-Beauce region. A characteristic feature of the ecomuseum is its decentralized spatial structure. The museum is represented in the territory of the Haute-Beauce by several so-called "antennas," or associated groups (cf. chapter 3.1.1.5). The antennas, together with the administrative and service center, form the ecomuseum.

The Ecomusée de la Haute-Beauce is a private museum. It is a nonprofit corporation, which through intensive motivation and recruitment campaigns, particularly in the initial phase, had over 1,700 members (family membership!) at the time of this study. Although at the beginning outsiders were also accepted into the corporation, the membership was basically confined to the citizens of the Haute-Beauce. Membership must be renewed every year by acquiring a membership card. The annual membership fee of $2 (Can.) is within everyone's means. In addition to the membership fees, the Ecomusée de la Haute-Beauce is financed both through contributions by the population and by local and, in exceptional cases, outside businesses (44.3 percent, 1981-1985, Gariépy, 1986, p. 75) and through subsidies (55.7 percent, 1981-1985, Gariépy, 1986, p. 75)[4].

---

[4] Not included in this number: a) a subsidy of $154,000 (Can.) in 1983 for the construction of workshops and exhibition space, and b) a subsidy of $180,000 (Can.) in 1985 for the Maison du Granit project.

The fact that the separate villages of the Haute-Beauce belong to various administrative units confers the advantage that the museum can apply to four different administrative districts for grants to carry out its numerous activities. Since the museum is recognized as an "organisme volontaire d'éducation populaire" (OVEP-a voluntary public education body), it also receives grants from the provincial ministry of education. For example, it received $21,000 (Can.) in 1986-87 to carry out continuing education programs. Because the activities of the Ecomusée de la Haute-Beauce are widely diversified, it can apply for project-related grants from various other ministries (agriculture, environment, hunting, fishing and leisure, science and technology, energy and resources).

Until 1983 the staffing of the Ecomusée de la Haute-Beauce was financed mainly through job-creation measures (for example, "Canada au travail"). Even today the museum falls back on job-creation measures. As a rule, the contracts have a duration of six to eight months, followed by several months of unemployment. During this time the employees receive unemployment benefits, which makes it possible for them to continue their employment for the museum with virtually no change-until the beginning of a new period of job-creation measures.

By taking advantage of various government job-creation programs, it is at least possible to place the same people under contract time and again, and thus a certain degree of continuity is guaranteed. However, the period of unemployment is a burden on those involved. Guy Baron, for example, expressed his frustration and a feeling of being exploited as a consequence of years of selfless, unremunerated employment for the museum (cf. Baron, 1987, p. 11).

Since September 1983, the Ecomusée de la Haute-Beauce has been a government recognized museum, i.e. one accredited by the Ministry of Culture of the Province of Quebec (cf. Ecomusée de la Haute-Beauce, 1984b, p. 1)[5]. Since then it has enjoyed a regular annual subsidy of $68,000

---

[5] As grounds for this step the Minister of Culture at the time, Clément Richard, in an interview, stressed first of all the model character of the Ecomusée de la Haute-Beauce (Doter le Québec d'institutions muséologiques de prémière importance 1983/84).

(Can.). The granting of this subsidy is conditioned on the contribution of an additional 30 percent of this amount by the citizens of the Haute-Beauce. Through this subsidy the Ecomusée de la Haute-Beauce now has a regular budget to ensure that basic functions are carried out. Basically, the money is used for the salaries of the director (on a 12-month basis) and two employees (on the basis of eight months a year). Although the latter still live from unemployment benefits for four months a year, this guaranteed annual subsidy provides a certain safeguard.

Up until now, the Ecomusée de la Haute-Beauce has not felt the governmental influence that might be associated with the subsidy. Despite this, Baron refers to the subsidy as a "half poisoned gift." A problem is the amount of energy needed for proper management of the large amounts of money and for the implementation of the corresponding activities (for example, organizing workshops and renovating exhibit spaces). Hence, at times, the burden of work has shifted onto the service center. In this way, not enough time remains for decentralized promotion in the region, i.e. work with the users and the public.

The core staff consists of around ten employees who work regularly at the museum and perform specific functions. At the time of the study, paid employees consisted of:

> Director (Maude Céré)
> Bookkeeper and technician (Luc Lafontaine)
> Motivator (Denis Hovanec)
> Two researchers (Guy Baron, Jacynthe Roy)
> Two graphic designers (Johanne Badeau, Paul Bolduc).

However, in addition to the employees, volunteers from the population are supposed to be included increasingly in the management and direction of the museum and its various activities. This is done in order for them to begin the learning process and someday take over the management of the museum. On this subject, Mayrand commented:

By definition and in accordance with our objectives… administrative and organizational education was one of the priority objectives. In order to be independent, these people needed to take themselves in hand, to set themselves objectives and to be capable of managing the objectives collectively, something they had never done.

For this purpose, the Ecomusée de la Haute-Beauce has a complex participation structure. The population (in the sense of the participants) may influence the museum through various kinds of decision-making authority set out in its corporate statutes (cf. Ecomusée de la Haute-Beauce, 1983a).

Once a year a general membership meeting ("assemblée générale") takes place, with an average participation of 100 to 150 persons. These meetings are used primarily to review finances and report on museum activities. In addition, the general framework for future projects is laid down in coordination with the members who are present.

An important characteristic of the Ecomusée de la Haute-Beauce is its decentralized structure[6]. In some localities linked to the museum, local committees or "associated groups" or "antennas", had already come into being before the founding of the ecomuseum on the basis of local initiatives. Others were formed only on the initiative of the museum: the Tourism and Cultural Action Committee in St. Hilaire, the Tourism and Cultural Committee in St. Sébastien, the Cultural Committee in Lac Drolet, the Heritage Society in Ste. Clothilde and the Crafts House in St. Honoré. With regard to the establishment of the committees, Céré noted:

> Well, in some cases, when there is already a sociocultural committee in place, it is that committee that becomes the link to the ecomuseum, but sometimes it is just a few individuals who get together and create a small nucleus. After a few activities, when it becomes strong enough, its

---

[6] After the research phase concluded (1985), some structural reforms were carried out in the ecomuseum. These will be explained at the end of the present chapter (3.1.1.4).

incorporation is brought about, its independence. What would be desirable is that there be 13 completely independent committees.

These committees are formally independent of the Ecomusée de la Haute-Beauce. They apply for subsidies to carry out local activities and reach their decisions independently at local meetings. The members informally choose one to three members to represent their village in the users' committee ("comité des usagers"), which is a critical component of the structure of the Ecomusée de la Haute-Beauce. The formation of the users' committee was proposed by Mayrand in 1983 at the establishment of the ecomuseum. The committee meets at least once a year, preferably before the general meeting, and the number of participants can vary from 15 to 50 (Mayrand), because, in addition to the selected representatives, interested observers are also permitted to attend. In addition to the representatives of the population, the director has an official seat on the users' committee. An elected chairman presides over the committee. The users' committee is a point of contact, or interchange, between the ecomuseum and its users, and because of that, it is a place of intensive motivational work. Within the framework of the meetings (Céré):

> ...the exhibitions are planned, the subsidy requests are planned, the 13 villages are brought up to date, the latest word is given on what is happening in the intra- and extra-regional bodies, the cultural councils, the development councils. Information is shared in this regard... It is with them that all our programs are determined.

In addition, the users' committee nominates five members of the ecomuseum's board of directors ("conseil d'administration"). They constitute one representative for each of the five zones the Ecomusée de la Haute-Beauce is divided in (Les Vallons, Le Grand Lac, Le Grand Plateau, Les Crêtes, Le Coeur; cf. Baron, 1986).

The rest of the members of the twelve-person board of directors are chosen at the annual general meeting, with the exception of the director and one representative of the parish of St. Evariste who is automatically entitled to a seat. The members choose the president, two vice presidents, the secretary and the treasurer of the Ecomusée de la Haute Beauce. In addition, both the employees of the museum and a number of permanent observers are entitled to take part in the board meetings, albeit without voting rights. The board of directors meets around five times a year and from two to 25 persons take part in the meetings (Mayrand).

The main task of the board of directors is to manage the museum's financial affairs. In addition, as official representative of the members, the board influences the development of programs in the spirit of the recommendations expressed by the members' meeting. In this process, the museum workers and the executive committee make concrete proposals in the first place.

An executive committee controls day-to-day operations, prepares for the meetings of the board of directors and develops concrete proposals. It consists of five to six people (Mayrand), … **who finally develop the work material, prepare the documentation and are strongly supported by the workers themselves.** The leading member of the executive committee is Mayrand, the initiator and present president of the Ecomusée de la Haute-Beauce, … **who is often something of the great thinker, who sees things more in the long term**-evaluation of Denis Hovanec, which is shared in principle by all the other respondents. The other members of the committee are the two vice presidents, the secretary and the treasurer- thus, the same individuals who hold board positions. The museum director participates in the meetings of the executive committee by invitation, but does not have the right to vote. The basically participation-friendly structure described in this section addresses a quite important element of the Ecomusée de la Haute-Beauce. The various activities and programs of the museum are simultaneously the result of this structure and the means for its implementation and change. This connection is clear in the model of the "triangle of creativity of the ecomuseum of the Haute-Beauce" (cf. Rivard, 1984a, p. 43; cf. figure below).

In this regard, Céré (1985, p. 12) explains: "The creation process of the ecomuseum began with an interpretation initiative taken up by specialists. Its power of diffusion made it possible to sensitize the population to the ideas of identity and appropriation of the heritage-action in order to be able to release clearly the sense of territorialization. Thanks to the techniques of creativity, the ecomuseum was produced. Through a phenomenon of retroaction, this population itself can now interpret what it is and determine the directions of its development."

The triangle of creativity of the ecomuseum of the Haute Beauce:

<u>Interpretation</u>

<u>Retro-action</u>   <u>Sensitization</u>

<u>Ecomuseum</u>   <u>Creation</u>   <u>Territory</u>

Overall, Céré (1985, p. 56) is correct in speaking of the structure of the Ecomusée de la Haute-Beauce as a "participation structure." From a formal perspective, the museum does have a democratic structure. Many paths exist for the population to participate at various levels of museum activities, and to use the ecomuseum as an instrument for its purposes.

Public participation is a crucial element of ecomuseology, in general, and occupies a prominent position at the Ecomusée de la Haute-Beauce. Problems associated with participation, however, have emerged at the Ecomusée de la Haute-Beauce, which require detailed discussion.

In regard to participation, doubts exist on the efficiency of the museum's democratic

decision-making structure, because strict limits have been placed on real participation-up to the present time, in any case. Hovanec and Létourneau maintained that potential citizen participation in the museum's activities was limited from the outset. Because the population largely consists of agricultural and forestry workers, these have relatively little free time.

For those in other occupations, with more free time, a large number of local groups exist that they can join. St. Sébastien alone, a village with a population of 200, has nine institutions of this kind, in which some of the same people tend to participate over and over.

The situation posed a certain obstacle for the formation of a local committee of the Ecomusée de la Haute-Beauce (Hovanec).

The core group of active individuals includes 25 or 30 people who regularly participate in the ecomuseum's varied activities, i.e. in conception, research, education and programs (Hovanec). I believe emphasis is placed on participation in the sense of "letting oneself be included" and less on independent activity stemming from one's own initiative. Exceptions, however, are occasionally found at the level of the local committees.

While the local population has a certain autonomy, at the Ecomusée de la HauteBeauce, the volunteer staff I interviewed (with one exception) stated they take action only when the initiators request them to perform specific tasks. Ginette Fortin, for one, said:

> Maude has always asked me when there was something to do, she would call and say "can you help us" and I would go there.

Or Létourneau:

> When they have needed help and I was available, I would go there, perhaps to organize various activities, perhaps to help with something big, but I would do what I could.

For Létourneau, volunteer work at the Ecomusée de la Haute-Beauce appears to be synonymous with readiness to help out:

In the museum they have their employees, but it happens that motivation work has to be done at a certain time, or there are people visiting, things like that.

Candide Dubord, on the other hand, is not convinced that it has to be this way. She stated:

You participate to help them…but our participation…it's going to be partial…I wouldn't feel that it belongs to me and that it is my area of work and I have to do it.

She later vented her displeasure with this unsatisfactory state of affairs:

You feel you're put on the shelf to be taken off when there is a need and then put back on right afterwards.

Now the question naturally arises: why do people remain in this passive position? The reasons are complex and varied for the interested citizens themselves. First of all, the work of the ecomuseum, its tasks and possibilities, have not yet penetrated the consciousness of the population of the Haute-Beauce (cf. chapter 3.1.1.2). In this respect, Hovanec said:

The rest of us say this is a tool for the population, but the people don't know it's a tool. It's like with me, if I have a tool, but I don't know how to use it. The situation is a little like that for the people, I think. They know that the ecomuseum does things, you can participate and they actually do, they set out to, and they do more, but this is still not something they feel more strongly than that.

The assessment that the population lacked the necessary knowledge and capabilities in order to take initiatives itself and have people from its ranks occupy leading positions was by and large shared by the volunteer staff who were questioned. In statements such as, "I am not a specialist" (Létoumeau), "… none of us are experts or specialists… we don't have the education" or "… I don't think that there is a formula yet for taking on that duty and carrying it out adequately" (Létoumeau) a feeling of subordination is clearly expressed. This contradicts the partner-like, egalitarian working conditions that the Ecomusée de la HauteBeauce boasts about. Ginette Fortin assessed their capabilities differently than did Létoumeau:

> It takes someone like that to run this. You cannot improvise around there. You have to have knowledge these aren't small matters. Take me, I wouldn't be capable, even if I wanted to, I think that I couldn't keep that up for long.

The population discharges its responsibility by delegating it, from an unjustified sense of inferiority, to specialists whose authority enjoys almost unlimited recognition. Those questioned expressly emphasize how necessary it is to be guided by persons in authority for anything to happen.

The lack of responsibility keeps the population in its relatively passive position, which can be gathered from Dubord's statement:

> He [Mayrand] is the one who has an interest in this moving forward, whereas it isn't like that for the rest of us, we just help, it isn't our job. We're not the boss. That means that when we're not our own boss, we help when we want to… Since this is not our own responsibility, we wait, we wait until we're told and, if the others are tied up with something else, nothing moves ahead.

Those who try to influence decisions after participating several times frequently feel overtaxed or simply overrun. They have too little prior information and too little available time-the agenda is too extensive-for them to discuss the project proposals thoroughly and carefully weigh their decisions. With regard to the lack of information, Lorraine Charest believes the people would really like to be fully informed, but they do not try sufficiently hard.

Occasionally, however, the day-to-day work governed by events and time pressure result in participants' expressed wishes being disregarded or they simply not being consulted. Hovanec identified one of the basic principles of the ecomuseum and its attendant problems:

> ...that things are done in the rhythm of the people, according to what the people want, and this, I think, may often be the greatest problem, particularly with respect to specialists and thinkers. For my part, I find that they are frequently perhaps a little disconnected from the people's everyday life and this is what gives rise to the danger at a given moment that the thinkers are finally too far off from the population.

This problem further justifies the cautious reserve of the population. Proposed projects, even if based on identifiable needs, far exceed in kind and extent the imagination and capabilities of those concerned.

Caution also characterizes many residents of the region for another reason: The fact that the Ecomusée de la Haute-Beauce project was created by outsiders and will be further advanced by them obviously gives cause for skepticism.

A further problem in the acceptance of the Ecomusée de la Haute-Beauce results from the fact that the staff-with the exception of Jacynthe Roy and Luc Lafontaine-does not consist of locals (Mayrand):

> The main characteristic is that the majority of those people do not come from the region, which currently poses a problem.

Another difficulty appears to lie in the fact that the staff of the Ecomusée de la Haute Beauce is made up of volunteers and paid employees. Therefore, a difference in status ensues that is reinforced by sociodemographic characteristics. Contrarily to the initial phase, in which a predominantly volunteer staff was employed, a core group of permanent employees has existed since 1983. While, on the one hand, the formation of a staff of professional employees certainly has advantages in terms of efficiency, on the other hand it has led volunteers to feel superfluous and without responsibility. "Let the 'others' do it: they know more and they're better able to!"

As indicated above, this inequality is reinforced by sociodemographic characteristics. The paid employees are individuals 28 to 35 years of age, some of whom have a university education in the fields of geography, art history, history or education. The division by genders is quite balanced. The group of volunteers, on the other hand, is made up predominantly of women 45 to 60 years of age, with little or no higher education. This reflects the common stereotype **that cultural endeavors are a matter for housewives** (Fortin).

Through intensive and regular contact as well as active exchange of information, it may be possible to achieve convergence and perhaps create a common basis. Some time has passed since the intensive sensitization phase and the museum has turned its attention to other priorities. Thus, employees note with regret that the museum has strayed too far from its basic principles.

Hovanec, for example, said:

> I find it's like we're in neutral. I find that people have even been a little overtaken by events. There was the first period, sensitization was going on, the people were being made to understand a little about what was happening [...], but we are dedicated to being a development ecomuseum [...]. Sometimes people find this interesting, but frequently they are reticent, afraid, often you even have projects that are beyond them. [...] maybe you are no longer concerned with people following the movement. [...] I find there has been a distancing from the popular will, from popular participation.

Luc Lafontaine echoed these feelings:

I find that more attention should be paid to our users' committee. I think that the ecomuseum is above all for the population. There are big projects, but in the end they don't touch the population.

In the meantime this "being in neutral" seems to have been overcome. There was a change in the museum's management in early 1986. Gradually the president of the Ecomusée de la Haute-Beauce, Pierre Mayrand, made a renewed effort to activate and involve members of the corporation, whose numbers had shrunk from 1,700 to around 800, and recruit new members (cf. Le conseil d'administration de votre musée, 1987).

In connection with this initiative, the ecomuseum's structure was changed to create five new committees, each chaired by a member of the executive committee:

Development committee (Pierre Mayrand)
Program committee (Guy Baron)
Finance committee (Rénald Lessard)
Committee for the establishment of the Maison du Granit (Jacques Fortin)
Personnel committee (Lucille Létourneau)

These committees meet about twice a month. The chairmen are required to find people to participate both from the board of directors and the interested population.

Although the users' committee is formally still in existence, it no longer functions de facto for lack of initiatives on the part of the "users". The new structure is intended to motivate people to participate. A project created by the development committee, for example, strives for a radical decentralization of resources and responsibility (cf. Mayrand, 1987). This project was first presented to various local groups in the form of a working paper in February 1987, and was later submitted to the members for their approval within the framework of an extraordinary general meeting. In addition to the director of the service center, two other directors were named in the region (Denis Hovanec and Guy Baron), so that the

Ecomusée de la Haute-Beauce is now led by a directors' group (without a corresponding change in the bylaws). The two additional executive positions are supposed to be occupied by alternating representatives of the various villages on a rotating basis. The division of the territory of the Haute-Beauce into five zones was abolished.

Instead, the local committees are given greater autonomy and now directly name five members of the board of directors from their ranks (Pierre Mayrand, conversation of 8-7-87).

It was not possible to evaluate the result of these new initiatives by the time the present work was concluded. However, the implementation of unrestricted public orientation, through the involvement of the population, is coming about in a slow and cumbersome manner. Hovanec stressed (in a conversation of 1-7-87) that the same people still cooperate actively in the new committees, while new interested individuals can be recruited from the ranks of the population only with difficulty. He further described present participation as extraordinarily fragile, and seriously questioned whether an effective bridge can ever be built between the ecomuseum and the population.

In any event, one should not expect direct success from the new attempts at mobilization. On the basis of years of endeavors, Hovanec came to the conclusion that the population may cf. no reason for a concerted action like the Ecomusée de la Haute-Beauce and feels no need for mobilizing innovative forces because, in principle, things as a whole are going all right from its point of view.

In any case, the introduction of effective participation and self-management is a lengthy operation consisting of very small steps.

3.1.1.5 Activities and programs

The various activities and programs of the Ecomusée de la Haute-Beauce are based on a concept of overall cultural action, that is, on action that embraces the changing relationship of humans to their physical and sociocultural environment, linking the past to the present and the future. Historical reflection-given relatively great emphasis-is the point of departure for coping with the present.

In contrast to the traditional museum, the main area of work of the Ecomusée de la Haute Beauce is not collection or conservation, but rather the motivation of the population of the Haute Beauce, i.e. public-directed educational action for the purpose of coping with the present and the future. All other areas of work are subordinated to motivation. The basis for the museum's educational program is not created simply through collection, conservation, documentation, research and public programs, but rather motivation is partly carried out within the framework of these working processes by involving interested citizens in them.

A common element to all areas of work of the Ecomusée de la Haute-Beauce-differently from the traditional museum-is the secondary importance of objects. The collection, conservation and presentation of objects are not ends in themselves, but communicators of content and sources of motivation, as Mayrand underscored:

> The priority, if the object is used, is never the object. In my opinion, it exceeds the object, it goes beyond the object. The object frequently becomes an accessory... and this is not in any pejorative sense, but this is truly a link with the other thing that is important and that is the human being.

The museum has a single collection, Napoléon Bolduc's collection referred to above. It consciously desires to acquire no other collections. The Ecomusée de la Haute-Beauce seeks rather to stimulate the population to preserve in situ and care for works, objects, buildings or natural spaces that are of significance to the region's heritage (cf. Trudel, 1984, p. 111).

Although the museum does not wish to expand its collection, it does carry on collection activity by systematically bringing together the records of the "collective memory." In separate interviews the citizens of the Haute-Beauce are asked about their life memories. The so-called "collective memory" is then produced from the comparative, theme-related analysis of the interviews. In this way the Ecomusée de la Haute-Beauce devotes itself to the everyday history of the Haute-Beauce, an area that is ignored by official historiography. Popular history focuses on the inhabitants' perception of the direct everyday world and their specific regional identity.

One of the initiatives that served to stimulate local historical research and thus to generate an awareness of everyday history and identity was the "Ancestral Home" program. In each of the various villages working groups explored the history of the oldest family still living in the house of its forebears. Céré explains:

> This awakens awareness of the quality of the habitat for the village as a whole. The people have to make a search, for which of the families is the oldest. Once they have chosen it, this awakens the awareness of others as to the value of the architectural heritage of the local people's environment.

Exhibition activity, one of the main functions of the Ecomusée de la Haute-Beauce is also guided by this basic thought. First of all, the administrative and service center in St. Evariste, the museum proper, houses a kind of reception room, the so-called interpretation center. There, a museum educator ("animateur") presents basic information on the Haute-Beauce region using maps, illustrations and oral explanations. This, in turn, leads to the permanent, special open-air exhibits and local interpretation centers.

The first permanent exhibit of the Ecomusée de la Haute-Beauce comprised the entire Bolduc collection, which was presented in the various rooms of the former presbytery (cf. Ethier, 1981). On display was a representative cross-section of the regionally specific, everyday material culture of the 1920s and 1930s. By confronting their past, visitors (or "users") were supposed to encounter part of their identity (Céré, 1985, p. 22f):

This collection of one thousand six hundred ethnographic objects thus becomes the triggering element or pretext permitting the population of the Haute-Beauce to express its feeling of belonging and of pride.

In addition to the permanent exhibit, thematic special exhibits are regularly carried out in the museum's main building in St. Evariste. These are listed below in chronological order:

1. "Christmas traditions in our families" (December 1980)
2. "The woman through baptismal clothing" (spring to autumn 1981)
3. "How the citizens of the Haute-Beauce have appropriated their environment" (spring to autumn 1982)
4. "The masterpieces of the Haute-Beauce" (spring to autumn 1983)
5. "The symposium on animal art" (spring to autumn 1984)
6. "The ecomuseum celebrates" (summer/autumn 1985)
7. "The language of the tool" (summer 1986 to spring 1987)
8. "The world is small: family portrait" (summer to autumn 1987)
9. "Gallery of exploration" (summer to autumn 1987)

Initially exhibits were constructed with the active participation of interested citizens, based on a course in "people's museology" to be given every year but which actually has occurred only twice. They were taught by Céré: the first in 1981, in connection with the exhibits "The woman through baptismal clothing" and "The maple with open heart"; and the second in 1983 during the exhibit "How the citizens of the Haute-Beauce have appropriated their everyday environment."

The three-month course consisted of a theoretical and a practical part. Over the course of six evenings, the following topics were discussed (Céré conversation of 1-22-87):

- Introduction to museology and the history of the museum
- The cultural and natural heritage ("patrimoine")
- Exhibit design and production

- Motivation, museum education
- Publicity work

In addition to acquiring basic museological knowledge, participants carried out practical work related to specific exhibit projects.

Two individuals from each village who had been selected in open meetings took the courses. Participants functioned as multipliers, forming working groups in the village and passing on their newly acquired museological knowledge. Thus, the courses were an effective means of sensitizing the population to the possibilities offered by the ecomuseum.

In 1984 a subsidy from the provincial ministry of culture allowed the Ecomusée de la Haute-Beauce to renovate its lighting system, install a security system to protect against fire and theft, and acquire equipment to control temperature and humidity (cf. Trudel, 1984, p. 113). The renovation also created a larger exhibit space for showing the Bolduc collection. A selection of objects-small, in comparison to the previous permanent exhibit (550 out of 1,600)- was installed in so-called "environments," from which the visitor is separated by plates of glass. Four subjects were treated in these scenic exhibits: "keeping order," "work," "the hearth," and "rest." They provided the visitor with an overview of everyday life in earlier times.

Although the population was consulted through the users' committee and had the opportunity to make specific proposals, the results did not meet expectations. Involved citizens were disappointed and felt deceived because they realized that, although their proposals were heard, they played a minor role in the actual shaping of the exhibit. The Ecomusée de la HauteBeauce, which in principle intended to relate to the real life of the citizens of the Haute-Beauce and views itself as a mirror of the population, did not achieve its purpose with this exhibit.

Dubord expressed the sense of disappointment:

> I did not find that year's exhibit attractive and I did not send anyone to see it. ...They say that this represents us, ... this does not represent us at all, at all, at all, these are not our ideas, this is not the way we see this... Maybe

it's because I don't understand their idea, but you cannot say the people wanted this and that this represents the people.

That is not true.

In connection with the newly formed permanent exhibit, Létourneau makes a distinction between the needs of the "people from here" and those of the "real" public. Although the new exhibit is "beautiful," it does not speak to the local public, it is not faithful to the public because of its intellectuality. She questions whether the programs of the Ecomusée de la Haute-Beauce must necessarily have a professional character, knowing from her experience that activities and exhibits of a folk character are far more popular with the public than the cold and displeasing sparkle of professional exhibits. Maude Céré, one of those principally responsible, admits mistakes were made.

In 1987, in order to reawaken the interest of its public and once more include the population in its actions, the Ecomusée de la Haute-Beauce organized a number of courses and project related workshops in the area of people's museology (cf. Les ateliers de l'Ecomusée, 1987). The gradual inclusion of citizens in specific work processes is seen as the best means for a radical public orientation. In order to make exhibits interesting and accessible to the public, the Ecomusée de la Haute-Beauce also carries out a number of motivational activities (cf. Hovanec, 1987). Several examples that follow shed light on this area of the museum's work.

Within the framework of the educational preparations for the first permanent exhibit, Céré put together two companion collections of materials, the so-called "educational packages," which were used to carry out motivational work in the schools of the Haute-Beauce (cf. Céré, 1982b; 1985, pp. 25-33; Céré, Audet, 1981, Locas, 1982). Each of these consisted of a transportable mini exhibit packed by hand, in the form of a triptych. The first version, intended for the fifth and sixth grades, called "The presence of man through the object: the hand," consisted of a box that opened to form a three-part mini-exhibit.

The first wing of the exhibit contained several key words on the theme of "museum," which students were encouraged to discuss. Reproductions of museum objects were attached to the second wing to clarify what work is performed with the hand. The third wing showed examples of what the students themselves could do with their hands. The second version, "The perception of objects through the Napoléon Bolduc collection," was similarly constructed for the first through fourth grades and was aimed at familiarizing the students with museum objects by testing their powers of visual and tactile recognition. Motivation work through the use of the educational packages in the schools was supplemented by museum visits and subsequent evaluation lessons. A total of 1,735 students took part in the program.

Overall, Céré evaluated this educational program as being relatively costly. The high level of expenditure and the realization that a program of this kind had to be repeated every year in order to maintain interest led the Ecomusée de la Haute-Beauce to refrain from large-scale direct cooperation with the schools for some time.

An important part of the museum's exhibit-based educational activities are guided tours.

This motivation work was carried out partly by volunteers and partly by paid museum employees. The volunteer activities played a significant role particularly in the initial phase, for example, in connection with the exhibit "The woman through baptismal clothing."

Despite this positive experience, motivation work by the volunteers led to organizational problems. In the meantime, employees of the service center had taken over the museum's educational service, while the responsibility for motivation work in the local interpretation centers continued to fall on the volunteer staff.

An important part of the supplementary program involved the organization of round tables to reinforce exhibit themes, for example, in connection with the exhibit "The woman through baptismal clothing". Using the exhibit as a point of departure, citizens discussed various questions related to women, such as childbirth and family life. The

Ecomusée de la Haute Beauce used events of this kind to go beyond historical contemplation to confront issues related to the present and prospects for the future.

An exhibit-related activity emphasized by many other museums - mass-audience (as opposed to scholarly) publications - is relatively underdeveloped in the Ecomusée de la Haute Beauce. Catalogues, brochures and leaflets with supplementary information have been produced only rarely. Here a public relations innovation should be noted: since 1987, the Ecomusée de la Haute-Beauce has published a quarterly bulletin, Muséambule, which is sent gratis to some 6,000 households in the Haute-Beauce and is intended to keep the public up to date on the museum's activities (Muséambule, 1986, p. 1).

Another means for making the Ecomusée de la Haute-Beauce known and popular to the population was the organization of celebrations and social evenings, both of which were generally well received.

However, the Ecomusée de la Haute-Beauce doesn't demonstrate its closeness to the citizens only in the area of public relations and exhibit-related activities. A more elementary component of an open, decentralized museum is its representation in all parts of the territory, as Céré (1982a, p. 216) explained: "…decentralization is necessary so that the people will feel clearly that the museum belongs to them, that it is their tool, that there they can create, realize themselves, develop, recognize themselves. The museum has to be everywhere at once."

Within the framework of the decentralization program, called "Creative Haute-Beauce, territorial museum", the museum set up small open-air exhibits (cf. Musée et centre régional d'interprétation de la Haute Beauce 1982b; Céré 1983, Renaud, 1985). The purpose was essentially to show the population that the museum is not confined to St. Evariste, but rather that the ecomuseum is an undertaking that is geared to the entire region and that each person has a place in it (Céré). The open-air exhibits should be seen less as exhibits than as monuments or identification objects to mark the territory. Mayrand (cited by Davallon, 1986b, p. 106) characterized the exhibits as "a form of expression, conceived and carried out by a collective, in an open-air space, representing the history and aspirations of a population and making the environment dynamic." The first exhibit of this kind was opened in 1980 in St. Hilaire de Dorset.

In 1981 the two "gateways" to the Haute-Beauce region in St. Romain and St. Victor were marked with appropriate plaques. Other open-air exhibits were set up in 1982, for example "at the foot of the hill" in Lac Drolet and "angular stone of the Haute-Beauce" in St. Sébastien. Up to 1984 the exhibits that followed were:

"From landscape to folklore," Ste. Clothilde
"The vales of progress," St. Ephrem
"Plateau of maple," St. Benoit
"Plateau of agriculture," St. Honor
"The wind in the sails," Lambton.

The activities in the individual villages were supplemented by a comprehensive special exhibit ("exposition de synthese") in the museum in St. Evariste: "How the citizens of the HauteBeauce have appropriated their environment."

When visiting the open-air exhibits, as I did in 1984 in connection with "the first international workshop on new museology and ecomuseums," one gets the impression that these are relatively static monuments whose current utility is not so readily obvious - with the exception of marking territory, as mentioned above. In fact, this aspect is treated by the initiators as being of secondary importance. Of more fundamental significance is not so much the end product as the working and learning process that leads up to it (Mayrand). In the case at hand, this is the sensitization of the population and the accompanying territorialization of the HauteBeauce as a region within the framework of becoming aware and stimulated by dealing with a specific task - the marking of territory. Besides forming a regional awareness in the participants, setting up these exhibits also served the purpose of learning certain basic techniques, **which were the**

carriers and germinators of the future, leading to other actions, much more important than these" (Mayrand).

There was no doubt that interested citizens of the various parishes financed and constructed the mini-exhibits themselves. The question arises, however, whether the exhibits were conceived independently, as the initiators maintain. Whether the open-air exhibits were imposed or desired and conceived by the population must remain an open question.

A further means of decentralization were the so-called 11 "antennas" and associated groups, which have already been addressed. Small local interpretation centers supported by their respective local associations, they have no permanent collections. Objects on display are lent by the population on the spot and, after the exhibit is closed, are returned so that their owners and users can preserve them in situ.

The first antenna, established in 1983 in St. Hilaire de Dorset, was the "Maison des Gens de St. Hilaire." Although associated with the ecomuseum, it is wholly owned by the tourism and cultural action committee.

On the one hand, it houses a small permanent exhibit on the village school, the "école du rang." In addition, various special exhibits are held in this interpretation center, their themes mostly exploring the local collective memory. A more important task of this local interpretation center is genealogical research. The tourism and cultural action committee in St. Hilaire has drawn up the genealogies of the most important local families and made them available to the general public in a small exhibit in the Maison des Gens de St. Hilaire. Not only was genealogical research carried out on the spot, but efforts were also made to contact former residents of the village who had moved away.

There are other local interpretation centers in Ste. Clothilde and Courcelles. The latter -the expo-train in Courcelles - consists of a restored railroad car intended to house special annual exhibits on themes "associated with the railroad in central Quebec and its economic and social impact on the region's population and landscape" (text of the exhibit, recorded in October 1984).

Baron stated that, because the interpretation center was created without the involvement of the villagers, their lack of understanding expressed itself in the form of vandalism.

The Maison du Granit is to be another antenna on a larger scale (cf. Ecomusée de la Haute Beauce, 1984, p. 1), "a polyvalent interpretation and cultural center, a major tourist attraction, an ecological, cultural and commercial showcase" (cf. Céré 1987). After those responsible had launched the idea of the Maison du Granit, village meetings took place in those parishes involved in the project, St. Sébastien, Lac Drolet and Ste. Cécile de Whitton (in the area adjoining the Haute-Beauce).

The site of the Maison du Granit, a former granite quarry, was determined a long time ago. A subsidy of $180,000 (Can.) had already been promised to the museum in January 1985. The planning phase was completed in January 1987 and thus the implementation of the Maison du Granit interpretation center may now be followed with interest.

An important characteristic of the Ecomusée de la Haute-Beauce is its opening toward the outside, that is, the constitution of a widespread network of contacts with institutions and persons within and beyond the Haute-Beauce. In this way new perspectives and horizons are opened up to those involved and the danger of chauvinistic nostalgia for the homeland is lessened.

In the course of this external orientation, the Ecomusée de la Haute-Beauce has set up a program of partnerships and exchanges with two other ecomuseums: the Ecomusée de la Maison du Fier-Monde in Montreal and the Ecomusée Breton du Coglais in France. An active interchange has developed with the French ecomuseum, in particular. Apart from its obvious sensitization effect, this interchange has also considerably expanded the personal horizons of the participants.

In connection with the museum's regional orientation, collaboration with other institutions is of particular significance. The character of the institutions envisaged, as specified in the ecomuseum's statutes (Ecomusée de la Haute-Beauce, 1983a, p. 2), extends from "cultural, touristic, educational and recreational bodies of the region" to "administrative and economic authorities of the region, in particular ... the regional county municipalities and the ministries responsible for the development of the agroforestry region." For example, cooperation with the cultural institutions of the traditional Beauce region takes place within the framework of the Société du Patrimoine des Beaucerons (Heritage Society of the Beaucerons) and the Réseau des musées de la Beauce (Network of Museums of the Beauce), which was founded at the initiative of the Ecomusée de la Haute-Beauce and includes, in addition to the ecomuseum, the Musée Marius Barbeau in St. Joseph and the Musée et centre d'exposition Méchatigan in St. Georges (cf. Trudel, 1984).

In the economic area, the Ecomusée de la Haute-Beauce has thus far cooperated with the following institutions, among others:

> Conseil de Développement de la Chaudiere *(Chaudiere Development Council)*
> Municipalités régionales de comté *(Regional County Municipalities)*
> Union des producteurs agricoles *(Agricultural Producers Union)*
> Syndicats de production de l'acériculture *(Maple Production Trade Association)*
> Associations féminines *(Women'sAssociations)*
> Association touristique du pays de l'érable *(Tourism Association of the Land of the Maple)*.

The continuing cooperation between the ecomuseum and the Paysmage Company is intensive and fruitful. This is a group of young people who are concerned with the preservation of nature and the development of tourism, **the action group for the discovery of the landscape in Quebec** (Baron). Baron, a Paysmage worker and the main cooperating partner with the Ecomusée de la Haute-Beauce, outlined the objectives of the group as follows:

> ...one of its objectives, the main one, was to make it more possible for the largest possible number of Quebecois, also for people from the region, to

enjoy the landscape, to enhance its value. The best way of protecting it is to enhance its value, for people to find it beautiful, to profit from it.

For example, a park in the center of Courcelles and a trail on Mont St. Sébastien were established in cooperation with Paysmage. A further aspect of the ecomuseum's public orientation, which is already clear from the various cooperating partners listed above, is its diversification of activity and perspectives. Although the Ecomusée de la Haute-Beauce is primarily a cultural institution, it does not shy away from economic development. On the one hand, the museum and local interpretation centers create a limited number of jobs.

On the other hand, the museum endeavors to make people familiar with the producers of the region to increase sales of local products. One of the first initiatives of this kind was the traveling exhibit, "The maple with open heart," which featured in shopping malls and at agricultural fairs, for example, the International Maple Products Festival. Producers cooperated in the exhibit and also carried out promotional work at exhibit sites, where visitors learned about the overall development of maple culture from the past through the present and into the future (new technologies, effects of acid rain). The exhibit did not limit itself to technical aspects but also examined ecological, economic and cultural factors. Céré characterized this approach as "ecosystemic."

In general, the emphasis of the ecomuseum's economic-related activities is related to tourism. The museum's varied offerings are geared to making the Haute-Beauce an interesting destination for visitors. In addition to the local public, to which the museum is primarily directed, it also aims to stimulate weekend and short holiday visits. Museum workers associate the discovery and understanding of their own region with endeavors to open it to others.

One of the first initiatives in this respect was the establishment of the "integrated tourist routes through the countryside." The Ecomusée de la Haute-Beauce has developed a network of selfdirected walking and driving tours that enable visitors to familiarize themselves with the main attractions of the Haute-Beauce (cf. Trudel, 1984, p. 112). A walking tour was laid out for each of the five zones of the ecomuseum. The starting point for each is the service center, where the visitor receives a short introduction to the region's characteristics. A project to create a regional park in the Haute-Beauce with hiking and cross-country ski trails was being planned.

For local people queried, tourism and the hope of a regional economic revival are two of the main motivations for their work with the Ecomusée de la Haute-Beauce. They see. tourism as an alternative to the declining forest industry. However, the ecomuseum does not wish to encourage tourism on a large scale. Rather, it is seeking a form of "adapted" tourism, a small scale type of tourism, as René Rivard remarked:

> They do not want these to be people who burn up the miles, who don't talk to anyone, who do not respect their environment.

Monique Pomerleau characterized the ecomuseum as "a new form of tourism." The restoration and conversion of a historic mill into an interpretation center form the core of a project to create a tourism center in Ste. Clothilde, a village of 600 inhabitants. These measures are to be supplemented by the establishment of cultural walking routes and cross-country ski trails, presentations of plays and musical dramas in the mill, the creation of overnight accommodations, campaigns to beautify the village, etc.

The preceding overview gives a representative cross-section of the various activities and programs the Ecomusée de la Haute-Beauce provided during its seven years of existence.

Problematic aspects have already been referred to in individual cases. To conclude this case study, 1 will indicate how the those interviewed valued the "overall cultural action" of the Ecomusée de la Haute-Beauce.

3.1.1.6 Evaluation

The Ecomusée de la Haute-Beauce has not carried out a systematic evaluation of its effectiveness. In the meetings with museum workers, personal impressions and comparisons provided some assessment. However, those in positions of responsibility and the paid employees, in particular, consider that it is necessary and desirable to carry out evaluations.

In practice, however, the Ecomusée de la Haute-Beauce does not have the time, money or appropriate specialists to critically evaluate its activities. In order to bridge the current gap in evaluation studies, Hovanec proposed to hold round-table discussions with visitors so as to obtain some direct feedback:

> ...maybe this is not a scientific evaluation, but at least you will find yourself together with local people discussing this, and that will make it possible to find out their perceptions.

A current assessment of the activities of the Ecomusée de la Haute-Beauce can be made only through a comparison of the statements of the individuals I interviewed. With respect to the effectiveness of the activities and programs described above, a distinction needs to be made between two levels: the individual and the social. At the former level, the ecomuseum makes a real contribution to individual participant. For example, Lorraine Charest speaks of a "personal opening" and of the "great personal satisfaction" she has derived from her work in the museum. Ginette Fortin believes:

> There is an enrichment all along the line.

Guy Baron remarked:

The ecomuseum, in my opinion, is a body that has enabled a certain number of people to place a value on themselves and to express themselves and feel good inside their skin.

Maude Céré said something similar:

There are women who would say, 'I woke up this year, I did guided tours for whole bus loads, I was capable, I could express myself well, I wouldn't tremble, everything worked out fine, my ideas were clear, and it's the ecomuseum that made it possible for me to do that.' When you can say that, you tell yourself this is a success, it's fantastic.

Up to now the effect of the Ecomusée de la Haute-Beauce on social development has been limited. Hovanec said: For me, the five years that have passed have not really been socially relevant, in the sense of improving or changing a lot of things. However, the beginnings of social changes can be found in the area of territorialization of the region, that is, in the creation of a regional cohesion. People from the region who were questioned stated that, since the ecomuseum opened, they had become more familiar with their own neighborhood and significantly more knowledgeable about the region.

Expanded geographical knowledge and cooperative work in the Ecomusée de la Haute Beauce have instilled in participants a regional awareness and feeling of mutual belonging, as stated by Denis Hovanec. All of those asked expressed themselves positively and without reservation about the new regional cohesion.

The Ecomusée de la Haute-Beauce gives the population the possibility of discovering itself, the cultural and natural heritage of the region worth preserving, and local and regional values. It affords the opportunity to become conscious of the specific regional identity of the Haute-Beauce region. Guy Baron made this clear:

...this was the first time that the world of Courcelles saw itself. This is a world that had never seen itself. They watch television, but they have never seen themselves. They see the world of Montreal, but they have never seen themselves. I think that the ecomuseum makes it possible - and this is its great success - it makes it possible for people to see themselves. And they don't like to see themselves poor and forgotten in some corner, [...], they like to see themselves with a certain pride.

The emphasis of the activities is placed on imparting value to the population and its region. The exhibitions consequently lack critical perspectives. Those in positions of responsibility stressed that, at first, before taking up more provocative subjects, all the themes were consciously chosen to strengthen the population's self-awareness and confidence. Hovanec remarked:

...it is certain that the first five years revolved around giving value to the heritage and all of that, but this is a mechanism for triggering other things. In the end, it was necessary to begin with something very prosaic, something truly very close, in order to develop more afterwards.

Maude Céré states further:

First it was necessary to make exhibits that the people liked. [...] it is important to start with relatively simple subjects that the people like, and then to slowly evolve.

Thus far the Ecomusée de la Haute-Beauce has not carried out critical, problem-oriented exhibitions and activities. Problematical points are dealt with "in passing" in order not to be provocative.

According to Baron and Paul Bolduc, the Ecomusée de la Haute-Beauce has been too past oriented up to now. They feel that the emphasis should be more on the present and the future, and thus, open up new perspectives.

In order to increase its impact on the region's social development, the Ecomusée de la Haute-Beauce would not only have to orient itself more toward the present and future, but also have at its disposal more human and financial resources as well as stronger backing from the population.

The Ecomusée de la Haute-Beauce receives an average of 6,000 visitors a year. Around 50 percent of the visitors can be attributed to the local and regional public. As discussed in detail above, there is a core of 10-20 people who work with the museum continually. Grouped around this core are some 250 supporters who occasionally work for the museum in a wide variety of areas. By reaching this level of participation, the Ecomusée de la Haute-Beauce has produced an excellent result.

The volunteers whom I interviewed state unanimously that they became increasingly involved through their participation in the ecomuseum's activities, finally assuming roles in the various committees and, particularly at the local level, carrying out their own projects. It should be emphasized, however, that women such as Ginette Fortin, Lucille Létoumeau and Monique Pomerleau should be counted as part of the museum's active core, its "guiding spirits" (Létoumeau). These are women with an exceptional amount of initiative and readiness for action who understand how to put things in motion. This explains why the local committees in Lac Drolet, St. Hilaire and Ste. Clothilde - the committees within these women's field of action - carry out numerous activities and enjoy relatively good popularity with the local people. However, Céré states:

> But things aren't that way in all the villages, for example. There are still people who expect the ecomuseum to come to them to do something.

Overall, those surveyed agree that the Ecomusée de la Haute-Beauce is still not well enough known in the region and that an increase in active participation would be extremely desirable. New initiatives in this direction and the problems connected with them were mentioned earlier in the previous chapter. One critical problem should be stressed again: the dominance of Mayrand and Céré with respect to the initiation, planning and organization of the various activities and programs of the Ecomusée de la Haute-Beauce. Jacinthe Roy on this subject:

> ...Many people - and even us, if it comes to that - identify the ecomuseum with Maude and Pierre. There is no doubt that they are the ones who started it, but they should take themselves in hand and disengage a little more.

And Létourneau on the same subject:

> They run things well. In the end they are the parents of the project, they are the ones who have moved this forward [...]. Since it is their dream, they are the ones who most want it to advance.

If the Ecomusée de la Haute-Beauce is to make real progress, the population must cut loose from the umbilical cord and take the museum's future into its own hands. It cannot be foreseen at this time whether this will happen. It appears the way to autonomy is still long and arduous.

Great efforts have been made since the establishment of the Ecomusée de la Haute-Beauce.

Something has been achieved, but occasionally there is doubt whether the ecomuseologia concept can be realized 100 percent (Hovanec). On May 16, 1987, the Ecomusée de la Haute Beauce invited citizens and specialists associated with the museum to a round-table discussion in order to take stock and in this way impart new impulses. The discussion reflected quite realistically the central problem of the Ecomusée de la Haute-Beauce: participation and, in that connection, relationships between the museum and the community. In conclusion, let us cite a reflection by Mayrand (written comments on the interview, December 1986), in which he makes clear that the development of the Ecomusée de la Haute-Beauce is an open question, the answer to which should continue to be pursued attentively. According to Mayrand, it is increasingly apparent:

...that ecomuseology is a process that is continually in question, that the ecomuseum is realized in steps, that these steps do not follow a linear progression: there are breaks, moments when things stop, leaps forward, undercurrents, work that is sometimes long and imperceptible. This is why one should avoid making summary judgments... The ecomuseum is a path one must constantly return to, a building of which it is difficult to foresee. Whether it will have a roof, even whether there is a need for it. The ecomuseum is an open question for a population.

The dynamics and openness of the ecomuseological concept will become clearer in the next chapter, where the example of the Ecomusée de la Maison du Fier-Monde will demonstrate the adaptation of the ecomuseum to an urban context.

3.1.2 Ecomusée de la Maison du Fier-Monde

3.1.2.1 Montréal Centre-Sud[1]

The present-day Centre-Sud, consisting of the parishes of Ste. Marie and St. Jacques, is Montreal's oldest working-class district, called by its inhabitants the "Faubourg à m'lasse" after the sugar factory (Méthot). Proximity to transportation routes (St. Lawrence River and railroads) was the decisive factor in establishing a wide variety of industries, for example beer, rubber, sugar, textiles and wood (cf. Maison du Fier-Monde, 1985a, p. 10f). In the19th- and up to the mid- 20th century, Centre-Sud was a lively and expanding cultural and industrial center - the heart, so to speak, of French-Canadian Montreal (cf. Desrosiers, Lafleur, 1981, p. 66f; Soucy-Roy, 1977).

In the last 30 or 40 years, however, a serious reversal has taken place in Centre-Sud (cf. Gonzales, Joseph, 1984): businesses and cultural institutions have closed or moved away. The declining economy of Centre-Sud has had social consequences. Between 1966 and 1980 the population decreased approximately 50 percent; today it totals 37,000. Twenty percent are unemployed and welfare recipients, 26 percent low-income workers, and twenty percent pensioners (Desrosiers, Lafleur 1981, p. 11; cf. Centre St. Pierre, 1984). The unemployment rate in Centre-Sud is double that of Montreal as a whole, while per capital income is half (Binette). Its poor socioeconomic position creates pressing problems for inhabitants, as cited by Binette:

---

[1] If the origin of statements is not further specified, they are summaries I have made of the available material. When I refer to Binette, Méthot or Fontaine without further information, they are René Binette (2-6-85), Bertheline Méthot (2-7-85) and Arme Fontaine (2-7-85).

The most elementary needs - paying the rent, eating, finding a job - these are the urgent problems. There are so many unemployed, so many welfare recipients, that is the number one problem. What do you eat this weekend? …The problems are not five years from now, the problems are right there, today and tomorrow. They are immediate problems.

Centre-Sud is a dead or dying neighborhood of the underprivileged, ruled by unemployment, poverty, loss of orientation and resignation.

While the area had to struggle against economic and social decline, its selection as the site of highway and large construction projects further affected its viability, destroying a significant part of the residential area and closing schools, markets and businesses. According to a brochure of the Maison du Fier-Monde (1985a, p. 14): "… the strategic position of Centre-Sud as a communication axis was to cost the area dearly, part of it being sacrificed to transportation."

The present-day Centre-Sud is bounded by two main highways on the north and south, by a railroad line on the east and by the university and Montreal' s business and trade center on the west. However, the city is not only the neighborhood's boundary; it also threatens further destructive advances into the residential areas of Centre-Sud in the forms of elegant office and bank buildings and their occupants, who require businesses, restaurants and living space.

Citizens of Centre-Sud have introduced countless initiatives in the past 15 to 20 years in order to counteract these tendencies toward the destruction of traditional living spaces and estrangement of residents from their neighborhood. These measures attempt to counteract the effects of the prevailing catastrophic socioeconomic situation in one way or anoother, and to support the population in reclaiming possession of its neighborhood. Binette speaks of approximately 50 so-called "community groups" in the neighborhood today (cf. Maison du FierMonde/Habitations Communautaires Centre-Sud 1982; Bottin Pop…. 1983).

3.1.2.2 Origin
The Maison du Fier-Monde, a neighborhood museum

The Maison du Fier-Monde project began in June 1980 through the citizen initiative "Habitation Communautaire Centre-Sud" (cf. Binette, Cloutier 1983, p. 5), and intended to establish residential cooperatives ("coopératives d'habitation"). However, the organization did not deal merely with the creation of favorable housing conditions, or, as Binette says:

> …a place where you live well is not only a house, it includes something else.

Sociocultural institutions were needed to breathe new life into the neighborhood. Hence the idea of creating a neighborhood museum, an idea proposed by outside social workers and so-called "animateurs" (motivators) active in the citizen initiative (Desrosiers, Lafleur, 1981, p. 12).

It is important to note here that, although the origin of the Maison du Fier-Monde belongs in a certain sense to a citizen initiative, the project goes back to the efforts of a small group of people who occupy a special position in the community as a result of the know-how they acquired through their education. Méthot remarked:

> Take me personally, I would not have put it in a favorable light, because I would not have known how. Naturally, at the conceptual level, there is someone who lived in the neighborhood, who had done higher studies, he had traveled, who had thought at a certain moment that perhaps, with all there is in the way of objects of value in the neighborhood at the individual level, buildings, everything else, it might be possible to make a museum… This happened to us at a certain moment, something was put down on paper… After that, it was accepted by the Habitations Communautaires.

The result was that a group of interested citizens founded, together with the leading members of the Habitation Communautaire Centre-Sud, a so-called "museum committee." The planning committee developed the first ideas and proposals for the establishment of a neighborhood museum in consultation with outside historians and museologists (cf. the working paper Projet du musée de voisinage... 1980 and Compte Rendu... 1980; Quelques Notes... 1980; Notes de Parcours... 1981; Maison du Fier-Monde no year). As justification for this way of proceeding, the working paper states (Projet du musée voisinage... 1980, 4): "Ideally, the project should be prepared and directed by the citizens of our neighborhood. But one should have no illusions: it will not be the great mass of the citizens who are interested in the project from the beginning. And this is normal! A man who has lost his pride cannot find the way out by himself. Particularly if this lack of pride is reinforced by the shame of living in a neighborhood of 'poor people' [...]. In the initial phase of the project we will therefore need outside help to demonstrate the need for the project and its feasibility. Once this demonstration has been made, we will request the acceptance of the citizens. It is certainly at this stage that our fellow citizens will begin to participate."

The objectives of the Maison du Fier-Monde were formulated as follows in the initial phase of the museum committee (Desrosiers, Lafleur, 1981, p. 14):

> Through the creation of an ecomuseum, to make the presentation of heritage into a tool for education and collective action;
> To create a commercial space (public market, restaurants, shops) where the population of the neighborhood could meet;
> To create a space that will serve as a rallying point for meetings of all kinds.

At the beginning of the museum committee's work[2], a document on the history of Centre Sud (1840-1960) was prepared with the financial support of the Quebec Ministry of Cultural Affairs. This was to serve as a basis for further planning. It was published in December 1980 (Les

---

[2] With respect to the activities of the initial phase, see Echéancier, 1981; Maison du Fier Monde, 1982c, 1982d, 1982f; Projects et taches, 1982.

Habitations Communautaires Centre-Sud 1980). In the spring of 1981 this document resulted in the first historical exhibit on the eating and dressing habits of neighborhood residents: "Du marché d'hier au musée de demain" (From yesterday's market to tomorrow's museum). This first public appearance of the Maison du Fier-Monde was a great success.

Also in 1981, a publication was released in which the museum project was explained in detail (Desrosiers, Lafleur, 1981). In December 1981 another exhibit was opened – a traveling exhibit called "La Maison du Fier-Monde" organized by 20 "people's groups." The planning committee was simultaneously a promotion committee. One of its most pressing tasks was to make the Maison du Fier-Monde project publicly known and accepted by Centre-Sud citizens.

The Ecomusée de la Maison du Fier-Monde

In May 1982 the museum was renamed the Ecomusée de la Maison du Fier-Monde[3], because the basic principles of ecomuseology – identification with a territory, participation of the population and decentralization – roughly corresponded to those of the Maison du Fier-Monde.

The Ecomusée de la Maison du Fier-Monde explained this fact in leaflets distributed to the public: "The Maison du Fier-Monde is interested in the past and bears witness to history, which is done in order to take control of the future. Thus, the Maison du Fier-Monde offers a mirror to the population of Centre-Sud. The Maison du Fier-Monde is a museum that belongs to the citizens; it therefore speaks to everyone. It is a meeting place where the population expresses its experiences. This is what an ecomuseum is!" (Maison du Fier-Monde no year, leaflet II). "Essentially and differently from a traditional museum, the ecomuseum maintains organic ties to its environment. Specifically, this means that the very life

---

[3] Hereafter, the name "Maison du Fier-Monde and the Ecomusée de la Maison du Fier Monde are entered under "Maison du Fier Monde."

of the ecomuseum, its exhibits, its activities and its overall choices are a function of the environment in which it was created, of the history of that environment, of its characteristics, its concerns, its forecf.able future etc. [...]." (Maison du Fier-Monde no year, leaflet l).

However, renaming the Maison du Fier-Monde neighborhood museum the Ecomusée de la Maison du Fier-Monde was based not only on conceptual correspondences with ecomuseology. Binette presents further grounds:

> We are a true ecomuseum [...]; we meet the criteria. Except that you can certainly say that there are also strategic advantages [...] that is, [from] joining the Association of Ecomuseums in Quebec, to participating in that whole movement that is developing [...], that is the thing to do to a certain extent. If the train is pulling in, you get on it. Thus, there are also reasons that are really of a strategic nature.

3.1.2.3 Conception and objectives

The Maison du Fier-Monde was intended to be a meeting place for the population of Centre-Sud, a place to confront the past and to analyze and discuss it. It is one of the few educational institutions in Quebec that deals exclusively with labor history.

The name Maison du Fier-Monde (House of the Proud People) is to be understood programmatically. This museum sought to engender pride and self-respect among neighborhood residents. By imparting knowledge of their historical roots, the Maison du Fier-Monde wished to empower the citizens of Centre-Sud and enable them to control their future in a spirit of self-confidence. By analyzing the neighborhood's history, the Maison du Fier-Monde helped citizens carve out "identification markers," that is, clues to a sense of belonging and responsibility.

Here, history is not pursued for its own sake, but rather to connect the past to the present and future (Fontaine). History and cultural heritage are seen as tools for future development. A position paper (1984a, p. 1) refers to the nature of the Maison du Fier-Monde as a tool: "The Maison du Fier-Monde, at the same time a tool for recalling the past and an opportunity for meetings and public events, is the favored means of showing the way forward in order, on the one hand, to arouse in the citizens of Centre-Sud true pride in belonging to a neighborhood with such a rich and generous past and, on the other hand, to give these same residents a unique opportunity to participate fully in the future of their neighborhood."

One speaks of the future of the neighborhood, not development. Indeed, the term "development" does not appear in the discourse of the Maison du Fier-Monde's workers. When asked, they said it was difficult for them to define development positively because measures for so-called neighborhood development in the past worked only to their disadvantage and contributed to their neighborhood' s destruction.

Disregarding the word's negative connotations, Binette and Méthot express themselves hesitantly regarding what development of the neighborhood might ideally mean. According to Binette, development must be based on the needs of those who have to struggle with direct existential problems. For Méthot, development in the interests of the population of Centre-Sud means first of all concrete improvement of basic living conditions for those whose income is permanently below the poverty line and particularly for single childrearers. Méthot described these families' distress:

> ... the lowest rent in Centre-Sud is $270 a month[4]. Heat and light are not included, so that brings the rent up to $300-350 a month. If the woman or man who is alone with two children gets $600 a month and half of it goes to pay the rent, the heat and the electricity, nothing is left to eat on. Nothing is left for recreation, nothing is left to clothe the children, to clothe themselves, but nevertheless they need a minimum of clothing.

---

[4] Dollar amounts refer to Canadian dollars.

The Maison du Fier-Monde originally wanted to make a contribution to improving the living standard of part of the population of Centre-Sud by creating jobs. In its initial phase, consideration was given to integrating the museum into a complex of businesses, restaurants and a market (cf. Desrosiers, Lafleur, 1981; Notes de parcours... 1981). However, this ambitious plan had to be discarded because of the constrained financial situation, and in fact the museum itself had to fight continually for its own survival. The possibilities for the Maison du FierMonde itself to create jobs were extremely limited (cf. section 3.1.2.4), so that no impulses in this regard can be expected from the Maison du Fier-Monde.

Nor does the provision of concrete offers of help to the population figure in the acknowledged objectives of the Maison du Fier-Monde. It does not view itself as a social welfare or charitable institution:

> The mandate is not to solve short-term problems or severe problems. (Fontaine).

There are further reasons for this. In the first place, the Maison du Fier-Monde had to avoid entering into competition with already existing service groups. On the other hand, the Maison du Fier-Monde, with full insight into the need for such services, was convinced that excessive support was not in the citizens' interest.

Thus, the Maison du Fier-Monde avowedly wished to contribute only indirectly to coping with the concrete problems of everyday life and neighborhood development. Through its work in the area of awareness building, it sought to create the prerequisites for local control over future development. Citizen-related development implies for the workers of the Maison du Fier-Monde (Binette) **... the environment taking charge of the environment.**

3.1.2.4 Structure and organization

Since 1984 the Maison du Fier-Monde has had its permanent headquarters in the former St. Eusebe Elementary School[5], where various citizen initiatives have formed the Carrefour St. Eusebe (the St.-Eusebe Crossroads). In addition, the Maison du Fier-Monde is represented in the Centre-Sud neighborhood by two so-called "antennas": the rue Olivier-Robert and the Polyvalente Pierre-Dupuy (cf. section 3.1.2.5).

The Maison du Fier-Monde is a private museum not recognized by the government. The establishment of an independent association (literally, a "corporation") of 60 to 70 citizens accompanied the renamed Ecomusée de la Maison du Fier-Monde (cf. Maison du Fier-Monde, 1982g). Some of the requirements for membership are that the members be citizens of CentreSud, if possible, or at least that they show a special interest in the neighborhood, and that they be of age. The association's bylaws (Maison du Fier Monde, 1982a) established the structure of the association and the principles of its decision-making hierarchy. The society meets once or twice a year in a membership meeting, which is attended by an average of 25 to 30 people. The bylaws (Maison du Fier-Monde, 1982a, p. 2) state: "The general meeting of the members is the supreme authority of the corporation." In addition, projects are also proposed and discussed by the museum workers and (to a limited extent) by the members. Finally, decisions are reached on projects for the following year (Maison du Fier-Monde, 1985b).

In addition, the membership meeting chooses a museum board ("conseil d' administration," literally "board of directors") that is mandated with making decisions on the association' s business on behalf of its members: "The board of directors shall exercise, [...], the powers

---

[5] As long as the Maison du Fier-Monde has existed, those responsible for it have been concerned with creating an appropriate permanent residence for the museum. The negotiations have broken down time and again and the failures have had to be borne. A detailed account of this is given in the "Bilan du project de l'école Plessis" (Maison du Fier-Monde, 1984c).

delegated to it by the general meeting, [...]" (Maison du Fier-Monde, 1982a, p. 5). The board is accountable to the membership.

The museum board consists of a chairman, the deputy, a secretary, a treasurer, an adviser and the coordinator of the Maison du Fier-Monde (the only non-elected member of the group). Elections are held once a year for only part of the board members. The chairman's and deputy's terms of office are two years (Méthot). In addition to the actual voting members of the museum board, each museum worker and each member of the society has the right in principle to take part as an observer in the meetings of the board.

Immediately after the association was formed, the board met every week to set all the machinery in motion. Since then, meeting frequency has settled down to once a month. The board deals primarily with administrative matters (Binette), related, for example, to obtaining and managing project resources, recruitment of museum workers or finding a permanent home for the Maison du Fier-Monde.

The board recruited a coordinator to represent its interests and decisions in everyday relations with the other museum workers and report back to the board. At present the coordinator not only receives and carries out orders and makes reports, but also makes many decisions, either independently or in consultation with the workers. The museum workers attend staff meetings at least once a week, at which they discuss all current matters and develop proposals for the board. At the time of my research, the staff consisted of a motivator, a researcher, and a coordinator.

The personnel situation of the Maison du Fier-Monde is lamentable, mainly due to lack of financial resources. Because the Maison du Fier-Monde is not accredited by the government, it has no regular annual budget, but is essentially dependent on project-linked subsidies by the federal and provincial governments and on job-creation measures.

The peculiarities of job-creation measures have quite specific personal consequences for the workers of the Maison du Fier-Monde (Binette):

The three people who work here, Berte, Anne and I, are actually not workers, we are unemployed. We are volunteer unemployed persons within an organization for 40 hours a week. Because we are unemployed persons within an organization, our unemployment insurance benefits are raised to an amount that is quite interesting, but the fact remains that we are unemployed and are considered to be actively seeking employment, just like any other unemployed person.

The financing of the Maison du Fier-Monde through projects and job-creation measures creates a considerable level of insecurity with regard to the museum's continued existence. It is more and more uncertain how the museum will be funded a half year from now. In 1983-84, the museum went through a serious crisis that resulted from financial difficulties. From May 1983 to February 1984 the museum had no permanent paid employees. Binette on this subject:

And at that time, it was on the verge of completely failing.

Since they have been employed at the Maison du Fier-Monde, René Binette and Bertheline Méthot have worked two-thirds of their time on the basis of temporary contracts and one-third on a volunteer basis without pay. This has been possible only because of their extraordinary motivation and readiness to contribute.

Their personal experience with unpaid employment makes them refuse to systematically involve volunteers:

It must be said that the word "voluntary" is itself not a word that we like a lot, nor is it a philosophy that we like. [...]. We don't try to go looking for people in the neighborhood.

Unpaid employment is essentially limited to the five members of the museum board and the two main members of the staff (periodically employed). Apart from this hard base of colleagues, who work without remuneration at various levels and invest a lot of time and work in the Maison du Fier-Monde, the museum does not intend to extend further the unpaid employment of its members. In view of the constrained social and economic position of most of the residents of Centre-Sud, Binette and Méthot felt that it was exploitation to let people work regularly without adequate pay.

Binette demands rather formation of a permanent paid staff and, in this respect, also reflects the position of the museum board. The institution needs a team of permanent employees to ensure continuity and coordination of the work of the Maison du Fier-Monde. Binette says:

> It takes a minimum of paid permanent staff to be able to do a lot of things. […]. It takes a team of paid people to bring the people together. Because volunteers are ready to give you an evening, a day, a weekend, perhaps two weeks of vacation, but they do not want to do the whole thing from A to Z. It takes paid people to do the dull things, the things that nobody wants to do. That is normal, those are our jobs […]. People are interested in mounting an exhibit or putting up a mural, that is an extraordinary experience, but that takes at a minimum someone who can coordinate all of this.

A further reason for the small number of volunteers is a certain cautious, waiting reserve the population has toward this new institution. Méthot says:

> Maybe one day they will be ready for it, but at the present time they are still very fearful, because the Maison du Fier-Monde is new, it is too new for them.

Concern about including the citizens in the work of the Maison du Fier-Monde and about integrating the museum into the life of the neighborhood is one of the essential characteristics of the Maison du Fier-Monde. Méthot says:

What is important for me is to make the history of the neighborhood with the people of the neighborhood, for them and with them.

Where the inclusion of the citizens in the work of the Maison du Fier-Monde is concerned, what is understood is not so much regular unpaid employment, because of the reservations discussed above, but rather the various forms of citizen involvement that Binette and Méthot refer to as participation, which they specify as follows (Binette):

> There are people who are members of the Maison du Fier-Monde who come to the general meetings, who participate by giving an interview when the oral tradition is being recorded, by giving their photographs, by being promoters of the Maison du Fier-Monde in their circle, by coming to the exhibits. For us these are different levels of participation. The goal is not to bring people to give so many days a week or so many days a month.

First of all, participation is to be found at the decision-making level, that is, participation in the members meeting and the museum board. However, participation in the board, in particular, requires an expenditure of time and work that only a few citizens of the neighborhood are actually able to make. Anne Fontaine, who was secretary of the board for a period of time, observed:

> ...the most difficult thing there, no matter the group, is to combine your life with volunteering. If you do things as a volunteer, that's o.k. at first, but in the long run it is tiring, it demands a lot [...]. This is a problem with participation. In any event it is hard for me to combine my life at home, another job, volunteer work here, other activities and my family.

Méthot described the extreme case:

>...it is hard to participate when you are hungry. It is hard to participate when you know that tomorrow you may not have food to give to your children.

Furthermore, Méthot said the citizens of Centre-Sud are generally not sufficiently informed to commit themselves actively to the work of the Maison du Fier-Monde.

Even if these obstacles are overcome and the citizens do participate, their actual influence on events is limited. Because of their involvement in everyday matters and their continual presence, the coordinator and employees have a relatively strong position on the board and at the members meeting. In practice, the content is predominantly determined by the employees.

Practical experience makes employees familiar with arguments, hypotheses and the potential for solving problems. This gives them a head-start when it comes to the museum board and membership, which means that initiatives and proposals come less from the community (that is, from the members of the association) than from the museum staff. Thus, although the population formally has all possibilities of participating on the basis of the association's structure, its real participation at the level of initiatives, proposals and decisions is relatively small. Binette remarked:

> If you are there all day, 35 hours a week for a certain number of weeks, it is certain that you have a power that is real.

Despite these limitations, the members meeting remains the official participatory body of the Maison du Fier-Monde. An effort is made to make the meetings as attractive as possible to induce members' involvement.

A broader level of participation that differs from attending meetings involves making photographs, documents, objects and interviews available to the Maison du Fier-Monde. In this way, residents supply the raw material for exhibit projects, for example, but without participating further in their conception and implementation. In the end, it is the Maison du Fier-Monde's workers who produce something from this material and present the finished product to the population.

Although the population contributes in some way to the exhibits, it still remains a consumer with respect to the end product. Still, according to Binette, a simple museum visit is a form of participation:

> ...there is also another level of participation. This is quite simply to come to the Maison du Fier-Monde, to cf. an exhibit and afterwards, around a cup of coffee, to discuss what was seen, to talk about what the neighborhood was, of what it has become and where it is going... There are so many ways of participating, at a minimal level, that is, to come once, to come cf. what the museum is.

3.1.2.5 Activities and programs

The activities of the Maison du Fier-Monde include research, collection and documentation, as well as communication through exhibits, sound-and-slide shows and neighborhood tours, in which educational guides from the museum play a special role (Binette; cf. also Maison du Fier-Monde 1982c; 1982f; 1983c; 1983d; 1984a; 1984d; 1985c; 1985d; 1985e; 1987).

Museum activities are basically oriented toward imparting knowledge to the public. Research, collection and documentation are not ends in themselves, as in many traditional museums, but relate to an exhibit, a sound-and-slide show, a neighborhood tour, a publication, etc.

The Maison du Fier-Monde does not have a collection in the traditional sense. Objects are not housed in a museum setting, but are lent by the citizens to the Maison du Fier-Monde for exhibits. The collection proper consists largely of photographs and written documents that citizens have made available to the museum. The museum collection will find its way into the documentation center of the Maison du Fier-Monde, which is under construction (cf. Maison du Fier-Monde, 1983a).

Research and collecting at the Maison du Fier-Monde emphasize the so-called "collective memory," the commonly experienced history of the neighborhood's residents, the collective life history of the neighborhood, so to speak. Basically, the Maison du Fier-Monde endeavors to have this narrated history inform its programs so that visitors can identify with their content.

Up to now, research has been carried out by various people within the framework of job creation measures. Citizens rarely take an active part, that is, participate in the studies as researchers. Frequently the research breaks new ground, since up to now, who has been interested in the history of a French-Canadian working-class neighborhood? Thanks to the research carried out by the museum, a piece of everyday history is written down and a piece of the "culture des autres" (the other people's culture) is rescued from oblivion.

In 1987 the Maison du Fier-Monde began a long-term research and exhibit project in cooperation with the University of Quebec at Montreal. The goal was to prepare a systematic history of industrialization in Centre-Sud (cf. Maison du Fier-Monde, 1986a), for which the community was to play an active role in researching and writing.

The Maison du Fier-Monde parallels the approach and experiences of Sven Lindquist (1978; 1983; 1985), who conducted popular historical research in Sweden. The work of the increasingly numerous history workshops in the German Federal Republic also provides some interesting ideas in connection to this. At the moment, the organizers are primarily interested in how these groups function in detail, how they work (Binette, conversation of 11-20-86). The Maison du Fier-Monde is seeking, in the form of a systematic educational program, to introduce the citizens to the methods of historical research so that they will be in a position to research and write their own history under the guidance of the museum. Johanne Lemieux states (1987, 15):

"Within the framework of this project, we are focusing on a research and education methodology that will enable the residents and workers of the neighborhood to produce their own knowledge of their history. In this way, the citizens will be able to participate in all the stages of research and writing."

The research material - the historical evidence - is not well ordered and readily on hand in a museum or documentation center of labor history, but rather is found in the streets, houses, drawers, attics and minds of the residents of Centre-Sud. The main task of this research project was to encourage the population to discover these things for themselves and make them usable in an exhibition or other program.

The most important tool for the Maison du Fier-Monde is the exhibit. A total of six exhibits have been mounted since it was formed:

1. "From the market of yesterday to the museum of tomorrow" (4-24 and 25, 1981)
2. «Maison du Fier-Monde» (12-12 and 13, 1981)
3. "Rue Olivier-Robert" (May 1982)
4. "Workers' housing" (May 1983-December 1984)
5. "Between the factory and the kitchen" (December 1984- November 1986)
6. "A trip to Centre-Sud" (opened 4-9-87).

A particular characteristic of the ecomuseum relates to the physical and social environment of the neighborhood, to such an extent that its activities partly go beyond the four walls of the museum proper ... so that decentralized actions are carried out throughout the territory (Binette). Therefore, besides the exhibits and activities that accompany the exhibits, neighborhood walking tours form a significant offering of the Maison du Fier-Monde. There are three tours:

1. Visit to Centre-Sud
2. The beautiful streets of the neighborhood
3. A walk around St. Anselme

Two maps give an initial overview and the itinerary of the tours (Maison du Fier-Monde no year [a], leaflet l; 1985a. p. 62f). Accompanying brochures published by the Maison du Fier-Monde furnish more detailed information (Maison du Fier-Monde, 1982e; 1985a).

These walking tours not only track the hidden beauties of the neighborhood, they emphasize the social dimension of the mute witnesses of history, which are presented in the form of streets, houses, factories, churches, schools, parks, etc. Basically, the history associated with one building or another is sought. What did this or that mean for the residents of the neighborhood? What effect did it have on their daily life?

Moreover, history is not pursued here for its own sake, but rather functions as an instrument for coping with the present. The point of departure is the present, the image of the neighborhood today and its current problems. Apart from historical buildings, the program also includes structures and institutions that play a decisive role in the history and present-day reality of Centre-Sud residents, that is, primarily, the large construction projects and social institutions referred to earlier.

The so-called "antennas" are of significance in connection with the presence of the Maison du Fier-Monde in the neighborhood. At the same time, they can relate to groups associated with the museum and to their programs. Méthot compared the Maison du Fier-Monde and its "antennas" to a tree:

> For me, it is as if I had a large tree and there were branches on it. A tree that does not have many branches is not very strong, it is sick. The more antennas there are, the stronger the tree.

In 1981 the rue Olivier-Robert became the first "antenna." Some of its residents, under the guidance of a resident historian, got together to research the history of the street, in part by analyzing documents, but more by questioning the people who lived there. The results resulted in a public exhibit and a sound-and-slide show. In addition, the history of the neighborhood also finds its way into a wall painting that artists have put up in cooperation with the residents of the rue Olivier-Robert. The painting not only beautifies the external appearance

of the street, but also makes concrete references to the historical, present-day and future reality of the residents' lives. On this subject, Cloutier, Binette state (1983, p. 10): "This mural is thus in a certain way an immense mirror in which the people recognize themselves and in which they are proud to recognize themselves. For the Maison du Fier-Monde, which uses territorial identity to remake, and pride to re-find, the keystone to the future of the population of the Centre-Sud neighborhood, it is easy to understand that the execution of this mural is an important gesture that directly records its steps to restore value to the past and the present."

Another "antenna," the Polyvalent Pierre Dupuy secondary school, established close contacts with the museum. Both antennas serve to create links between the neighborhood and the Maison du Fier-Monde.

However, the action plan of the Maison du Fier-Monde for 1985-86 (Maison du Fier Monde 1985e, p. 3) stated that links to the antennas had recently been neglected, because the programmatic emphasis lay in other areas. It has not been possible to include the antennas in decisions at the level of the museum board. The Maison du Fier-Monde has other priorities for the immediate future.

Binette explained (11-20-86) that while close ties with the museum's surroundings were important – for example, in connection with the history project – creating official antennas with representation on the board was of secondary importance. He stated further:

> The people are interested in participating in activities, but are they interested in sitting on a board of directors? Power belongs to those who do the job.

It should also be noted that all resources – time, work and money - must be used to make the Maison du Fier-Monde functional, productive and known.

Publications make up an important aspect of public relations work. On the one hand, they are intended to be easily read, in order to reinforce an exhibit's themes, for example, but on the other hand, they serve as a motivational tool (Maison du Fier Monde 1984b, p. 5) within and outside the context of school lessons (cf. e.g. Barrette, 1986). Thus, these materials are used not only by schools and youth groups, but also in other citizen initiatives, provided they address appropriate themes (Binette, conversation of 11-20-86).

Another aspect of public relations work is publicity in the form of invitations, posters and leaflets. In this connection, the employees of the Maison du Fier-Monde consider it important to adopt a uniform design or layout, thereby giving the museum a long-term public image and supporting its recognition. The Maison du Fier-Monde also draws attention to itself in the media (cf. Maison du Fier-Monde, 1985f), particularly in the neighborhood newspaper La Criée and on the radio. The Maison du Fier-Monde increased exposure through celebrations at exhibit openings, the issuance of a publication, and holding a members meeting.

Finally, cooperation with other citizen initiatives and groups active in the neighborhood provides the Maison du Fier-Monde with a certain neighborhood presence. Occasionally the museum organizes evenings of discussion or entertainment with other community groups.

Moreover, it supports these groups when their activity corresponds to the objectives of the museum. (Binette, Méthot).

Publicity is not intended to increase visitation senselessly. The Maison du Fier Monde is clearly uninterested in attracting "casual customers" who would merely improve attendance statistics. The entrance to the St. Eusebe School does not even have the smallest sign that indicates the presence of the Maison du Fier-Monde on the third floor. Seriously interested visitors must already know where they can find the museum.

The target the Maison du Fier-Monde wants to attract is clear: in principle, all interested members of the public, including neighborhood residents and outsiders. Participants in neighborhood tours have been primarily strangers, that is, non-resident visitors, although the tours were intended to make local residents more familiar with their neighborhood. Binette believed it was a problem of motivation. The residents of Centre-Sud are given unlimited priority by the Maison du Fier-Monde. Binette noted:

> The Museum of Fine Arts does not address itself to the people who live around the Museum of Fine Arts. No kind of museum addresses itself to the people around it, while here we are defined in relation to a neighborhood.

Within the neighborhood, the Maison du Fier-Monde targets a variety of population groups, with students constituting about half of the visitors (Binette, conversation of 11-4-86). With respect to the makeup of the public, Binette stated:

> Our exhibits are seen both by elderly people and by nursery schools, it is the type of motivation work that changes. A visit to an exhibit is carried out in one way with nursery schools, in another way with the elderly, in another way with secondary schools, in another way with a women's group. The way of motivation is very flexible. […].
> People are not left to tour the exhibit just any way […]. We are not a museum where you buy your ticket and take the tour.

Méthot is in charge of education and interpretative materials for exhibits. As a housewife, mother and former waitress, she has no formal training in cultural work but has acquired the necessary knowledge through years of working on various citizen initiatives (Méthot). Her work includes leading visitors through the exhibit, answering questions, giving explanations. In connection with that, she motivates visitors over a cup of coffee to tell their own exhibit-related stories, share them with others and become aware of how their lives are conditioned by history. Both exhibits and motivation work strive to put individual experiences in their historical and social context.

3.1.2.6 Evaluation

Apart from mandatory final reports to the project's financial backers (cf. Maison du Fier Monde, 1983c; 1983d; 1984d; 1985c), the Maison du Fier-Monde makes no systematic evaluation of its activities.

However, the employees of the Maison du Fier-Monde endeavor to assess, as fully as possible, the success or failure of their efforts to meet the needs of the public. Measures of success include the degree to which the museum is known as well as attendance figures. In a survey of neighborhood groups conducted by the local newspaper La Criée (circulation 25,000), the Maison du Fier-Monde enjoys the highest degree of recognition, about 15 percent of respondents (Binette).

Considering the circumstances, the number of visitors is satisfactory. About 150 people attended the last exhibit opening - "Between the factory and the kitchen" (Binette). In total, about 3,700 people visited the exhibit (Binette, conversation of 11-4-86). Regarding this number, it should be noted that the Maison du Fier-Monde has no casual public. With few exceptions, visitors – be they groups or individuals – make an appointment and are led through the exhibit by the motivator. Hence, the visit has a quality that is often not possible in larger museums with larger attendance. Often visitors not only look at the exhibit, they also view the sound-and-slide show on the history of workers' housing in Centre-Sud and take a neighborhood tour (Binette, conversation of 11-20-86).

Another gauge of success are the personal reactions workers encounter as a result of direct contact with visitors taking the guided tours. In the course of conversations with museum visitors, it is possible to determine their impressions of what they were shown. Méthot explains:

> ...people recognize themselves, and they talk and talk and talk about the things that are there...They wanted to talk about them. I was able to ask two questions and they talked, simply talked, 1never asked each of them to talk in turn, they would all talk together, they would tell each other about it... But this stirred them up. When they were shown how this took place

during the years they were exploited. When they are shown the exhibit about women, they realize how they have been exploited and they want to say it. I find that this produces gasps and cries on the spot, that's what happens and you don't have to do anything else.

And, of course, this accords with the objective of the Maison du Fier-Monde to be primarily a meeting place, a place where ideas are exchanged, where people recognize themselves in their shared history, where they discover their own qualities and strengths and begin to be conscious of future possibilities.

Anne Fontaine stresses that no short-term changes in living conditions result from dealing with everyday history:

> ...they're not going to leave here with a job. These aren't things that are going to straighten out their problems.

Méthot also expresses something similar:

> History doesn't give them something to eat, but at least it gives them pride every time they come to cf. an exhibit.

She further observes:

> This re-awakens their pride. They are content, they are happy to talk about it. This makes for a pride they did not have before and they say: "You are proud, you didn't think about being proud." This is where the objective of the Maison du Fier-Monde has its appeal, because our objective is to re-awaken pride and I think we have done so.

On the other hand, Binette admits self-critically:

> It would be pretentious to think that we have really changed things in the neighborhood, let alone change the course of history.

All in all, the Maison du Fier-Monde, through its various activities, has attained the original objective that it has kept throughout the six years of its existence (Maison du Fier Monde 1985a, p.3): "The Maison du Fier-Monde wants to reveal the history of the neighborhood to its residents. The main reason is to enable the citizens to understand the current situation of the neighborhood in light of the past, but without being a devotee of the past, since the Maison du Fier-Monde aims to take charge of the present and future of the neighborhood for those who now live there. We want to revive pride in the Centre-Sud neighborhood and create a place where the citizens can meet."

Further work in this direction is supposed to be done in the course of continually consolidating the institution and expanding its offerings. The museum hopes the population will play an increasingly active role in the direct study of its own history. The first steps toward this end may be found in the three-year project to study the industrialization of Centre-Sud (cf. above; cf. Maison du Fier-Monde, 1986a).

3.2 The neighborhood museum in the United States

3.2.1 The Anacostia Neighborhood Museum

3.2.1.1 Anacostia[1]

In 1967 the renowned Smithsonian Institution established the first neighborhood museum in the United States, the Anacostia Neighborhood Museum. It is located in the Anacostia section of Washington, D.C., an area inhabited primarily by African-Americans.

The founding of Anacostia dates back to the American Civil War (cf. Hutchinson, 1977), after which the federal government assigned the wooded and hilly land on the outskirts of the district to the freed slaves who had fled to Washington (cf. Marsh, 1968; Thomas, 1972). Until World War II, Anacostia was basically a rural community (Thomas, 1972).

Isolated from its white neighbors, a small, stable African-American community developed, both socioculturally and physically (cf. Marsh, 1968, p. 12). Then, as now, the Anacostia River separated the community from the rest of Washington. Although bridges have been built connecting it to the rest of the District of Columbia, the river continues to represent a psychological barrier. Anacostia is ...**across the river-hidden away and remote from 'official Washington'** (Thomas, 1972).

After the end of World War II, Anacostia experienced a considerable population growth and accompanying changes. People displaced from other parts of the city by urban renewal programs in the fifties found homes in Anacostia (Thomas, 1972). Seventy-seven percent of housing in

---

[1] If the origin of statements is not further specified in the following text, they are summaries I have prepared from the available material. When I refer to certain quotes without providing any further details, these are statements made in interviews with: Dean Anderson (2-25-85), Zora Felton (2-28-95), Caryl Marsh (2-27-85), Rebecca Welch (2- 26-85), Edward Smith (2-26-85), James Mayo (2-26-85). All direct quotes from interviews are in bold.

Anacostia today consists of apartment houses, in contrast to 20 percent apartment houses in the rest of Washington (cf. Kramer, 1973). For the most part, housing units are in deplorable condition and, according to Thomas (1972), lack the most essential public facilities (cf. Department of Urban and Regional Planning 1973): "Many apartment complexes were erected on inappropriate and unsuitable sites without adequate planning for sewage, streets, sidewalks, recreation areas, transportation or erosion control. [...]. Many apartments are very badly maintained. Garbage and trash are often handled in an unsightly and unhealthful manner. Rats and cockroaches are still a major problem."

Anacostia today, with more than 100,000 residents, is one of those predominantly African-American urban centers of North America (92 percent, according to Rebecca Welch, a historian in the research department) in which slums and great social and economic problems define everyday life. Although a not insignificant portion of Anacostia's population can be classified as middle class, Anacostia, albeit not a slum, is on the whole an underprivileged neighborhood, many of its residents living on the fringes of society. With regard to the socioeconomic situation of Anacostia's residents, Edward Smith believes:

> I think a major concern in this community now is simple survival.

Apart from poor living conditions, unemployment is one of Anacostia's greatest problems. Over half the residents are of working age, between 18 and 65 years old (Thomas, 1972). Because of the low level of training and education, Anacostia primarily has an unskilled and underqualified work force, for which there is little demand in Washington.

Soon the Washington municipal subway system will connect Anacostia to the rest of the city. Some people interviewed hope this will spark an economic revival. But for the present, as Thomas says (1972), "Anacostia's five frustrations – housing, unemployment, education, drug abuse, crime" – are still all too present. The poor social conditions, that is, the combination of inadequate housing, poor education and unemployment, are determining factors for the resulting problems, such as drug abuse and crime, which arise from feelings of hopelessness (Thomas, 1972).

So how did a museum come to be founded in this neighborhood, which clearly lacks the essentials of institutional development? What does such a museum stand for and what special tasks has it undertaken in the poor conditions discussed above?

3.2.1.2 Origin

In contrast to the Maison du Fier-Monde, which exists in a similar socioeconomic context, the first impetus for founding a neighborhood museum in Anacostia came from outside, that is, from the Smithsonian Institution, located in downtown Washington D.C.

According to Newsome, Silver (1978, p. 182), the highest concentration of "museums, nature centers, parks, botanical gardens, and historic sites" in the country can be found in Washington. But most of the traditional institutions, including the Smithsonian Institution, have long failed to direct their services to a broad public embracing all strata of society. In the mid-sixties, criticism of the elitist nature of traditional museums and of the associated discrimination against a significant portion of the population intensified. John Kinard (after Vuilleumier, 1983, p. 94), the founding director, summarized the charges against established museums: "[...] they stand accused on three points: 1) failing to respond to the needs of a great majority of the people; 2) failing to relate knowledge of the past to the grave issues confronting us today or to participate in meeting those issues; and 3) failing to overcome not only their blatant disregard of minority cultures but their outright racism which is all too apparent in what they collect, study, and exhibit and in whom they employ."

Seeking to change this situation, a conference on museum and education took place in August 1966 supported by the Smithsonian Institution and the U.S. Office of Education (Marsh 1968, p. 11 f). The discussion centered on how the enormous educational potential of the more than 5,000 American museums could be effectively used (cf. Larrabee, 1968).

One of the first people to take the initiative was S. Dillon Ripley, the Secretary of the Smithsonian Institution. In November 1966 a report he delivered at a conference in Aspen, Colorado, appeared in Washington newspapers. In recognition of the museum's growing social and political responsibility, Ripley (cited in Marsh 1968, p. 12) recommended to the gathered museum officials "to try taking their museum to the people." The background of Ripley's efforts is explained as follows by Caryl Marsh, who played a decisive role in founding the Anacostia Neighborhood Museum[2]:

> I think it was a very personal thing of Mr. Ripley's. [...]. The Smithsonian was referred to as the nation's attic. So the ideas were to get the stuff out and make them available to people. And I think, during the sixties with the general social ferment and the pressures for civil rights, a man like Mr. Ripley was influenced by all this and he thought that it would be a good idea for museums in general to make some effort to move out into the community. [...], he thought that these museums on the Mall were very big and very formal and very restricted and he wanted to loosen things up. And he suggested among other things to take the museums to the people.

The Smithsonian undertook the first efforts in this direction in Washington, D.C., and publicly expressed its interest in providing so-called mediating agents at local level, which were to perform the role of a mediator between the population of a given area and the sponsoring institution – in this case the Smithsonian. Kinard (1973, p. 12) calls

---

[2] Marsh is a social psychologist who worked for the District of Columbia Recreation Department before she began working for the Smithsonian on the Anacostia project.

this kind of institution the "mediatory museum," a category which also includes the Anacostia Museum.

Marsh and Charles Blitzer, the Assistant Secretary for History and Art of the Smithsonian Institution, surveyed various parts of the city to identify interested citizens and find a suitable location for the mediatory museum. They did not carry out this work without resistance from the established Smithsonian staff, as Marsh recalls:

> [...] basically, the people on the Mall, the curators and the administrators, they thought it was a terrible idea.

However, the Smithsonian staff's acceptance of this project mattered little. Of greater concern to Marsh, based on her experience as a social psychologist, was orienting the future museum to the interests and needs of the envisaged target group:

> [...] I was thinking more about the nature of the relationships that had to be established among groups of people to make this new institution acceptable and to make it an institution that was controlled by the users rather than by the government.

In the course of innumerable conversations Marsh had with representatives of the various social groups and institutions, her ideas for the museum gradually took shape. An important step in this exploratory phase was a meeting with a group of African-American employees of the Smithsonian Institution (predominantly security and cleaning personnel). Marsh describes this meeting as follows:

> We sat and talked and I told them about the idea of a museum that would reach out beyond the Mall and I said, did they think that there would be any interest. And they were very enthusiastic, they thought it was a good idea, it would be useful. And I said o.k.: "What would it be like?" And so in trying to figure out what it might be like, they began to ask questions. The

first question was: "Who would control it, who would the director be?" So I said, well, the director would be whoever the people in the neighborhood choose. They didn't really believe me, but I wasn't sure myself at that time, but it was what I would recommend and let's see what would happen. Then they said, well, what would happen, if, on a hot day, children came and they were barefoot and they weren't properly dressed. So I said, well o.k., what do you think should happen, what is the correct thing to do? Well, they said, if they were orderly and as long as they had shirts on, that would be all right. What they were afraid would happen was, that children who were very poor would be turned away. And so I said, no, that's important not to do, because it has long been a tradition in Washington that when the schools would take a bus full of children to a Smithsonian museum, they would not permit children who were not well dressed to come into the bus.

Several areas of Washington expressed an interest in being the site of the planned museum.

After the Smithsonian Institution held round tables and negotiations with numerous representatives and community groups of these areas, the choice fell on the Anacostia neighborhood, with the support of the Greater Anacostia Peoples' Corporation (cf. Kinard, 1968, p. 3). Marsh observes:

> [...] they said that Anacostia deserved the museum, because it didn't have street lighting, it didn't have schools, it didn't have playgrounds, it didn't have sidewalks. So they said: "We deserve the museum."

Although the initiative first came from the Smithsonian Institution, the establishment of a neighborhood museum in Anacostia was not a unilateral process. From the beginning, it was the intention of Ripley to involve the population in the process of creating the museum. Ripley himself (1972, p. 182) said: "Involvement can only be created if it is their museum. It must have the active participation of the people who live there." Thanks to project coordinator Marsh striving tirelessly to bring the museum close to the affected population by having an active exchange with relevant community groups, the population of Anacostia took an interest and actively helped in the project, at least initially.

After selecting Anacostia as the site and subject matter of the "neighborhood museum," intensive planning began. Every citizen taking part in these sessions automatically became a member of the advisory committee of representatives of the more important segments of Anacostia's population – citizen and youth groups, tenants' committees, schools and the police (cf. Marsh, 1968, p. 12; Kinard, 1973, p. 13), as well as others, which Marsh classifies as very responsible middle-class people. In early 1967 the advisory committee met for the first time to discuss the implementation of the Anacostia neighborhood museum.

Planners found a suitable site for the museum in an old abandoned movie house, the Carver Theatre, renovation of which had active community participation (Marsh, 1968, p. 14): "Under the overall direction of the Smithsonian's Office of Exhibits, beginners and professionals of all ages worked side by side during the summer of 1967, stripping the interior of the old movie theater, scraping, plastering, painting, laying the new floor, making curtains and transforming a weedy [...] vacant lot into an outdoor exhibit area. As the formal opening date drew near, the building occasionally stayed open all night and the neighborhood residents stopped by to help with the installation of the exhibits."

The Anacostia Neighborhood Museum opened in September 1967. To what extent this museum, initiated by outside representatives of the white cultural establishment, has integrated itself into the neighborhood and how this at first empty hull of the neighborhood museum in Anacostia was filled with meaning, structures and activities, will be discussed in the following sections.

3.2.1.3 Conception and objectives

Unlike the previous Canadian examples, the Anacostia Neighborhood Museum has been in existence long enough to examine its accomplishments and trends. Its objectives and the way it sees itself have changed constantly during its 20 years' existence. The crucial steps in this process will be sketched below.

Originally, planners conceived the Anacostia Neighborhood Museum to be a mediatory museum. As an experimental demonstration of the "outreach" concept (Museums Aid Citizens 1970, p. 10), it was intended to mediate between the traditional, established Smithsonian museums and the African-American public they did not reach. That is, it was supposed to help break down barriers to access and create interest in visiting the large museums located only a few miles away. By functioning as an outpost, so to speak, of the Smithsonian in a marginal urban community, the museums and exhibits of the large Smithsonian museums were to be brought nearer to people living in Anacostia (Anderson):

> And a decision was taken, it was an experimental decision, let's open a kind of storefront museum, one that has no collections of its own, but one which could exhibit in a neighborhood in Washington the kinds of things that we are doing down here on the Mall and maybe begin to attract local residents who otherwise would never go to the museum.
> Perhaps, if they get into the Anacostia Museum they may even start coming downtown and cf. the rest of the Smithsonian.

Toward the end of the 1960s, the objective of the Anacostia Neighborhood Museum shifted under the strong leadership of its director, John Kinard, so that the concept of a mediatory function with respect to the Smithsonian receded more and more into the background. In contrast to the Smithsonian, in whose national museums African-American cultural representation was practically nonexistent, the Anacostia Neighborhood Museum devoted itself increasingly to the needs and life of its African-

American neighbors. It offers a reappraisal and presentation of African-American history and culture as well as the history and current situation of Anacostia.

These thematic missions have assumed prominence in the way the museum sees itself. Kinard's arguments (1972a, p. 155f) clarify the importance of the changed concept: "The neighborhood museum exists to serve the people of the area of which it is a part [...]. The neighborhood museum concerns itself with an analysis of the community and its history. It poses such questions as where did we come from, who are our heroes, what is our heritage, who are we as a people? What have we done to better ourselves and the community in which we live? What are our social, economic, political, and educational assets and liabilities? [...]. So we must begin with where the people are in the circumstances in which we find them. The urban industrial centres have their own history. In Anacostia it is one of crime, drugs, unemployment, inadequate housing, sanitation, rats, to mention but a few of the problems [...]. The museum must be a living institution. It must provide a place where neighbors are encouraged to meet and talk; call attention to urgent problems; inspire people to do the best they can, sponsor programmes in the performing and visual arts; and participate in the development of a variety of interests from alcoholism and local archaeology to ornithology and urban planning."

Anderson, at the time of this study, also stressed the special role of the Anacostia museum as a neighborhood-related educational institution:

> An educational resource for Anacostia means telling people in Anacostia about their own history, about how they can improve their lives, what they can be doing for their neighborhood, where it came from, what it is now, where it might go.

In addition to providing knowledge and skills, the Anacostia Neighborhood Museum aimed to increase feelings of self-worth among residents. Examination of African-American history was intended to generate self-awareness and self-confidence so that current and future problems could be tackled and solved. The Anacostia Neighborhood Museum, thinking of itself as a "mechanism for change in the inner city" (Kinard cited in Museums Aid Citizens 1970, p. 11), wanted to contribute to the solution of existing socioeconomic problems and to the development of the neighborhood by conveying knowledge, perspectives, identity and confidence in the population's own capacity to change. But although most museum employees sought to improve living conditions in Anacostia, concrete economic development was not included in the objectives of the museum. It could demonstrate possible solutions and actions, but refrained from actually organizing and coordinating them in a directed way. In this respect, Kinard (1972c, p. 2) stresses: "The Anacostia Museum is neither a missionary project nor an idealistic effort to eradicate poverty but a serious attempt to create a museum that reflects the achievements and failures, the aspirations and hopes of a people who are defined by geography."

He further stated (interview for program "Contrechamp," Radio Canada, 10-10-84, St. Evariste, Quebec): "The people can pick and choose. [...]. It's not for us to push and shove them around. It's for us to offer them opportunities that they can understand, and a unique understanding of what the problem is, then people can make their own decisions and get the credit for making their own decisions."

By limiting itself in advance to goals indirectly related to development[3], the Anacostia Neighborhood Museum's effectiveness as an instrument of community development was minimal, while the urgent problems of the neighborhood grew worse over time. Mayo, for example, states that in Anacostia the problems of 15 or 20 years ago are still rampant: unemployment, housing problems, crime and addiction. Regarding the latter, Mayo believes:

---

[3] The museum's 15th anniversary brochure (Anacostia Neighborhood Museum 1982a, p. 10) described the objective as "to help enrich the mind."

We cannot survive the drug problem, the drug problem is overwhelming, it's totally out of control.

Edward Smith assesses the situation similarly:

This community still has the same problems that they talked about in the late 1960s and early 1970s.
In light of this relative ineffectiveness to shape political ideas, Smith believes:

I would say what we really need is a shot in the arm economically to solve many of the problems that we are dealing with. [...]. My whole argument would be that most of our problems are economic.

When asking what the museum's current objectives are, so long after the civil rights struggles of the sixties and seventies, one notes decisive changes in its goals and self-perception, changes that reflect the altered context of contemporary history. The question is hardly one of social problems and development, or even of relevance to the neighborhood. Retreat appears to have been sounded; answers to pressing problems turn out to be correspondingly meager:

I would hope that people who come here leave with a heightened awareness of African-American history and culture. (Zora Felton); I think people ought to have some sense of who they are and where they came from. (Rebecca Welch); I think that anything a community can do, that improves the level of awareness of history and culture, is important. It's important for them to have a real insight into the history...
... I think it gives them role models, people they can look up to. (James Mayo)

The museum's turnabout from being an instrument effecting social changes to a "cultural stimulus" (Smithsonian Institution, 1986,

p. 102) is all too clear. The generally held objectives of increasing and imparting knowledge lack concrete references to the reality of the life of Anacostia's population and already point to the new way that the Anacostia Neighborhood Museum promises to go, namely that of a "National Museum of African-American History and Art." This problem will be addressed again in the following sections. But first we need to cf. how the above-mentioned conceptual changes affected the structure and organization of the Anacostia Neighborhood Museum.

3.2.1.4 Structure and organization

At the time of this study the Anacostia Neighborhood Museum had two buildings: the converted and renovated Carver Theatre, centrally situated on King Avenue, and a branch in Fort Place that it opened in 1975. This branch, some distance "up the hill" from the main building, is surrounded by middle-class residences. By 1987 the Fort Place building had expanded to include a new exhibit and office complex. All the museum functions were consolidated in a single location (cf. Smithsonian Institution, 1986, p. 102; McQuaite, 1987).

As part of the Smithsonian Institution, the unique Anacostia Neighborhood Museum is a semi-governmental institution. Initially it – along with the Smithsonian's publications service and its TV and radio services – was part of the administrative responsibilities of the office of the Assistant Secretary for Public Services. In 1983-84 it became part of the History and Art Division. This shift afforded it some degree of recognition as a museum, while setting the course for its possible evolution into a national museum.

The Anacostia Neighborhood Museum is financed through a fixed annual provision from the Smithsonian, as well as through project-related subsidies from the Smithsonian and other donations (cf. Kinard, 1968, p. 25). Anderson speaks of a regular annual allocation of almost one million U.S. dollars. Rebecca Welch stresses that the Anacostia Neighborhood

Museum, in contrast to other similar institutions, has …an economic base that is much more secure … because we have better funding as part of the federal government's funding of the Smithsonian.

Thus, as a consequence of being a part of the Smithsonian Institution, the Anacostia museum has a relatively large staff for a local museum: 18 at the time of this study. Apart from the administration (the director and secretariat), which forms a separate unit, the museum consists of three departments: research, exhibition design and production, and education (cf. Anacostia Neighborhood Museum). The structure of the Anacostia Neighborhood Museum is made clear in the following organizational chart:

Office of the Assistant Secretary for History and Art
Office of the Director·········· Administrative Services
Research Department --- Exhibitions Department --- Education Department
Production Branch --- Design Branch

In the Research Department, multi-year exhibit research projects are directed by historian Louise Hutchinson. The Exhibition Design and Production Laboratory conducts workshops where graphic designers, photographers, carpenters, printers, etc., create exhibits under the direction of exhibit designer James Mayo. The Fort Place building houses, in addition to the exhibition and administration spaces, the museum's education department, where Zora Felton organizes and implements exhibit-related activities.

The presence of the above-mentioned departments, personnel, and technical equipment, makes the Anacostia Neighborhood Museum substantially different from other small museums in the country.

Moreover, for work the Anacostia Neighborhood Museum cannot do, the extensive services of the Smithsonian Institution are available (Welch). Although firmly integrated into the Smithsonian Institution, the museum has shown independence in a number of respects. For example, all leading positions are occupied by persons who have worked there from the beginning and have neighborhood connections. For instance, the director, John Kinard still resides in Anacostia (Newsome, Silver, 1978, p. 183).

Because during the museum's first years many staff members resided locally and participated in numerous neighborhood initiatives beyond their museum work, the Anacostia Neighborhood Museum is frequently characterized as a "community-based museum" (Welch).

The relatively close ties between the museum and the neighborhood were further strengthened by the fact that the population of Anacostia could, and did, participate, first in the conceptual and initial phases, then through the founding committee, and the official advisory committee which began in 1972 (Newsome, Silver, 1978, p. 184). The function of the advisory committee was to receive ideas from the population and introduce them into the museum's work (cf. Smithsonian Institution no year, p.71ff). Numerous interested citizens volunteered at the outset in the museum's various departments. Apparently, in the early years, the Youth Advisory Council of local children and youth, played a special role in cooperation with the population (cf. Anacostia Neighborhood Museum, 1972, pp. 47-49).

But all this has changed. The closeness of the Anacostia Neighborhood Museum to the citizens has considerably diminished, and even with the best will in the world one can no longer speak of it as a "community-based museum." Mayo believes:

> It's community based, because it started here and I think its roots are here,

but these roots appear to have gradually dried up.

Today most of the employees of the Anacostia Neighborhood Museum live outside Anacostia, with the exception of the key personnel named above. Things stand similarly with the about 15 (Welch) to

20 (Mayo) members of the advisory committee, whose influence has apparently fallen off drastically.

Anderson believes that the committee has not officially met since he assumed his position in 1983. For him the present-day advisory committee is an embarrassing farce. Also, from the viewpoint of the Smithsonian Institution (Anderson), there is too little community participation. It can also be inferred from the statements of the employees in the museum's three departments that they have no interchange with the advisory committee and that the citizens have no influence on their substantive work, either as decision makers or as participants.

Although there is no exact information regarding the decision-making process, informant statements indicate its hierarchical character. Possibilities for resident and staff participation must be characterized as extraordinarily limited.

With respect to the staff's influence on the museum's current activities, Welch indicates that employees go to the director with proposals from which he selects what he personally considers appropriate:

Our director decides what exhibitions we do and the staff does them.

Mayo points out that previously this was quite different.

Why and how this change took place remain open questions. However, the changed decision-making machinery could be further strengthened by providing the Anacostia Neighborhood Museum, as the Smithsonian Institution wishes, with an advisory body partly made up of outside scholars.

On the basis of what has thus far been said about the structure and organization of the Anacostia Neighborhood Museum, its experimental nature ceased a long time ago. Originally planned as a democratic neighborhood museum, the Anacostia Neighborhood Museum, in its twenty years of existence, has evolved into an established cultural institution with fixed structures. It is, therefore, closer to the traditional museums of the Smithsonian Institution than to the "écomusées" or "museos integrales" with which it is always associated by representatives of new museology. Although for a long time the museum retained "neighborhood museum" in its title, recently "Anacostia Museum" has supplanted it in the museum's official publications. This occurs, for example, in the catalogue for the Anna Cooper exhibit (Hutchinson 1982, p. XIV) and in a leaflet for the "Out of Africa" exhibit (Anacostia Neighborhood Museum, 1979). When the museum moved to its new building in 1987, its name officially changed to "Anacostia Museum" (McQuaite, 1987, p. 1), "… because the museum serves a public beyond its immediate environment and has obtained a national and international reputation."

Respondents confirmed and did not view unfavorably the change of direction from an experimental neighborhood museum to a traditional museum. At the time of my research, serious consideration was being given to moving the museum from its original building on King Avenue and having all the departments located in Fort Place. In the meantime, this has taken place.

Visitor complaints on the crime associated with King Avenue were cited as one of the reasons for the move (James Mayo; cf. Rodriguez 1984/II). The Anacostia Neighborhood Museum, once problem-oriented and committed to the community, has become the leisure-time sanctuary of the new Anacostia Museum. Now, it is beautifully situated in a park with picnic tables and benches. The museum is distinguished primarily by its pleasant outside appearance and setting: no noise, no dirt, no heat and … no more life, just the worshipful, sterile atmosphere of a proper museum.

Long-term plans of the Anacostia Neighborhood Museum include erecting a new museum near the anticipated Anacostia subway station, to provide better links to downtown Washington (James Mayo). Together with the National Park Service and a military museum, the Anacostia Museum is envisioned as forming part of a museum island that will be the equal of the traditional museums on the Mall.

It must be asked whom this is supposed to serve. Certainly not the citizens of Anacostia, the neighborhood public in the first instance. The outward changes are only a reflection of the profound shift of emphasis within the Anacostia Neighborhood Museum. The neighborhood museum is beating a retreat from a problematic area. By moving to Fort Place, it cut itself off both spatially and structurally from the Anacostia population. Whether its activities and programs have also lost their explosive force and relevance to the citizens will be explored in the following section.

3.2.1.5 Activities and programs

As a "branch" of the Smithsonian Institution, the Anacostia Neighborhood Museum was originally planned not to have its own collection nor perform the collection activity of a traditional museum. All exhibits consist of loans from the Smithsonian or other institutions.

Welch stated:

> We don't have a mandate to go out and collect, we don't have an acquisition budget, we don't have any official authority to build a permanent collection.

The internal division of the Anacostia Neighborhood Museum into the three departments named above shows clearly that the present emphasis of the museum's work is in the areas of research, exhibits and education.

In its initial phase the museum established the Center for Anacostia Studies, devoted both to research into the history of Anacostia and its present-day problems (cf. Thomas, 1972). The center cooperated closely with the Anacostia Historical Society, founded in 1974 and independent of the museum. The museum's research department has greatly expanded in recent years through the employment of several historians, which has given research work as a whole a more professional character (cf. Hutchinson, 1975).

Each research topic relates to a concrete exhibit project. Increasingly, the research department has devoted itself to subject areas that go beyond the local horizon or may be only remotely related to Anacostia. Rebecca Welch observes:

> ...there is a difference between our early focus, it was very much more community oriented. [...], the kind of activity brought into the museum was really focused on the people who lived here rather than taking a topic that is of national importance.

Welch cites the increasing institutionalization as the reason for the changed orientation of the topics dealt with by the Anacostia Neighborhood Museum:

> ...when you have a research department, that means that you are going to build in topics of projects for which research is required as opposed to perhaps the kinds of projects that are community-service oriented which don't require the same kind of research component.

But the establishment of a research department alone cannot explain the shift in thematic emphasis, since nothing prevents it focusing on neighborhood and problem-related research. It seems to me that the crucial factor is the influence of the newly employed scholars, who did not have any community orientation.

The scholarly orientation of the research toward exclusively historical themes without local reference was accompanied by new research methods. Based on the example of the exhibit "The Anacostia Story," Welch explains the earlier practice as follows:

> "The Anacostia Story," I know, was very much pulling from the community in terms of records and information and oral history and there was an oral history project here at one point.

An extensive oral history project constituted part of the exhibit series "The Evolution of a Community" (cf. Thomas 1972). Present-day research practice, however, relies increasingly on traditional sources and methodologies to the exclusion of the citizens of Anacostia. In fact, "The Anacostia Story" of 1977 was the last exhibit to use local resources to tell a local story.

Under the changed conditions, developing a theme takes about two or three years (Mayo).

Because of the time-consuming scientific preparation of the exhibits, the Anacostia Neighborhood Museum today mounts far fewer exhibits than in the past. In contrast to about eight exhibits a year in the initial phase, for some time now the museum has produced only one exhibit a year (Mayo).

Between 1967 and 1984 the Anacostia Neighborhood Museum mounted 52 exhibits (Anacostia Neighborhood Museum Exhibits and Events, 1984; cf. also Kinard, Nighbert, 1968; 1972, Anacostia Neighborhood Museum, 1972; 1977a; 1982a).

Exhibit themes fall basically into four areas:

- Current problems in the neighborhood
- The history and culture of Anacostia
- African-American art in general
- African-American history in general.

Rather than discuss each exhibit individually, several have been selected for their exemplary value.

When we consider the original objectives outlined in section 3.2.1.3, it appears logical for the museum to focus on present-day problems in its exhibits. One outstanding example is "The Rat" (Anacostia Neighborhood Museum 1970f).

In the late sixties, a group of children tending the museum's small zoo called attention to the devastating effect of rats on the community (cf. Anacostia Neighborhood Museum 1970f, pp. 3-5). To provide visitors with information on rats – their behavior and the health threats they posed – and on possible steps to combat this problem, the Anacostia Neighborhood Museum created the exhibit "The Rat" in 1969, in cooperation with concerned local residents (cf. Kinard, Nighbert, 1972; 1973:13). Zora Felton explains (Anacostia Neighborhood Museum 1970f, p. 5): "The exhibit is the effort not of any single individual, but of a community to cast a harsh and proper light on rats and to expose to increased public scrutiny and action of this curse that affects other communities such as ours across the country."

The exhibit on rats is mentioned repeatedly as a prime example of socially relevant, current, problem-related museum work and is considered to be evidence that the Anacostia Neighborhood Museum even today can make a contribution to improved living conditions. It was intended that others of a similar nature should follow, according to Kinard (interview for the program "Contrechamp," Radio Canada, 10-10-84, St. Evariste, Quebec): "[...] we have tried to do a number of things with regard to [...] urban problems, the problem of drugs, crime, unemployment and the whole lot that you find in cities."

Kinard refers here to the second part of the exhibit "The Evolution of a Community," which had the subtitle "Urban Problems" (cf. Thomas, 1972; cf. Kinard, Nighbert 1972, 105f). A list of museum exhibits, however, includes no other exhibit title that refers to the above-mentioned problems. Nor does Kinard's article (Kinard, 1985), in which he calls the neighborhood museum "a catalyst for social change," cite any other specific examples.

When asked to what extent and in what form the Anacostia Neighborhood Museum has dealt with current problems, apart from the exhibits "The Rat" and "The Evolution of a Community, Part II," no one could (or would) reply. Therefore – with the reservations referred to – I conclude that these two exhibits, which took place 18 and 15 years ago respectively, were the only exhibits that attempted to address pressing, current neighborhood problems. Exhibits that were originally planned on subjects such as "Unwed Mothers," "Consumerism," "Roaches and Flies" and "What People Can Do to Improve the Community" (Smithsonian Institution no year, p. 42f) did not, in the end, materialize.

On the other hand, the subject of "the history and culture of Anacostia" was represented relatively strongly up to 1977. In addition to the exhibit "The Evolution of a Community, Part I" (cf. Thomas, 1972), the exhibit "The Anacostia Story" may be cited as an example. Using numerous documents, this exhibit presented the history of Anacostia from 1608 to 1930. It began with the original Indian inhabitants and proceeded through the arrival of the white settlers and slave owners, the Civil War, the first black settlers, to the development of Anacostia in the 20th century, with particular emphasis on the social history of the African-American population. In this regard, Kinard notes in the preface of the exhibit publication (Hutchinson, 1977, p. X): "This catalogue is designed to include accounts of the little-known men and women of achievement rather than to exclude them. It has been written to inspire a sense of pride and to heighten the aspirations for dignity and self-assurance of every person, no matter his station in life."

Although the exhibit dealt primarily with events prior to 1930, present-day references are made. Thus, Hutchinson writes at the end of the catalogue (1977, p. 137): "Today, Anacostians continue to petition (and maybe pray) for a better delivery of municipal services. Now, as then, they are concerned about land speculators and land use; the quality of education; adequate health care and care for the aged; and the preservation of community history and pride. For people who have an awareness and a sense of yesterday will have a tomorrow."

In addition to the historical exhibitions, several art exhibitions were mounted that were also devoted to Anacostia, for example "John Robinson. A Retrospective" (cf. Anacostia Neighborhood Museum, 1976), "Phil Ratner's Washington" (cf. Anacostia Neighborhood Museum, 1978) or "Here, Look at Mine! John Robinson/Francis Lebby" (cf. Anacostia Neighborhood Museum, 1982b). They featured artists whose work is closely related to Anacostia, stressing, among other things, the community's aesthetic, positive contributions.

With exhibits on "African-American art in general" that go beyond the local Anacostia context in terms of coverage and featured artists, the museum is addressing primarily a local audience. Of particular importance in this regard was the collaboration with the D.C. Art Association, an artists' group "dedicated to foster and promote visual arts through community involvement" (Anacostia Neighborhood Museum, 1974). Since the late sixties, the Anacostia Neighborhood Museum has cooperated with this group to occasionally exhibit works by D.C. African-American artists. By presenting art that traditionally belonged in elite galleries and established museums and showing it in the neighborhood as a form of creative analysis of the present, the Anacostia Neighborhood Museum wishes to take away art's elitist character and make it something everyone can experience and possibly apply.

The opening exhibit of the new Anacostia Museum, "Contemporary Visual Expressions" (cf. Driskell, 1987, McQuaite, 1976b), was also devoted to Washington artists. With this exhibition, the museum both revealed present practice and emphasized the kinds of exhibitions that were to be expected from the new museum.

The exhibits on African-American history, which are particularly stressed in the museum's exhibit schedule, are also detached from the direct reality of everyday life in Anacostia. They are aimed increasingly at a supraregional audience (Welch, Smith), while still endeavoring to make new areas of knowledge and experience accessible to local residents.

At the time of this study, the museum was preparing an exhibit on African-American history and had just shown "Climbing Jacob's Ladder: The Rise of Black Churches in Eastern American Cities, 1740-1877" (1987). The exhibit only marginally concerned Anacostia directly – aside from its African-American theme – dealing with the history of African-American churches not only as religious institutions, but as agents of political, educational and social welfare activities. When Smith developed the concept of the show and did research for it, he wanted to show ...

what developed from black churches to liberate not only the spirit of Blacks, but also to liberate them socially and economically as well.

This cross-section of the Anacostia Neighborhood Museum's exhibits shows the two primary characteristics that distinguish the neighborhood museum from the traditional museum. In the first place, the exhibits are treated in an unconventional way, oriented toward the neighborhood, as Mayo specifically emphasizes. This is true, at least, of the first ten years of its existence.

In the second place, the Anacostia Neighborhood Museum was the first institution in which exhibits were made by African-Americans for African-Americans about African Americans, and thereby this institution has assumed the role of forerunner.

Some of the exhibits produced by the Anacostia Neighborhood Museum are redesigned as traveling exhibits after they close. According to Mayo, the Anacostia Neighborhood Museum is the first institution that has ever done traveling exhibits on African-American history. It has thus played a leadership role, showing others what is possible and practical. In many cases SITES (Smithsonian Institution Traveling Exhibition Service) organized the traveling exhibits. This was the case, for instance, with "Art of Cameroon," "Black American Landmarks," "Black Wings," "Black Women," "Ethiopia Christian Art of an African Nation" and "Out of Africa" (James Mayo). In other cases, the Anacostia Neighborhood Museum itself draws up the loan contracts. In addition, Mayo reports a new program: to develop and tour mini-exhibits consisting of three or four exhibit tables cost-free to community institutions.

The costly and sometimes extensive exhibit catalogues published by the museum are produced to order by the Smithsonian Institution. The catalogues, in part scholarly publications, such as "The Anacostia Story" (Hutchinson, 1977), "Out of Africa" (Hutchinson, 1979) and "Anna Cooper: A Voice from the South" (Hutchinson, 1982) form an important component of the Anacostia Neighborhood Museum's communications activity, providing detailed background information on the various exhibits.

Apart from the catalogues, which are largely the product of the research department, the museum's education department led by Zora Felton has published a large number of exhibit-related visitor aids, for example, "A Visitor's Guide to 'Anna Cooper: A Voice from the South'" (Anacostia Neighborhood Museum/Educ. Dep., 1981). In addition, the education department arranges group tours to interpret the various exhibits and conduct neighborhood excursions in cooperation with the local public library (cf. Felton, no year).

But the major emphasis of the education department's work is collaboration with the schools. The museum holds teachers' workshops and has developed exhibit-related teacher resource and instructional materials for various grades, for example "Frederick Douglass. A Fighter for Freedom (1817?-1895). A Resource Unit for Intermediate Students" (Anacostia Neighborhood Museum/Educ. Dep. 1979); "Here Look at Mine! Teachers Resource Packet" (Anacostia Neighborhood Museum/ Educ. Dep. 1983); "Black Women: Achievements Against the Odds. Teacher's Resource Booklet" (Anacostia Neighborhood Museum/Educ. Dep. no year).

The education department provides material for widely diverse target groups, for example, small children, schoolchildren, families and senior citizens (Zora Felton), and organizes events (apart from regular exhibits, some five to ten events take place every month, cf. Anacostia Neighborhood Museum, 1983a; 1984a; 1985; 1986), the Anacostia Neighborhood Museum's education activities are directed primarily to teachers and students at various grade levels. While exhibits are geared to all levels of visitors, the museum's current public actually consists predominantly of children and young people who visit the museum with their school classes (Mayo).

In the early 1970s, the Anacostia Neighborhood Museum made an interesting offer to go beyond exhibits and related educational material, and establish a so-called Speakers' Bureau for community groups active in Anacostia to invite specialists to give talks. It offered a spectrum of some 60 subjects covering health care, political theory, labor and unemployment, education, nature study, religion, race discrimination, culture and history, housing, communications and economics. The program's brochure (Anacostia Neighborhood Museum 1970e, no page) says the Speakers' Bureau "[...] offers to the community a resource of information that can augment individual growth as well as further development of the community."

To conclude, the extent to which the above programs have contributed to fulfilling the museum's objectives and how the employees and the public have reacted to the various changes will be addressed in the following section.

3.2.1.6 Evaluation

Thus far the Anacostia Neighborhood Museum's work has not been systematically evaluated (Felton). Only visitor comment cards provide some information on public reactions. These comments are collected and typed. They are provided to all museum workers (cf. Anacostia Neighborhood Museum, 1972; 1984c). Up until now only a single systematic study has been done to find out how the local public as a whole reacts to the changes in the Anacostia Neighborhood Museum (shift of emphasis, moving the museum) (Rodriguez 1984/I, II). I have based what follows on this material and on statements from my interviews.

When assessing the public orientation and scope of the Anacostia Neighborhood Museum, it is necessary to distinguish between the initial phase and the current situation. From what has been said, it may be concluded that the museum, particularly at the beginning, was a lively focal point of Anacostia. As a place for exhibits, workshops, discussions and music presentations and as a meeting place for a variety of citizens' organizations, this neighborhood museum succeeded in interesting and activating a not insignificant part of the Anacostia's residents (cf. Marsh, 1968, p. 15). Kramer (1973, no page) gives the number of visitors for 1971 as about 94,000, while Newsome, Silver (1978, p. 182) give the number of visitors for 1974 as 69,500.

However, as already indicated in section 3.2.1.3, the museum has had no lasting effect with respect to improving the living conditions of the disadvantaged population of Anacostia. This may be based, in part, on the fact that, despite all good intentions and the museum's high promise, not enough neighborhood-oriented activities have been carried out. In addition, the Anacostia Neighborhood Museum has not successfully created the preconditions regarding structure and content that enable resident participation in the museum's work on a permanent basis, rather than merely as passive consumers. For this reason, the following statement by Ripley (1972, p. 183) cannot be true in its absolute form: "... it has, with the help of its Neighborhood Advisory Committee, become involved with the community as an innovative pace-setter, experimenter, and expert on local conditions."

Andersen believes the fact that the museum was not initiated from the outset by the community or its representatives reduced its relevance to development.

Smith says the main purpose of the Anacostia Neighborhood Museum has always been to emphasize the positive elements of African-American history and culture by showing examples of success. Despite the continued existence of racial discrimination, the goal was to provide the public with self-confidence and self-awareness. However, with respect to the actual impact of the Anacostia Neighborhood Museum's activities and possible social changes, Smith has doubts:

> Now, how successful have we been doing that, in other words, how successful have we been in raising the consciousness of young Blacks, I think, is probably debatable. You can look around and you still have drug problems and problems with crime. I think that those problems can't be solved; I mean, they can't be solved by simply putting on an exhibit. They are basically economic problems and until we get some economic enterprises or some injection of money from somewhere to deal with these

problems, I think these problems will continue. About the best that we can say is that, hopefully, we have reached some people and raised their sense of self-worth.

Mayo stresses the impact the Anacostia Neighborhood Museum has had in taking African-American history and culture beyond the local framework to achieve more presence and greater recognition. Its impact is reflected, for example, in the Smithsonian's SITES program, which did not include a single exhibit on African-American history and culture during the 1960s. Today SITES offers a dozen such exhibits, all of them developed by the Anacostia Neighborhood Museum (Mayo).

Going beyond its direct local significance, the Anacostia Neighborhood Museum, as the first African-American museum, is assuming an increasingly important position within the national framework, which, with support from the museum's leadership (cf. Mission Statement..., 1981; Kinard, 1984) should be further strengthened in the future. A report of the study commission set up by the Smithsonian Institution (Report of Advisory Panel 1979, p. 4) states: "... the Anacostia Neighborhood Museum has evolved to a point where its leadership is willing to drop many of the community dimensions of the programs to become the National African-American Museum."

And later the report states (Report of the Advisory Panel 1979, p. 6f): "Its earlier community-oriented programs seem to have declined considerably, and been largely discontinued, while at the same time it has developed ambitions to history as its exhibition focus."

A survey of museum and community workers in Anacostia showed (Rodriguez, 1984) that the local public complains about the museum' s neglect of social concerns and lack of social relevance.

In fact, over the years, as the Anacostia Neighborhood Museum has become more established and more institutionalized, the frequently evoked "strong community ties" have been completely lost. The sharp decline in the number of visitors indicates a lack of popular support, compared to the initial phase (Smithsonian Institution 1984b, p. 1):

38,429 in 1981; 39,047 in 1982; 19,527 in 1983; and 17,419 in 1984 (up to 9-30-84).

Reference must also be made to the fact that the Anacostia Neighborhood Museum, with respect to the local population, is turning primarily to a middle-class public. The declining numbers of visitors led Anderson to a devastating conclusion:

> It does not indicate that the museum is so important to the residents of Anacostia that they have adopted it, that they rely on it for an important thing to do with their time. It's still ignored by most of the people who live over there.

For him, the scope of the Anacostia Neighborhood Museum is too restricted and he complains that not enough has been done to motivate the potential public.

If the Anacostia Neighborhood Museum is to maintain and possibly expand its character as a neighborhood museum, work with the local public is urgently required. A national museum certainly has other concerns.

But, despite the reservations cited, the employees whom I questioned appear to be tending away from the local public, although it is not clear how the new public is to be defined.

Gaither's remarks (1979, p. 2) show that there are thoroughly convincing reasons in favor of establishing a "National Museum of African-American History and Art": "The majority report raises the question whether ANM could be an appropriate vehicle for the Afro-American presence in the Smithsonian. It is pointed out that the obligation of the Smithsonian is to reflect Afro-American contributions throughout its museums. This is certainly true. It must be noted, however, that this obligation is not a new one, and that it has not been honored in the past.

Moreover, there is no guarantee that it will be fully honored in the future. One may not, therefore, close the matter of Afro-American presence in the Smithsonian by citing a moral imperative that has – by precedent – been neglected."

The need for a "National Museum of Afro-American History and Art" is not at issue here and would go far beyond the scope of this work. But it should be noted that the combination of a neighborhood museum and a national museum is a somewhat unhappy one and does not appear to hold promise for the future, even if Kinard (cited in Alexander 1983, p. C9) sees points of contact between them: "We are a community museum, but we are also local, national and international. .

…The aspirations, hopes and dreams of the people of Anacostia are no different from those of the people anywhere else." We must wait and cf. what path the Anacostia Neighborhood Museum will take in the coming years.

3.3 The integral museum in Mexico

3.3.1 Casa del Museo

3.3.1.1 First project[1]

3.3.1.1.1 The Zona Observatorio

The first Casa del Museo project was carried out in the Zona Observatorio community of Mexico City. During its experimental phase in the 1970s the area was markedly heterogeneous, consisting of five distinct neighborhoods, the so-called "colonias" of Pino Suárez, Bellavista, Real del Monte, Lomas de Santo Domingo and Unidad Santo Domingo. As Antúñez, Arroyo noted (1980, p. 1): "This area was selected because of its heterogeneous physical and demographic make-up. The further down the ravine, the lower the social status of the population, which ranges from upper middle-class to shanty town dwellers lacking all public services."

At the time of the Casa del Museo project some 6,860 families (around 43,000 people) lived in the Zona Observatorio, but only a portion of them lived there permanently (cf. Antúñez et al., 1976, p. 2). A representative random study (Antúñez et al., 1976), covering 10 percent of local families, indicates the following general demographic profile. With regard to age, there was a strong predominance of individuals under 35. The educational level was low, with corresponding high rates of illiteracy. The working

---

[1] The Casa del Museo experiment encompassed basically two projects. In order to preserve their separate identities and maintain the analytical structure of the previous case studies, the present chapter is divided into two subchapters. However, the limited material related to the Mexican example means the respective sections will be less detailed than the earlier studies. To avoid repetition, the second study will make reference to the first.
Where the statements' origins are not further specified, these are summaries I have made from the material. When I refer to certain people by name, without providing further data, these are statements of my interview partners: Miriam Arroyo de Kerriou (3-21 to 3- 24-85) and Cristina Antúñez (3-21 to 3-24-85). In contrast to general textual citations, all interview quotes are in **bold**.

population consisted primarily of manual workers. The proportion of casual laborers and unemployed was suspected to be relatively high (cf. Hudson 1977, p. 16). On the basis of this typical portrait of a third-world metropolitan suburb, Hudson reached the following conclusion (1977, p. 16): "It was hardly surprising that the Tacubayans[2] were not accustomed to making a journey across the town to the National Museum of Anthropology. They were, for the most part, completely unaware of its existence and, even if they had been put into buses and taken there, the marble splendors, the fountains and the well dressed visitors would have terrified them."

How was the Zona Observatorio selected to be an experimental area for the Casa del Museo? To what extent has the museum integrated itself into the context described above? What role has it played? These questions will be addressed more fully below.

3.3.1.1.2 Origin

At a conference in Santiago, Chile, the then-acting director of the Mexican Museo Nacional de Antropología e Historia was given the task of organizing an exhibit on modem Latin America in which the city-country problem, marginalization and the population explosion were to be given special prominence.

However, a study of the national museum revealed that precisely those population groups most affected by these problems would not see such an exhibit for the simple reason that they did not go to the museum. At the time of this study the group of Mexican museum visitors was made up as follows: 69% male, 31% female; 30% of the males were between the ages of 20 and 29; 38% were students, 21% professional classes, and 24% white collar.

---

[2] The Zona Observatorio is part of the larger Tacubaya area.

What to do? Instead of waiting for people to dare cross the threshold of the big museum, the idea came to take the museum to them. In the early 1970s an attempt was made to decentralize the Mexican museum system by creating local and regional museums, as well as school museums (cf., for example, INAH, 1978a; 1978b;1979a; 1979b; Peltier 1977; 1979; Larrauri, 1975; Ramos, 1977). The origin of the Casa del Museo experiment should be seen in this context (Antúñez):

> We took the National Museum of Anthropology out of its wonderful walls, very nice, very clean, very expensive, and we took it to the very poor and forgotten areas in Mexico.

Mario Vásquez created an interdisciplinary team to plan and implement the first Casa del Museo project (cf. section 3.3.1.1.4). The team made reconnaissance tours of the suburbs or "barrios" of Mexico City in order to find a site for the Casa del Museo. Because of its heterogeneity, the Zona Observatorio of the Tacubaya quarter was selected (Arroyo de Kerriou).

In 1973 the interdisciplinary Casa del Museo team extensively studied the Zona Observatorio in order to become more familiar with its residents and institutions, needs and problems, and to create some basis for carrying out the project (the study report is not available).

It is not known whether the community officially approved the planned museum project on this occasion. In any event, also in 1973, the Museo Nacional de Antropología e Historia erected the first Casa del Museo in the center of the Zona Observatorio.

3.3.1.1.3 Conception and objectives

No available document explicitly describes the concept and objectives of the Casa del Museo. The interview statements are also wanting in this respect. Coral Ordóñez García, one of the museum workers, even stated explicitly (1975, p. 72): "There is no logical arrangement about the Casa del Museo, nor has any definite policy line been laid down. We work on the basis of trial and error; we correct and alter, act on suggestions and listen to criticism; we experiment again and again."

However, the present study offers some of the museum's objectives and the image it had of itself. In essence, planners sought to integrate the Museo Nacional de Antropología e Historia into an underprivileged and marginal neighborhood by creating a branch there to make the educational possibilities of the museum understandable to a wide circle of residents and make the institution useful. Arroyo de Kerriou understood this as follows:

> A special objective of the Casa del Museo was to integrate the museum into the community, not the community into the museum, because they didn't go.

Ordóñez García discussed in greater detail the desired role of the Casa del Museo within its neighborhood: The Casa del Museo seeks to awaken the desire to know, and still more the desire to look around and ask questions; to get the people to raise their sights above and beyond a slum that has sprung up in a river-gully. It seeks to create common interests and thereby to weld a community together; it seeks to get all those living in the community to identify themselves with their country, their city and their section of the city, while appreciating its present-day historical context.

Planners hoped to demonstrate the museum's usefulness in the everyday life of the affected population through relevant programs and activities. Therefore, a further aim of the Casa del Museo, according to Arroyo de Kerriou, was **to present the past, but as a function of the present, to create and correct the future**. Peltier (1979, p. 104) states its educational contribution to the neighborhood development as follows: "Its aims are to educate the residents of this poor area, to contribute to the betterment of standards of living through permanent and temporary exhibits showing how the history and culture of the country relate to their own situation, and to help them understand their problems and find solutions."

The Casa del Museo team recognized that community integration and acceptance was a precondition and priority for development-related museum work. From the outset the Casa del Museo was planned as an experiment to test what resources are needed and to what extent a socially integrated museum, that is, an "integral museum," could be realized: questions examined in the following sections.

3.3.1.1.4 Structure and organization

As already noted, the Casa del Museo was a project carried out by the Museo Nacional de Antropología e Historia. Because it was incorporated into the established museum structure, a brief overview of Mexico's government museum system is needed (cf. Fernández, 1983).

Two institutes that report directly to the national Ministry of Education determine Mexico's museum system: the Instituto Nacional de Antropología e Historia (INAH), founded in 1939, and the Instituto Nacional de Bellas Artes, founded in 1947 (INBA). For the most part, Mexican museums are government museums that belong either to INAH or to INBA.

Larrauri (1977, p. 9) refers to the educational potential and social relevance of the museums: "INAH museums must be seen as key factors in heightening social consciousness. Ultimately, they aim to prepare individuals to act upon or influence those events which affect them personally or socially in relationship with their social and natural environments. The museums must present a realistic and critical view of events that will aid people in understanding present day situations and problems."

Although the Casa del Museo reported directly to the Museo Nacional de Antropología e Historia, it was in essence a specific type of local INAH museum and sought, above all, to achieve the social relevance specified by Larrauri. The original Casa del Museo consisted of three connected, corrugated iron structures that conformed to local style because of their building material (Ordóñez García, 1975, p. 77).

As a branch of the Museo Nacional de Antropología e Historia, the Casa del Museo had no collection of its own. Objects required for exhibits came either from the national museum or directly from the population, and were returned at the conclusion of each exhibit. In the traditional museological areas, such as collection, restoration, conservation and exhibit design and production, the Casa del Museo depended on the services offered by the Museo Nacional de Antropología e Historia. A lack of equipment did not take away from its preferred role as a center of presentation and motivation.

In the early phases of the project, the Museo Nacional de Antropología e Historia hired an interdisciplinary team to carefully implement the first Casa del Museo. In 1974 Miriam Arroyo de Kerriou (educator) and Cristina Antúñez (administrator) joined forces and, together with Coral Ordóñez García (architect) and Lydia Gonzales (social anthropologist), formed the museum's permanent staff.

In practice, however, the population was less informed and less involved than the model shows. For example, no official participatory body was formed. A certain degree of participation by interested people was achieved only through informal discussions with the population inside and outside of the museum (Arroyo de Kerriou). But the local population had practically no part in the actual working and decision making of the Casa del Museo. The Casa del Museo was virtually grafted onto the neighborhood and only afterward was the population invited through posters and word of mouth to visit the museum, that is, to consume what the museum was offering. Instead of beginning with the study, the first step should have been informational work and an effort to involve the local population in the working and decision-making processes.

During the initial phase, the Casa del Museo project was financed by the Museo Nacional de Antropología e Historia and INAH. But when Cristina Antúñez and Miriam Arroyo began working for the Casa del Museo in 1974, the cash box was almost empty. Cristina Antúñez, therefore, worked from time to time on another project, from which she obtained materials and equipment for the Casa del Museo (Antúñez).

In addition, the employees made an enormous personal investment in the project. When asked how the Casa del Museo was financed, Antúñez and Arroyo de Kerriou answered:

By us, by INAH and by us,

which sheds much light on the project's financial situation.

This way, the museum overcame occasional shortages. It should be highlighted here that without the extraordinary personal contribution of the employees this project would surely have come to a sudden end. In an article on the Casa del Museo, Antúñez and Arroyo de Kerriou (1980, p. 5) observed: "We would like it to be clearly understood that over the years we did everything possible to prevent this very important project from going under." Without the boundless enthusiasm of the project's staff it would not have been possible to overcome the numerous obstacles and adversities it faced.

3.3.1.1.5 Activities and programs

As noted above in connection with the museum's construction and outfitting, the Casa del Museo's work concentrated on presenting exhibits and providing educationally relevant material (cf. Ordóñez, p. 1975). In their study of the Zona Observatorio, the organizers attempted, among other things, to delineate the wishes and needs of the potential public with respect to the future museum. Arroyo de Kerriou explained, with regard to the preparation of the first exhibit:

They took the information from the research, they knew what people wanted to know, what the people wanted to learn and they prepared the exhibition.

This first exhibit was entitled "Where You Live" (cf. Antúñez et al. 1976, Appendix 2). Like its predecessor, the second exhibit, on "Origin, Nutrition and Schooling", (cf. Antúñez et al., 1976, Appendix 2) addressed the interests of the potential public. However, these first two exhibits were by and large produced by the staff in cooperation with the specialists from the Museo Nacional de Antropología e Historia, without community participation. In addition, the Casa del Museo held a few short-term exhibits, each lasting only a few days, such as "Día de Muertos" (cf. Antúñez et al. 1976, Appendix 2) relating to the festival of the dead in early November. Here, the staff made an effort to involve interested people in the exhibition process, as described by Arroyo de Kerriou:

> I interviewed the people who lived around the museum to know if they are still making these altars in November and I asked them to come to the museum to work with us.

Neighborhood women cooperated in constructing the altars of the dead in the museum. Hudson (1977, p. 16) described the atmosphere in the "hallowed exhibit halls" of the Casa del Museo as "delightfully informal." Smoking and playing were tolerated, and people could bring animals in with them. Arroyo de Kerriou added:

> The people could touch, the people could smell, [...]. They could talk in the museum, they could run if they wanted, it was a free place to make them comfortable.

While Casa del Museo did indeed emphasize exhibits, these were not its exclusive main objective.

In order to create more lasting relations with a wider circle of the public, the Casa del Museo supplemented exhibits with regular evening events, such as concerts and dances, film presentations and lectures, which related in part to current problems facing the neighborhood. Antúñez and Arroyo de Kerriou mentioned, for example, subjects such as "health precautions and health care" and "hygiene." All museum visitors received written information on these subjects. In connection with the third exhibit the museum also ran workshops for teachers (Arroyo de Kerriou) **…to ask them to come to the museum and to learn how to use the museum.**

In the course of the project in the Zona Observatorio, the Casa del Museo's workers noticed some conspicuous demographic patterns of visitation. First, the Casa del Museo attracted mostly children and youth, for whom the museum represented a pleasant meeting place. They found the simply made exhibits and plentiful supplementary activities attractive. The adult public, on the other hand, cf.med more skeptical and reserved, as Ordóñez García (1975, p. 72)

emphasized: "The adults who come, being less ready to accept any change in the way they live, look on from a distance, some of them with an air of indifference, others with tolerant smiles."

Because the establishment of the Casa del Museo in the Zona Observatorio occurred shortly before the Mexican elections, some residents suspected it was a tool of the ruling party to canvas votes (Antúñez). This community suspicion led museum workers to carry out an intensive "door-to-door" campaign to explain the foreign body called the Casa del Museo to the residents of the Zona Observatorio. They tried **explaining what the museum was trying to do, why we were there, and what we wanted from them** (Antúñez)-in order to awaken their interest, receive suggestions – **health and hygiene, they wanted to know about it** (Arroyo de Kerriou) – and break down psychological barriers. Making direct contact with residents, despite its expense, promised to increase the acceptance of the museum and hence community participation (Antúñez/Arroyo de Kerriou). Because of its favorable central location and good visibility, the Casa del Museo attracted a relatively large casual public (Antúnez).

Those attending regular supplementary events numbered between 20 and 100.

Antúñez/ Arroyo reported that, in addition, an indeterminate number of immediate neighbors followed the museum's activities from their windows or rooftops. Further information on the Casa del Museo's actual outreach is given in the following section.

3.3.1.1.6 Evaluation

The location of the Casa del Museo at the intersection of five distinct communities of the Zona Observatorio turned out to be unfavorable for the Casa del Museo, because of the conflicts that existed among these neighborhoods. The internal problems of the Zona Observatorio and the great distances involved aggravated the work of the Casa del Museo to such an extent that the project was finally terminated.

In order to obtain precise data on the effect and the effectiveness of the Casa del Museo, the museum team conducted an extensive evaluation study in the Zona Observatorio toward the end of the first project in 1975 (Antúñez et al., 1976). The knowledge gained was supposed to influence the planning and implementation of further Casa del Museo projects in order finally to develop a systematic "methodology" at the conclusion of the experiment (Antúñez et al. 1976, p. 1).

Results can be summarized as follows (cf. Antúñez et al., 1976, Appendix 2): Of the sample group of Zona Observatorio residents, 27 percent had visited the Casa del Museo once, 37 percent had heard of it, and to 35 percent the Casa del Museo was completely unknown. The degree of awareness of the museum was greater in the nearby "colonias" than in the distant ones. The strongest visitor group consisted of females (62.4 percent female visitors, 37.6 percent male) and with respect to age, individuals from 15 to 24 years old = 60.2 percent, 25-34 years old = 16.1

percent; 35-44 years old = 18.3 percent; 45-54 years old = 5.4 percent; and, aged 55 and older = 0 percent. Children and youth had an important multiplier effect: adults were largely encouraged to visit the Casa del Museo by their children.

Most of the visitors (75.4 percent) came out of curiosity. They took the greatest pleasure in the objects and exhibits that reflected their everyday reality (Antúñez et al., 1976, Appendix 2): "This response, related to the objects that most interested them, proves to us that the desire to know more about the place where they live is basic to planning the exhibits."

The evaluators referred expressly to the significance of this relationship between museum work and neighborhood reality (Antúñez et al. 1976, Appendix 2): "The statements made by the people who were questioned for more information regarding their neighborhood show that the Casa del Museo, by offering information on the Zona Observatorio through its exhibits, succeeded in stimulating the population and awakening its interest in knowledge of the origins, common problems and history of the community in which they live." Those who were asked said they wanted more opportunities to prepare exhibits and carry out exhibit-related activities.

An indicator that the Casa del Museo mattered little to the local population is the fact that there was practically no reaction when the Casa del Museo closed (Antúñez):

> I don't think anyone wrote a letter to the INAH crying because we left.

The closing of the Casa del Museo, like its opening several years before, was taken for granted by the residents.

In their final evaluation of this first Casa del Museo project, Arroyo de Kerriou and Antúñez complained primarily about its paternalistic structure, comparing the Casa del Museo with those charitable church institutions that operate without the participation of those affected, thus reinforcing their passivity. A paternalistic relationship between museum and community is not suited to implementing an "integral museum."

Building on and modifying this experience, a second Casa del Museo experiment began at another site under more favorable conditions.

3.3.1.2 Second project

3.3.1.2.1 Pedregal de Santo Domingo de los Reyes

A second Casa del Museo[1] experiment was carried out between 1976 and 1979 in the Pedregal de Santo Domingo de los Reyes section of Mexico City. Its relatively homogeneous population mostly migrated there from rural areas and was united in its struggle to settle urban land and receive a minimum of city services. Their squatter operation has been described as the most significant in Latin America: In a single night in September 1974 around 30,000 people occupied the area of Santo Domingo[2]. At the time of the Casa del Museo project, approximately 25,000 families (or about 150,000 to 200,000 people) lived in the neighborhood.

Because of their mutual concerns over land rights and city services, Santo Domingo residents, as Antúñez and Arroyo de Kerriou stressed, were highly organized. That meant that, like official political groups, there was a well-developed network of citizens' committees and self-help organizations in Santo Domingo. Each street chose its own street committee, the chairman of which was a so-called "natural leader" (Antúñez/Arroyo de Kerriou). And it was precisely at this level that the second Casa del Museo project began.

---

[1] No written documents exist related to this second project, either published or unpublished, apart from a two-page presentation in Antúñez /Arroyo de Kerriou (1980, pp. 3-5). Therefore, I have based my statements on interviews with Arroyo de Kerriou and Antúñez, as well as on the sources referred to above.

[2] When "Santo Domingo" is mentioned here and below, "Pedregal de Santo Domingo de los Reyes" is meant.

3.3.1.2.2 Origin

Those responsible for the Casa del Museo project learned from the Zona Observatorio experiment that, before setting up a Casa del Museo in Santo Domingo, a long promotional phase was needed to prepare and inform the population. This sensitization work began with the "natural leaders" of the community, those who occupied leading positions within the affected community (not to be confused with its political leaders).

Museum workers initially encountered mistrust and a chilly response in Santo Domingo, especially since presidential elections were again scheduled to take place soon. Thus, it took repeated and persistent inquiries to establish contact with the natural leaders. About 80 people attended the first information meeting explaining the Casa del Museo project, including the chairs of the street committees referred to above.

Subsequently, museum workers met with members of the citizens' committees in order to create broader support for the project. Informal discussions with groups and individuals constituted the most important sensitization work in Santo Domingo.

In connection with these intensive preparatory discussions, affected residents asked to visit a "real" museum to get a picture of what it was like (Antúñez). A weekend visit of many interested participants helped clarify for them the plans for the Casa del Museo (Antúñez, Arroyo de Kerriou, 1980, p. 3): "Contact with the community was made through its·natural leaders. [...].

Once the population had become aware of the Casa del Museo's aims, it decided the role the 'museum' should play in the community. Full explanations to the community members took place, so that they would understand what a museum was inasmuch as the majority had never seen one."

The preparatory phase lasted about six months, during which the Casa del Museo team held information meetings and carried out a large number of museum-specific activities in temporary quarters. This early phase served to familiarize Santo Domingo residents with the nature of museum activities and gradually helped integrate the museum into the community.

When the museum had to find a new space, community acceptance of the museum had gone so far that residents themselves proposed erecting the Casa del Museo in a corrugated iron building in Santo Domingo (Antúñez).

With local financial support, residents and museum staff laid the foundation and built the Casa del Museo. In this connection Antúñez and Arroyo de Kerriou stressed that it helped community relations that the museum personnel were not too good to pick up a shovel. Construction offered each group the opportunity to learn from and about each other as Arroyo de Kerriou stressed:

> …we learnt a lot from the people. We came with knowledge, but they have a lot of experience and their own knowledge.

3.3.1.2.3 Conception and objectives

While the primary objective of the Zona Observatorio experiment was to bring the Museo Nacional de Antropología e Historia nearer to a public that did not normally go to it, the Santo Domingo project sought to work with the residents of underprivileged neighborhoods to establish and support real community museums. Aside from this change, the objectives of the Casa del Museo in Santo Domingo basically corresponded with those of the Zona Observatorio project (cf. section 3.3.1.1.3).

The Casa del Museo in Santo Domingo saw itself as an educational institution related to present-day matters. However, the experience gained in the Zona Observatorio led the team to emphasize the fact that the Casa del Museo was not a welfare institution. They wanted it to be distinct from public-assistance organizations and to be a partnership between the museum and the community. As a result, Casa del Museo offered no practical help in coping with specific problems.

The Casa del Museo in Santo Domingo viewed itself first and foremost as an information resource for the local population to learn about development. The museum, however, did not intend to usurp decision-making responsibilities about development measures from those affected.

3.3.1.2.4 Structure and organization

The second Casa del Museo project also reported to the Museo Nacional de Antropología e Historia, and thus was formally integrated into the official Mexican museum system (cf. 3.3.1.1.4.)

The remaining staff of the first Casa del Museo project started the second in Santo Domingo. This included Cristina Antúñez (administrator), Miriam Arroyo de Kerriou (educator), Lydia Gonzales (social anthropologist) and Coral Ordóñez García (architect and city planner).

Although these museum workers represented various disciplines, there was no specialty-based division of labor in Santo Domingo. Rather, all four undertook tasks in all areas of the museum's work (Antúñez), including the areas of promotion and sensitization, exhibits and education. Like the first Casa del Museo, Santo Domingo was exclusively a center for exhibits and events. To a limited degree, it could avail itself of the resources of the Museo Nacional de Antropología e Historia.

Overall, the second Casa del Museo project had limited financial and material resources at its disposal. Much, therefore, had to be improvised. In constructing exhibits, for example, items and materials discarded by the national museum were used – including paper, metal and wood. Although improvisation at first presented some difficulty for the museum workers, Antúñez/Arroyo de Kerriou emphasize that the use of modest means contributed in the long run to the acceptance of the Casa del Museo in Santo Domingo (Arroyo de Kerriou). Antúñez observed that in this way they did not scare the public away with costly and unfamiliar technology.

At first the museum opened to visitors during normal business hours of 10 a.m. to 5 p.m. and for evening events. Because only a part of the adults could visit the Casa del Museo during the day, residents requested that the museum be open at unorthodox hours. Arroyo de Kerriou explained:

> Early in the morning, at 5 o'clock [...] we went to the milk line, because 700 families were there to buy milk and we went to show people what the museum is, what the Casa del Museo is, what exhibitions we had [...] and everything. [...] So, we were talking with the people. The problem was, people said, "Well, why don't you open the museum at 5 o'clock. Sometimes the father comes to take the milk, other days the children come and sometimes the mother comes, so why don't you open the museum?"

Because museum workers were ill disposed to showing up in Santo Domingo at 5 o'clock every morning, some local residents proposed that the keys be left with them (Arroyo de Kerriou). Thus, the community gradually assumed more and more responsibility for the museum and played an increasingly important role in all areas of its work. Interested individuals proposed the subjects to be addressed, planned and implemented exhibits, collected photographs, documents and objects and took charge (Antúñez):

> ...and people used to clean and paint everything, to change the exhibitions, they were world champions. [...]. It was a great experience. I think it was the most wonderful thing.

Although not organized in an official way, all Casa del Museo's exhibits in Santo Domingo had the close cooperation of residents.

Antúñez, Arroyo de Kerriou (1980, p. 4) remarked on the significance of this active community engagement: "Participation in this case was complete in both the planning and the implementation of activities. The difference between the two experiments was that in the second one not only was the community aware of the Casa del Museo but its participation was decisive in all our activities. It may be argued that this participation was obtained because of the intensive work to create awareness carried out by the team despite its small size and limited budget."

The Casa del Museo was essentially a time-limited pilot project, from which financial support was gradually withdrawn because of personnel changes in the Museo Nacional de Antropología e Historia and the INAH. For example, no new personnel were hired to replace the three workers who left in 1978 partly for personal reasons. Without backing and resources from the sponsoring institution, the project was gradually doomed to fail, despite the extraordinary engagement of the employees and the population. Government projects such as the Casa del Museo depend on the good will of the political powers. A change in leadership within a given sponsoring government institution can have devastating effects and put a sudden end to successful projects.

3.3.1.2.5 Activities and programs

The second Casa del Museo emphasized exhibits, the first of which - "The Origin and History of Santo Domingo" - was proposed and developed by a group of interested citizens of Santo Domingo after a visit to the Museo Nacional de Antropología e Historia during the preparatory phase (cf. above). Residents improvised the exhibit made up of their photographs and documents and prepared in cooperation with the museum staff. It occupied a common room of the local school where preparatory discussions had taken place.

In its first year the Casa del Museo mounted 14 small exhibits (Antúñez). Each theme was determined by participating community members and covered a broad spectrum of subjects, from historical topics, such as "Evolution," "The Aztecs," "The Birth of Jesus Christ/Christmas" and "The Mexican Revolution", to representations of the various ethnic groups living in Santo Domingo to current problems such as "Nutrition," "Home Construction," and "Health Care."

Wide-ranging possibilities for community participation existed, for example, in presenting the various regional cultures themselves (Antúñez, Arroyo de Kerriou):

> So the people [...] put up the things from their regions, they were complemented with dances and films and people making food, like the things they were doing in their homes. [...]. And they dressed, they received the people and went to the museum to give guided tours.

Antúñez stressed they were dealing here with a "living museum." Moreover, the Casa del Museo ran workshops both to accompany exhibits and to constitute a so-called "open school" for adults to acquire practical skills like knitting, home construction, cooking and furniture upholstery.

Concerning nutrition, the Casa del Museo not only conducted workshops, but at times also ran an information service that provided local women with daily information on which of the local markets had the lowest prices. Some of the local women themselves carried out the necessary inquires and price comparisons.

At times the Casa del Museo of Santo Domingo maintained a branch in the neighborhood of Ajusco-Hayamilpas a few miles away (also called "La Comuna" by Antúñez, Arroyo de Kerriou). There, some 50 families from Santo Domingo had established a new community and were asking for a Casa del Museo. They repeated some of the exhibits and workshops in the Ajusco branch after closing in Santo Domingo.

In addition to presenting exhibits and various supplementary events, museum staff lectured in the local schools, to which they also invited the students' parents in order to familiarize a wider public with the museum.

The development of personal contacts between museum workers and local citizens played a significant role in the integration of the Casa del Museo into the community. These contacts were strengthened by the museum workers' participation in local celebrations.

In many cases the contribution of the Casa del Museo team went far beyond actual museum activities. Because staff had easy access to all possible official institutions (owing to their social position), they were able, for example, to obtain important information that the residents of Santo Domingo needed for their struggle to acquire land rights (Antúñez/Arroyo de Kerriou).

In San Domingo it was really possible to develop a kind of solidarity and cooperation based on partnership between the museum and the community, leading to the social integration of the museum. The assessment of this second Casa del Museo project will be dealt with in detail in the following section.

3.3.1.2.6 Evaluation

In La Comuna, as in the Zona Observatorio, the Casa del Museo found itself in a power struggle among competing community groups, making the museum's work considerably more difficult. This finally led to cancellation of the second Casa del Museo project in Santo Domingo and La Comuna in 1979, and with it the end of the overall Casa del Museo experiment. Other factors included work-related sickness, exhaustion, and personal conflicts among the staff.

In the end, Arroyo de Kerriou, who ended up being the only employee of the Casa del Museo, returned to the Museo Nacional de Antropología e Historia in order to systematically evaluate the Casa del Museo experiment and perfect its methodology. In her reflections, Arroyo de Kerriou found that the modified way of proceeding in the second project had been largely suitable and successful, but a crucial weakness of the project became quite evident (Arroyo de Kerriou):

We were so busy working with the people that we didn't cf. one thing: we had to prepare the people to keep their museum with them, because they were carrying on the museum, they opened and they closed the museum, they paid all the expenses for the museum and they did the work, but we did not prepare the people to maintain their museum by themselves. So, we had to find the other part of the methodology. We had to prepare a group of people from the community as natural promoters, because we found that that was the way to work and that would be the kind of museum Mexico needed.

As Arroyo de Kerriou neared completion of her evaluation and had already come to certain conclusions, representatives of the community of Vicente Villa (Netzahaulcoyol City)
came to the Museo Nacional de Antropología e Historia and asked whether a Casa del Museo could be established in their neighborhood. To be more precise, it was the students of a secondary school who expressed interest in setting up such a museum. Intending to modify and test her revised methodology, Arroyo de Kerriou agreed.

Again, the process began with surveys and round-table discussions. Arroyo de Kerriou stated: And 1started talking with the students to present a program like the one in Santo Domingo, because I had to tell them what a museum is, what the program is, how we work and show what the work was and then I told them: "OK, we have to prepare five workshops, one for research, a second for production and mounting, the other one on promotion and diffusion, the other one on guided visits, and the other one for complementary activities."

These five workshops formed the crucial new element of the Casa del Museo methodology. Through them interested citizens could theoretically guide the museum and keep it alive on their own.

The third (and last) Casa del Museo project, however, never got beyond a preparatory phase. In 1980 the Casa del Museo project was finally terminated. After the experiment was concluded, Antúñez, Arroyo de Kerriou (1980, p. 5) expressed the hope that their experiences with the Casa del Museo would continue: "We may conclude that the Casa del Museo should be advanced from its experimental status and become established as a definitive program with its own funding and staff. The experience obtained is thoroughly sufficient for affirming its viability."

A thoroughly justified hope, because in the wake of the experiments of the 1970s, the INAH changed its policy, as is briefly sketched in the following citation (Ubicación del Departamento de Servicios Educativos, Museos Escolares y Comunitarios ..., 1984, p. 6): "In the face of the theories that have been held and in opposition to the general line of conceiving of museums as sanctuaries of art, as privileged places to exhibit only beautiful objects, the museums of the INAH imposed an anthropological and educational concept that considered culture in its broadest sense, without separating it from its material, economic and social contexts."

The methodology developed for the Casa del Museo pilot project, adapted and modified, forms the basis for the new Program for the Development of the Educational Function of the INAH Museums, which will be discussed in the following chapter.

3.3.2 Program for the Development of the Educational Function of the INAH Museums

3.3.2.1 Origin[1]

Two years after the 1981 termination of the Casa del Museo project, the INAH again attempted to establish museums that fulfilled their social mission at the local level. It formed the Departamento de

---

[1] If the origin of statements is not further specified in the following text, they are summaries I have prepared from the available material. When I refer to certain individuals without providing any further details, these are statements made in interviews with: Miriam Arroyo de Kerriou (4-1-85), Jesús Armando Ruiz, Elena Navárez de Ramírez, Manuael Váldez Durán (3-26-85), Gloria Parra Gonzales (3-27-85), Clara Elena Gutiéraz Miramontor (3-28-85). All direct quotes from interviews are in **bold**.

Servidos Educativos, Museos Escolares y Comunitarios directly under the Dirección de Museos y Exposiciones (cf. DESEMEC, 1985c, p. 1). In the beginning, the department consisted of only two employees, Arroyo de Kerriou and Cristina Urrutía. They first prepared a country-wide inventory of Mexican museums, with particular regard to their social functions.

The survey concluded that a large part of the Mexican museum system consisted of "dead museums" that ignored their responsibility to serve the public (Arroyo de Kerriou).

As a consequence of this negative outcome, a special program – the Programa para el desarrollo de la función educativa de los museos de la INAH (Program for the Development of the Educational Function of the INAH Museums) – was created in 1983 to remedy the prevailing problematic situation. In this way the following public-oriented INAH programs were combined and coordinated (Ubicación del departamento, 1984, p. 7; cf. Arroyo Quan, 1985, p. 1):

> "1. Educational Services. Consists of attending to the needs of students and nonorganized public groups in general; for this purpose, it relies on educational aids, such as guided tours, audiovisual aids, publications and complementary activities (theater, film, dance, etc.).
>
> 2. School Museums Program. These are museums organized and developed for the school community, in which students, teachers and parents participate; it repeats the study program, but also complements it.
>
> 3. Community Museums Program. Unlike the above programs, this program was implemented beginning of this year. It is based on the experiences of the Casa del Museo experimental project. Its purpose is to integrate the museum into the everyday life of the community through the participation of its members, becoming the transmission channel of their needs, concerns and interests."

3.3.2.2 Concept and objectives

The objectives of the new program are ... (Ubicación del departamento ..., 1984, p. 7):

"a) To encourage the full and voluntary participation of the population in the knowledge, recovery, conservation and enrichment of the nation's cultural heritage.
b) To expand the educational services that museums offer to the marginalized sectors of the population.
c) To transform the museums into dynamic cultural centers which, without losing their own characteristics, will make possible the participation of the users."

In an unpublished paper (Programa para el desarrollo ..., no year, p. 1; cf. Arroyo de Kerriou, p. 1986, p. 3f) two further objectives were added: "To contribute to the affirmation of the values characteristic of our national identity, and to transmit, through exhibits and activities complementary to them the full concept of culture, understood as 'the total product of human activity."

On the basis of prior experiences with local museum work in Mexico (the Casa del Museo, Local and School Museums), the officials of DESEMEC (Department of Educational Services and School and Community Museums) expressed an interest in implementing the concept of the "integral museum" in cooperation with a given population and creating a new kind of museum (DESEMEC, 1985c, p. 2):

"The new museum is a full reproducer, preserver and absorber [reproductor, conservator, y captador] of the culture. It is not limited to a single space, but can work with the totality of the community or with part of it. It is a communicator at all levels. It is clear, understandable and entertaining. It transmits to its public signs and forms through objects and images that are not alien to the social and natural milieu. The objective of the exhibit is to stimulate the visitor to observe and analyze its content by obtaining knowledge through objects, interpreting them within their social context, participating with initiative in the development of the museum, and expressing and communicating his culture."

As the name suggests, this new INAH program sought to develop a systematic program of the museum's educational work. Thus, the museum appears as an alternative educational institution. The theoretical frame of reference supplies the concept of "permanent education," as formulated and disseminated by the UNESCO leadership since the 1960s (Méndez, 1984, p. 9ff).

The starting point for implementing the program was a network of hundreds of school museums established in the 1970s, but the majority of which are no longer functioning. Arroyo de Kerriou placed them in the category of "dead museums". Through revitalization and remodeling, several of these school museums became community museums. Calling the museum a "community museum" depends on a definition of community that is not so much geographic as referring to a grouping of people with similar socio-economic and cultural backgrounds, common interests and needs. Members need not necessarily reside in the same location or neighborhood (Narvárez de Ramírez, Valdez Durán). A further attribute of "community" signifies the participation of the population as well as the integration of the museum into the mainstream community.

Because this constitutes a crucial aspect of the program, the original text is cited in full (INAH, 1985, p. 8f): "The community museum is one in which, through the active participation of the population, the function of community service is performed, since the themes that it develops are always tied to the interests and needs of the community. [...]. It promotes the recognition of the creative and decision-making capacity of the community to meet its needs and to recover the past common history in order to understand the current reality. The community museum disseminates the singular expressions and communication codes of the community for the purpose of preserving and conserving the social and territorial area. It strengthens the feeling of belonging to a group by integrating and bringing together its individual members. It gives impulse to the re-evaluation of its speech, traditions, customs, geographical conditions and forms of production and, in addition, promotes a happier relationship between communities, thus promoting cultural interchange. The community museum educates in the possibility of understanding and planning alternatives to everyday problems, and presents the past as a function of the present. It maintains a constant dynamism and changes exhibition activities in accordance with the suggestions of the collective."

It can be inferred from these statements that the transformed Mexican school museum and the Mexican community museum are distinguished principally by the following characteristics:[2]

1. These museums are public educational institutions in the service of society;
2. They are a network of local museums, each of which is responsible for a certain area;
3. These museums are oriented to the preservation of the cultural and natural heritage of an area's population, that is, they are past-related;
4. The past and its evidence are related to the current reality of the area and serve as a medium for coping with just this reality;[3]
5. Past and present are placed in relationship to each other and communicated in the form of exhibits and the events that accompany exhibits;
6. These museums are based on the participation of the population: that is, those parts of the population that are interested in being engaged determine the form and content of the museum's work.

---

[2] Armando Ruiz summarized the objectives of the program as follows: 1) to get people to know their particular cultural and natural environment; 2) to have them learn to value their patrimony; 3) to enable them to rescue this patrimony; 4) to disseminate this patrimony toward the interior of the community; and 5) to achieve the participation of the people so that they participate in the solution to their own problems.

[3] For Armando Ruiz, dealing with history is secondary. For him, the main concern of the community museum is **to show the people what they are in the present ... their own culture, their own way of living.**

In their claims, these museums correspond by and large to the concept of "integral museum" and relate therefore to the Casa del Museo experiments. At the same time, however, the emphasis on involving the community represents a further development in the organization and implementation of the sensitization process (promotion and motivation).

Basically, the community museum seeks to contribute to: a) the formation of a given population's identity by preserving and instilling awareness of its regional cultural and natural heritage (Valdez Durán); and b) the creation of a multifaceted national identity, as Arroyo de Kerriou (1984, p. 2) states: "The new museum is a tool that helps to find the national identity because it recognizes and engenders respect for the various regional cultures."

Specific community development work is not one of the direct tasks of a community museum, but rather it is a long-term goal, in which the museum plays an important role. It is accomplished by building awareness and identity.

The following section will look at how the program actually functions and what has been achieved so far, particularly those parts of the program that relate to school museums and community museums.

3.3.2.3 Structure and organization

The organizational framework for implementing the above-mentioned objectives is the Department of Educational Services and School and Community Museums (DESEMEC) with its four subdivisions. At the time of my study, they were not yet fully staffed. All members of the interdisciplinary team, with the exception of the department head and the two section chiefs, work on the basis of time-limited contracts.

The core of the program is a network of promoters and coordinators that links DESEMEC and the grassroots. They work with individual communities to establish museums and ultimately structure and organize the museum's work (cf. Peña, Ortega Almazán, 1986). Main tasks of the promoters include advancing the idea of establishing a community museum, awakening interest and identifying those persons and groups in the community who actively support the undertaking and ascribe to the program objectives described above. In so doing, it is up to the circle of interested persons, mostly volunteers, to decide how and when to meet the museum's objectives (Ruiz, Valdez Durán).

Promoters and coordinators interviewed for this study unanimously agreed that the decision on where a community museum would be established was made centrally by government authorities such as the INAH.

The role played by central control explains the program's emphasis on promotional work. The following quote from an INAH publication makes it clear: "... promotion is the spinal column in the work of the school and community museums. There must be promotion during the formation phase and it must continue throughout all the activities. It is a constant labor of personal contact and group organization work, a delicate and sensitive effort, like all interpersonal ties.

To promote is to sensitize, which means that the motivational work must be essential if one wishes to attain the objective, which is to make the community conscious of the importance and utility of the museum. When this premise has been satisfied, the museum will make an impact on the transformation of attitudes, on the past, present and future cultural production and reproduction"

At the time of my study, a total of around 50 promoters were active in the states of Chihuahua, Hidalgo and Jalisco. Without exception, the promoters are teachers who are released full or part-time from their school duties to do museum work. As a rule, they have worked for years as teachers in the same community where they are now carrying out promotional work for the local museum. This takes advantage of their basic knowledge of local conditions and contacts, with whom they enjoy a certain degree of trust.

With the exception of teachers who already had some museum experience in the above mentioned school museum programs, the teachers who act as promoters for a community museum have no previous museum training. Teachers who work in small places, as Gloria Parra Gonzales stresses, often occupy a central role in the community's social life and thus already perform duties related to education and culture that are similar to those of a museum promoter.

Promoters receive additional schooling and support through DESEMEC (1985c, p. 9): "The museum promoter supports and coordinates the community activities. The Department of Educational Services and School and Community Museums, which consists of an interdisciplinary team, enables, advises and assists all the museum promoters in order to facilitate their work and expand their possibilities for action."

Several times a year, DESEMEC issues an information sheet that serves as a discussion forum for promoters and the INAH team during the time between personal meetings (cf. DESEMEC, 1984a). In addition, the Educational Service offers the promoters various exhibits to make their work easier during the initial phase. Up to now the subjects of the exhibits have been "Mesoamerica l, the West of Mexico," "The Higher Caliber," "The Popular Culture" and "The Medicinal Plants of Mexico" (cf. Arroyo Quan, 1985, p. 4). The promoters also receive a folder with drawings to facilitate and support the promotional work, that is, an explanation of the aim and purpose of the museum and the way it functions.

DESEMEC also provides documents to help promoters plan and execute their local activities (cf. e.g. Abundis, 1984; Avalos y Pérez, 1985; Perea, 1986; Rivera, 1986). The central element of the promotional tools is the so-called "methodology" (cf. fig. 26; cf. Arroyo de Kerriou 1987b, p. 7-15), a kind of work-guide for promoters. With regard to this "methodology," Arroyo de Kerriou observed (1986, p. 8): "The methodology is based on the elements of social promotion adapted to the needs posed by the creation of museums. This methodology consists of techniques, methods and programs that foster change. In the case of the promotion of museums, it is necessary that the community adopt a participatory attitude in their development."

In February 1984 promoters were given a training course for the first time in Mexico City where they were introduced to the methodology. Another two-week course (in which I participated as an observer) took place in March 1985. There, 34 elementary and secondary school teachers from the states of Chihuahua, Jalisco and Hidalgo received their first training as promoters (cf. DESEMEC, 1985b). Through lectures, group work, general discussions and museum visits, the future promoters were familiarized with the following subject areas:

a. General history of museum development
b. Museum development in Mexico, with particular reference to the Casa del Museo
c. Social work, motivation
d. Group dynamics
e. Historical research
f. Museography, the principles and techniques of museum work.

Several coordinators also took part in the course acting as intermediaries between the INAH and the promoters. Each promoter reports to the coordinator with responsibility for his or her region. With the coordinator's assistance, each promoter draws up work plans for one week, one month and one year. The coordinator's principal tasks are to plan and manage the museum projects in the given region. In addition, coordinators also provide practical help when problems arise. Each of the three aforementioned states is further divided into various zones, with a coordinator responsible for the museums in each zone. At state level coordinators report to a supervisor.

The general course acquainted the future promoters with the program's principles, objectives and opportunities. While promoters have some leeway to adapt the program to different local conditions, they nevertheless adhere closely to the program, as Jesús Armando Ruiz stressed:

First, they have to inform us of whatever they do. Second, they have to fulfill the objectives of the program, that's very important. They have a certain freedom, because they cannot apply that program and its objectives like a recipe to each community just like that. So, they have to have flexibility, but they have to fulfill, I repeat, the objectives of this program.

3.3.2.4 Activities and programs

Up until March 1985, the time of my research, the program's activities were focused on the state of Chihuahua. According to Arroyo de Kerriou, in 1985, that state had two museums that were so far advanced in their work that they could rightly be called "community museums." One of them is in the city of Chihuahua and the other is in Ascensión. Arroyo de Kerriou (1986:13) also cites community museums in Autlán de Navarro, Jalisco, and Ixmiquilpán, Hidalgo, as "... clear examples of the new museum." At the time of my research, several school museums and community museums were under construction in Jalisco and Hidalgo. Arroyo de Kerriou (1987a) also states the scope of the program had considerably broadened since then. In the meantime, 75 promoters and 14 coordinators have begun working for 56 community museums in the states of Chihuahua, Jalisco, Hidalgo, Guerrero, Tlaxcala and Guanajuato.

Two examples from the state of Chihauhua may clarify the process of implementing the community museum:

Ouauhtemoc

Founded in 1750, Ouauhtemoc today is a predominantly rural community of around 40,000 inhabitants located in the Sierra Madre Oriental of Chihuahua. In 1984, on the basis of their experiences with three school museums, citizens of Ouauhtemoc and the municipal administration expressed interest in building a community museum. Through DESEMEC in the INAH, planners selected the local teacher

Clara Elena Gutiéraz Miramontor, who had already worked for the school museums, to be promoter and project developer.

Gutiéraz Miramontor named "identity building" and "development" as objectives of the future community museum. She wished to use local museum work as a counterweight to the inundation of Mexican culture by foreign influences, and to instill in the citizens of each museum site a sense of their own regional and national cultural identity. She hoped that by presenting local, regional and national history it would encourage them to resist the massive cultural and economic influences of the neighboring United States.

The museum's long-term objective is not only to build awareness and identify historical markers, but also to influence the present-day economic and social structure (Gutiéraz Miramontor):

> In a way that would be development, because it would help to create jobs for people and to reinforce the social and economic structure of the place.

Gutiéraz Miramontor gives no more detailed information as to how this will proceed. However, I find the tendency here to concentrate on defending against outside influences questionable. It runs the risk of losing the critical perspective of the prevailing structures within the community and the possibility of changing them. On the basis of admittedly meager statements, this suspicion concerns the problem of setting goals. However, this could not be proved factually, because at the time of the study the community museum project in Ouauhtemoc had still not gone beyond the preparatory phase.

The promotional phase consisted first of all in establishing contacts with the "natural leaders." In Ouauhtemoc, museum planners – as their Casa del Museo predecessors before them – mistakenly associated with the various political and religious groups (Gutiéraz Miramontor):

I have had many problems, many obstacles, beginning with the political ones in which several parties tried to appropriate the work for their promotion.

Despite these obstacles, the project went forward. Interested citizens formed 14 groups, the members of which reflected occupational niches: merchants, workers, farmers, bank employees, students, etc. Promoters met with these relatively homogeneous groups to familiarize them with the museum.

Citizens who had been encouraged to cooperate during this initial phase formed working groups of six members each. These working groups carried out various activities in preparation for the establishment of the museum. "The Mexican Revolution" was selected to be the theme of the first exhibit with particular emphasis on the local perspective. They collected material related to local history, conducted interviews and carried out work projects such as painting and carpentry.

Community participation had become a reality here for the promoters. By involving the population in the various aspects of museum work, Gutiéraz Miramontor wanted to create a so called "living museum." However, the available material does not indicate whether in the long run participation will go beyond selective involvement, because at the time of this study the Ouauhtemoc project had been in operation for only a few months.

For just this reason, it is hardly possible to evaluate adequately the community museum in Ouauhtemoc.

San Juanito

In 1905 plans to build a railroad brought about the founding of San Juanito. Located in the state of Chihuahua, it has 15,000 inhabitants. Today, its economy relies on forestry (Gloria Parra Gonzales). For its surrounding villages, San Juanito constitutes a regional trading center.

The objectives and tasks of the San Juanito community museum are relatively general. They concern principally protecting and communicating the local cultural heritage (Gloria Parra Gonzales):

> ... the program is first to get to know our cultural values, afterwards to appreciate and rescue them–this is the principal part of it, then, to conserve or preserve and afterwards to disseminate the heritage.

According to acting promoter Gloria Parra Gonzales, the community museum in San Juanito wants to sharpen in this way the population's awareness of its cultural identity so that **people are going to feel a little bit more related to the community and to the nation**. Here again the element of national integration appears listed among the objectives, which makes the community museum appear to be an extended arm of the Mexican national museums (on this subject, cf. also Arroyo de Kerriou, 1984, p. 2).

A private initiative by Gloria Parra Gonzales led to the establishment of the San Juanito community museum. As a teacher she had had to work far away from her home in San Juanito and wanted to be transferred there. The authorities released her from school service so that she might work as a promoter for a community museum in her home town, which she began in February 1985. She first approached the city administration and the leaders of the various local institutions in order to get some idea of possible starting points for her promotional work. As a next step, she contacted "natural leaders" and held informational meetings with interested citizens. In the beginning she had to establish trust among the residents, who had had poor experiences with projects of any sort.

At the time of this study, three groups of 60 members were at work on the San Juanito community museum. It is too early to tell how this cooperative effort will turn out, because by March 1985 the project had only been in existence for a few weeks. The participants still had not selected the subject of their first museum activity.

With regard to the informational meetings, Gonzales remarked that interest and involvement came first from the ranks of the underprivileged majority of the community.

On the basis of the composition of the citizens' committee, I believe that there is a good chance that the community museum in San Juanito, as opposed to that in Ouauhtemoc, will serve the great majority of the population. Since the project could only look back on a very brief history at the time of my study, results and possible problems have not yet become apparent, so that a detailed assessment of the San Juanito community museum must be deferred.

3.3.2.5 Evaluation

It is in Mexico that the social integration of museums has been most consistently developed since 1972. This involves preserving the cultural and natural heritage of a community and generating awareness of its own identity. With this as a foundation, museums could undertake at a later stage educational work directly relevant to development.

Apart from the similarity to the integral museum, one aspect must be emphasized: the readiness to learn from experience and make corresponding changes according to the prevailing conditions.

With the help of questionnaires regularly filled out by the promoters and coordinators, organizers continually evaluate the program itself and the work of the school and community museums (cf. DESEMEC, 1986a). Results form the basis of program modifications and improvements. I believe the experience gained over the years, the readiness to learn and the remarkably systematic nature of the program offer a sound basis for future success.

However, a problem exists in the fact that Mexican museology depends on government sponsorship and risks, therefore, possible control. A way to enhance the quality and credibility of the program would be to ensure that local museums were in a position to enable communities to develop their own programs of self-portrayal and self-determination. What community museums may accomplish in the future remains to be cf.n, but, whatever it is, should be carefully followed by museum professionals.

4. Claims and Reality of New Museology: Comparative Analysis of the Case Studies[1]

4.1 Objectives

Today most modern museums think of themselves as educational institutions in the humanistic sense. These conventional museums are basically static places of safekeeping where objects, not visitors, reign supreme and where the vast majority of visitors lack learned access to the collection. Thus, traditional museums frequently elevate preservation of a given culture to the status of an object in itself, while not denying the visitor a certain leisure and relaxation value. Despite the recent upsurge in museum education programs that help break down barriers to access, these measures frequently do not go beyond pure entertainment.

Unlike traditional museums, "new" museums preserve, document and study culture as a tool in a goal-directed educational process. It is a means to an end, namely that of providing the public with a way to attain its educational objectives. Identity building and coping with everyday problems are specific objectives that are supposed to lead to the general, complex objective of social development, in the sense of abolishing flagrant inequalities and disadvantages. The crucial distinction between the traditional museum and the "new" museum lies in the perception and formulation of a social task aimed at societal development.

The case studies, however, have revealed that these objectives still played no recognizable role in the initial phase of new museology. The Anacostia Neighborhood Museum and the first Casa del Museo were established as so-called intermediary museums. They were created as

---

[1] In the following comparative analysis, specific textual references to the case studies are generally not made. However, where it cf.ms appropriate, I have noted the case studies to which the remarks refer.

satellites of large national museums in order to address an otherwise unreachable segment of the public for the general, humanistic purpose of imparting knowledge. These experiments (as the intermediary museums were seen to be) intended to decentralize the national museums and integrate them as educational institutions into marginal, local communities.

Educational content in each case corresponded to that of the supporting institution. Specific goals related to the population were not formulated, so that the museum's social integration was fundamentally no more than an end in itself.

But after a relatively short time the experiments assumed independence and oriented themselves to their respective local contexts, which led–similarly to the case of the ecomuseums–to a general increase in the significance of educational goals such as identity building, coping with everyday problems, improving living conditions and effecting societal development. I believe the social integration and acceptance of the museum as a foreign body cannot be achieved without concrete objectives attuned to the target public. For populations not accustomed to museums, the museum must have a recognizable purpose related to the reality of their lives. What produces acceptance of the museum is its usefulness as recognized by the population in question.

The case studies have revealed that in practice each museum emphasized different goals. In all of them, pride of place in the hierarchy of objectives was to generate a feeling of community identity. Here one might object that in this regard there is little difference from traditional museums. In the end, an implicit objective of any museum–whether a technical, art or history museum, whether local, regional or national–is to set in motion identification processes in the passive visitor, be it by self-recognition in the objects exhibited or by aesthetic pleasure. But "new" museums are not content with this diffuse means of establishing identity. They go beyond this and understand themselves generally to be a practical instrument in an active search for identity by primarily marginal population groups. They seek cooperation with the community to determine its historical, present and possible future relationship to other sociocultural groups, which helps engender identity.

"New" museums have achieved a considerable amount in the area of identity building. One of their characteristics is that they generally work with disadvantaged and marginalized social groups whose identity differs from the "official" one, that of middle and upper classes. The Anacostia Neighborhood Museum, for example, was the first museum in the United States to devote itself to that particular African-American community's history, culture and current problems. In Mexico, community museums carry out identity-building with provincial populations within a framework of an otherwise strictly centralized museum system. Labor history and culture became for the first time the central focus of the Ecomusée de la Fier-Monde in Montreal. In addition to the case studies described here, there are other museums that exist on Indian reservations and in Inuit settlements in the United States and Canada whose purpose has been to study and preserve their history and culture and help them renew their appreciation of their traditions. Apart from ethnologists, journalists and a few engaged individuals, hardly anyone up to now has studied the specific characteristics of these groups, let alone help them establish their own local museums for the purpose of supporting core values. Rather these groups have been oppressed, assimilated, or ignored, and have lived on the margins of society.

While most museums studied here have equated identity-building primarily or exclusively with the affirmation of ethnic and regional identity, the Mexican community museums also strive to develop national identity to help the community achieve national integration. This has its roots in the prevailing social context and in the centralized governmental control of the Mexican museum system.

In Mexico, as in other countries with ethnically heterogeneous populations, use of the "new" museum may succeed in both affirming ethnic or regional identities and acting as an instrument of national integration. However, the "new" museum's nation-building objectives should not aim to impose a dominant unified culture. In large-scale, government-run museum development programs involve a basic danger which is that museums will be used as a political instrument by those in power.

If "new" museums really want to serve the interests of the above-mentioned groups, they must contribute to the self-determined identity search of these groups, and avoid acting as an extended arm of the government. Critics of neighborhood museums in the U.S. also emphasized this danger when they suspected that the 1960s' neighborhood museums merely reproduced the well-known repression mechanisms in a new guise–as a "device employed by the dominant white community to keep the cities 'cool' in summer" (Dennis, 1970, p. 16).

Conversely, another problematic aspect of identity-building work that must be guarded against is the encouragement of uncritical self-adulation. Because target groups often have a distorted or decidedly negative sense of their own identity, the "new" museums generally have a tendency, in their efforts to create a positive identity, to go to the other extreme, particularly with regard to their image of history.

Of course, history being a social reconstruction of reality and not the same as reality, it is easier to achieve historical accuracy through a critical approach than through the selective emphasis of only positive elements seen from a present-day viewpoint. Identity includes not only knowledge of one's strengths and "heroic deeds," but also a realistic assessment of weaknesses and mistakes, from which a community can learn and improve its social development. Moreover, self-critical identity building helps prevent chauvinism.

But identity-building should not be a "new" museum's only objective, it should contribute to the problems of coping with everyday life. Identity in the sense of historical knowledge, of orientation in space and time, of self-respect and the feeling of belonging to a sociocultural group is a basic precondition for action and responsible behavior. In general, "new" museums hope to influence marginal social groups so that they will structure their present and future in conformity with their specific cultural characteristics.

Identity as well as the self-awareness and self-confidence it embodies enable a population to cope appropriately with everyday life, which for some of the museums studied involves imparting useful knowledge and skills. These include, for example, making relevant current information accessible (Casa del Museo II), identifying current problems (Anacostia Neighborhood Museum in the early 1970s), and communicating working methods and forms of organization suitable for representing a group's interests before political decision-makers (Ecomusée de la Haute-Beauce).

In this respect, "new" museums go beyond the objectives of cultural educational institutions: The communication of identity and history, of knowledge and skills is seen by all of the museums studied as a step toward achieving the higher goal of social development, of changing a community's social reality.

As for goal-oriented development measures, the museums studied here either do not wish to enter this rough terrain (Ecomusée de la Maison du Fier-Monde, Casa del Museo I, Casa del Museo II, San Juanito community museum) or feel themselves powerless in the face of prevailing conditions (Anacostia Neighborhood Museum). Only the Ecomusée de la Haute Beauce has occasionally gone beyond identity building. It has undertaken concrete steps to stimulate the regional economy and improve the living conditions of residents. Although no lasting effects are apparent at this time, the Ecomusée de la Haute-Beauce intends to enter consciously into the process of social development.

Curiously, although proponents of new museology claim that museums need to contribute to social development, none of the individuals questioned was able to define clearly and comprehensively what they meant by development, that is, to detail what should be accomplished in the end. I believe this is a fundamental weakness of the "new" museums I studied. Because "social development" is undefined, no adequate, action-oriented strategies can be developed for achieving it and the results cannot be measured.

A solution may involve more modest objectives by having "new" museums confine themselves to identity-building as an indirect way of contributing to social development. By doing this, however, the "new" museum loses some of its innovative character that distinguishes it from traditional museums. If "new" museums really want to depart from the humanistic educational ideals of traditional museums and be effective in the social development process, the only acceptable alternative is for these museums to undertake the unquestionably laborious task of defining "development" as a goal.

This does not mean one definition of "development" must bind everyone.[2] Rather, each "new" museum must determine its political and ideological position in order to define what "social development" means in conformity with the local context, and how it will achieve it. Only on this basis can the museum put in place appropriate programs and action strategies.

Museums cannot solve a community's problems at one blow, even if they do formulate concrete development goals. Rather, museums should realize they have a proper place in the social development process. The Ecomusée de la Haute-Beauce is showing the first signs of this.

The objectives of the "new" museum set forth here raise certain basic principles that must exist and be respected so that social development objectives can be achieved.

4.2 Basic principles

Two basic principles underlie a museum's efforts at identity building, coping with everyday problems and effecting social development: territoriality in all areas of the museum's work, and a radical orientation toward the public.[3] The "new" museum claims to relate to a delimited, clearly comprehensible space and to act as a cultural educational agent

---

[2] Within the framework of the present work, the extraordinarily complex subject of "development" cannot be dealt with in a preliminary manner, let alone comprehensively. Therefore, it is addressed here only in so far as it concerns the "new" museum.

[3] Although these basic principles will be treated separately, they touch on all aspects of the "new" museum, hence the need for repeated references to them in the following sections

of development. It does so to serve the residents of this space. These two together–the territory and its residents–constitute the local context and determine the nature of the "new" museum, as the case studies revealed.

With respect to a radical orientation to the public, new museology claims that museums should be "grass-rooted," that is, that they should be founded through community efforts. In contrast to the traditional museum, which as a rule is established and run by specialists and administrators for the public, the "new" museum is distinguished by the fact that it is initiated and supported by the public itself of a given region or neighborhood. One encounters frequent references to the "entire population," which allegedly enthusiastically commits to the establishment of a museum–a "slight" propagandistic exaggeration in which the wish rather than the reality is truly father of the thought!

Museums are far from mobilizing the masses: a maximum of 10 to 30 people can be counted among regularly active nonprofessionals who take part in decision-making and museum work, the actual number generally closer to the lower limit. For the territorial units cited in the case studies, which have 15,000 to 200,000 residents, this means an extremely small percentage of participants.[4] None of the museums I studied owes its establishment exclusively to a community-based, grass-roots initiative. Instead, outside specialists and administrators played significant roles and brought ideas and initiatives to each population in question.

This state of affairs is not surprising since in general the majority of the populations concerned simply do not know what a museum is and how it could be used, or they have unclear ideas formed from a superficial knowledge of traditional museums. Most people are unaware of the significance of examining, preserving and imparting a given heritage.

Moreover, understanding of the structure, functions and possibilities of a museum to be an open educational institution is generally reserved to a few, and is frequently conveyed as a diffuse idea rather than as concrete and applicable knowledge. This explains why interested laypersons, if they

---

[4] Chapter 4.3 will deal with the overall problem of "participation" in greater detail.

take steps on their own, seek the advice and participation of specialists (Ecomusée de la Haute-Beauce) or, vice versa, why specialists approach a given population with ideas and initiatives (Anacostia Neighborhood Museum, Casa del Museo l, Casa del Museo II, community museums).

Thus, "new" museums hardly differ from traditional museums in regard to their origins, notwithstanding specialists' tendency to underplay their own role and emphasize that of the population. l believe museologists and involved scholars should, on the one hand, take a critical view of their specific role in the museum process, but on the other hand admit to it in a more courageous and self-assured way. Because the vast majority of the population is attached to traditional ideas of the museum, new museologists can serve as catalysts by pointing out the new, socially oriented possibilities of museum work.

The museologist communicates the concept of the "new" museum, which necessitates some simplification to guarantee citizen participation and cooperation (cf. section 4.3). A "new" museum cannot be ordered by decree. Unlike the initiation and concept phase, the implementation process of a "new" museum differs from traditional museums. The specialists (museologists, historians, educators, to name but a few) who either are appointed by interested members of the community or by local authorities, or who intervene on their own initiative consider it one of their main duties to identify prevailing community needs and gear museum work toward fulfilling them.

Accordingly, the actual founding of the museum in each case study was preceded by an exploration and promotion phase. Contact between museum staff and interested local residents aimed to create the widest possible "popular" basis for the museum. ln almost all the cases–with the exception of the Casa del Museo project–a participation and advisory structure in the form of associations (Ecomusée de la Haute-Beauce, Ecomusée de la Maison du Fier-Monde), committees (Ecomusée de la Haute-Beauce, Ecomusée de la Maison du Fier-Monde, Anacostia Neighborhood Museum) or working groups (San Juanito, Ouauhtemoc), etc., paralleled the information work on the nature and possibilities of the "new" museum (cf. section 4.3). In the case of the Casa del Museo II, already existing citizens' committees served as forums for sensitization and participation.

The sensitization phase–called "promotion phase" in Mexico– is distinguished by its reciprocal relationship between specialists and residents. This is expressed in the "triangle of creativity" in the Ecomusée de la Haute-Beauce, and in the "methodology" of the Mexican community museums. Continual interchange serves to convey a better understanding of the foreign body called a "new" museum to the broadest possible circle of the population. The process aims to modify and finally implement the museum together with involved citizens in accordance with their interests and needs. The process of interchange and modification does not end with implementation, though. The point is not to impose a firmly structured notion of the "new" museum, but to open it for productive adaptation to local conditions.

At its heart, the "new" museum pursues interchange and sensitization in order to produce coordination of the diverging concepts and working methods of specialists and citizens. The end is to produce an action-oriented synthesis. However, this communication process–as I have regarded sensitization–does not always proceed smoothly. Although useful as a starting point, interchange and coordination are made more difficult by various barriers that preclude meaningful communication. As an agent of social integration, the "new" museum still leaves something to be desired, despite the availability of appropriate mechanisms, in other words, the "new" museum is not only not "grass-rooted" (cf. above), but in many cases is not even as public oriented as several traditional museums.

These influential factors relate, however, to only one of the basic principles. If the "new" museum wishes to satisfy its claim to public orientation, the public under consideration must not be some amorphous mass public, but rather a clearly defined target group. Here the second principle of "new" museums–territoriality–comes into play.

All the museums I have discussed relate to a clearly delimited spatial unit–a neighborhood (Ecomusée de la Maison du Fier-Monde, Anacostia

Neighborhood Museum, Casa del Museo I, Casa del Museo II), a small town (Ouauhtemoc, San Juanito) or a region (Ecomusée de la Haute-Beauce)–each different in kind, size and number of inhabitants.

In addition to physical boundaries, a population's specific cultural (in the broadest sense) features determine the local or regional context. In this regard, the museum locations I have dealt with may be characterized as follows: The Ecomusée de la Maison du Fier-Monde is located in a declining industrial neighborhood of Montreal with a traditional francophone working-class population. The Casa del Museo II operated in a poorly cared-for neighborhood of Mexico City, to which groups from various rural regions of Mexico migrated in search of a new livelihood. The Ecomusée de la Haute-Beauce is in a rural region of Quebec with a francophone population of small-town dwellers who work in the crisis-prone sectors of agriculture, forestry and small industry.

These three geographic and demographic contexts are sharply defined and relatively homogeneous, which enables each museum to fulfill both basic principles of the "new" Museum–territoriality and radical community orientation. It should be recalled, however, that in the case of the Ecomusée de la Haute-Beauce, a territorial unit was first created for this purpose by the museum.

However, in regard to the Anacostia Neighborhood Museum, Casa del Museo I, San Juanito, and Ouauhtemoc, although the population in question also occupies a specifically defined geographical area, the communities are more heterogeneous–only part of the population can be considered "underprivileged." It is important to stress that although the majority of the population can be characterized as underprivileged, the area also contains a middle-class stratum. That means a portion of the population has other interests and needs, and is likely equipped with greater power.

Population heterogeneity and conflicting interests pose dangers for these museums. Either they wear down and succumb to competitive struggles and contradictory interests (Casa del Museo I) or they develop a strong tendency to become bourgeois, that is, to being taken over by the middle-class public–the traditional beneficiary of cultural and educational institutions (Anacostia Neighborhood Museum, Ouauhtemoc, San Juanito).

My research suggests that too heterogeneous a target group impedes the realization of one of the basic principles–public orientation. Not only must the physical context be clearly defined, the relative homogeneity of the historical, cultural and social background, as well as common problems, interests and needs, must also constitute a basic precondition of a "new" museum.

But should the museum find itself in a heterogeneous local context, it must exert a strong integrating influence and link together the diverse population groups so that it can work in the interests of the population as a whole. However, compromise solutions of this kind may significantly limit its scope of action, since those themes that relate, for example, to power relationships and social injustices are often precluded in advance.

Thus, to do justice to the concept of the "new" museum, planners should pay particular attention to the local context–consisting of a territory and its population–and determine precisely who and what these entities are. Ideally, feasibility studies should accomplish this as a first step.

4.3 Structure and organization

The "new" museum's objectives and basic principles referred to above must coalesce into organizational structures that can be implemented. They involve a low degree of institutionalization, financing through local resources, decentralization, participation, and team work by specialists and interested citizens working on an equal basis (cf. chapter 2).

Representatives of new museology reject institutional ordering in the "new" museum. I believe that this is based on a misconception. What one wants to prevent are strictly formulated structures that impede dynamic action. But it cannot be ignored that a museum is basically an institution, that is, a social entity characterized by certain patterns of order and rules and performing specific functions (cf. Hartfiel, 1976, p. 307f).

When a human activity–i.e., the preservation of a given heritage, for example–goes beyond selected individual actions, and people join together into working groups or in clubs to pursue a certain goal, they confer on themselves a certain organizational form. This can be considered the beginning of institutionalization. Actions are repeated and long-term, complex projects and programs are developed that involve larger numbers of people. Offices, documentation centers, stock rooms and exhibit spaces become essential.

This necessarily requires a more complex and more formal organizational framework, such as the creation of a museum (or some similar establishment). The group in question then adopts social controls (cf. Berger, Luckmann 1980, p. 59). In my view, therefore, every museum should be considered a social institution. It becomes an instrument that a society confers on itself in order to pursue, in an organized way, consistently determined goals and objectives that are considered socially relevant. With regard to financing projects, the creation of an institution naturally facilitates access to resources, for example, government subsidies.

In practice, the involvement of specialists is frequently associated with institutionalization, although society doesn't necessarily lose all decision-making power with the creation of the institution. The original individual influence on certain processes occurs within each institution through a participation structure (that as a rule is given) and corresponding control mechanisms (cf. below). It is characteristic of institutionalization, however, that individuals delegate tasks, authorities and decisions to the institution in order to take the load off themselves (cf. Hartfiel 1976, p. 308). Therefore, institutions have a tendency to become independent and viewed as an objective reality (cf. Berger, Luckmann 1980, p. 62ff). New museology wants to counteract this tendency, that is, the possible negative results of institutionalization.

In my view, museums, including "new" museums, are social institutions. If one speaks of a low degree of institutionalization in connection with the "new" museum, this can only mean that the institutionalization of the museum has not progressed so far that it has become an independent goal in itself. "New" museums must keep up a continual interchange with the population in question and be open to change. How much a museum distances itself from the community depends on the existing structure and the degree of citizen participation, which must be long-term. The community must look after its legitimate rights and be actively involved in the institution. "New" museums create structural elements as mechanisms to maintain openness and check institutionalization.

How the museum is financed affects the degree of influence and control. To be active sponsors of the "new" museum, the community must shoulder some or all of its financial support.

Comparative analysis of the case studies reveals great differences in methods of financing. The demand for self-financing, particularly in regard to the scope and professional standard of projects, is generally proving to be extremely unrealistic, since we are dealing with financially weak and underprivileged groups. Consideration of the case studies reveals that "new" museums–apart from isolated contributions in kind or money from the community–are largely government financed.

As an experimental project of the Museo Nacional de Antropología e Historia, the Casa del Museo I received its funding exclusively from it. The same applies to the Anacostia Neighborhood Museum, an "intermediary" museum within the institutional framework of the Smithsonian Institution. Of all museums considered in this study, the Anacostia Neighborhood Museum has by far the largest budget, is the best equipped and has the most employees. Although this financial cushion has enabled the Anacostia Neighborhood Museum to move beyond an experimental phase, at the same time it has fostered the growth of institutionalization (professionalization, clear administrative hierarchy and reduction in community influence). As a result, this had led to the former neighborhood museum becoming indistinguishable from a traditional museum.

The Ecomusée de la Haute-Beauce enjoyed independence from other institutions. It is the only "new" museum that was successful in financing itself from community contributions.

This applies, however, only to its initial phase. Fund-raising success presumably resulted from the fact that they created projects (the purchase of the Bolduc collection and the establishment of a museum) that the community valued. After their conclusion, however, community-based financial support declined. The museum proposed additional projects, but residents identified less closely with them and were therefore reluctant to contribute.

Now, as to some extent before, the necessary funds flow into the Ecomusée de la Haute Beauce through government subsidies. Ever since the museum gained government recognition, it has had a fixed annual budget, supplemented by project-specific grants either from the government or from corporations. The Ecomusée de la Haute-Beauce example indicates how the blessing of money brings with it increased professionalization and a distancing from the community, owing to its need to satisfy certain professional standards in exchange for government recognition. To stimulate community funding, the Ecomusée de la Haute-Beauce wants to encourage more locally based projects that appeal more specifically to residents and which they can identify with and wish to support.

In contrast to the Ecomusée de la Haute-Beauce, the likewise-independent Ecomusée de la Fier-Monde has no fixed budget nor permanent staff. Therefore, it exhibits a lower degree of institutionalization than previous examples. Because support initially came from a small group of citizens, it never attempted broad community financing, but depends exclusively on project bound government subsidies and work-creation measures. While this mode of financing slows the progress of institutionalization, it entails other problems, such as lack of continuity, absence of long-range planning and economic insecurity for the workers.

The Casa del Museo II differs from other case studies in that funding derived from the private resources of the population and staff contributions. Its experience demonstrates that a talent for improvisation and self-help can overcome financial bottlenecks. Low professional standards and modest, unassuming programs due to limited resources were seen as advantages because this reflected the everyday situation of the majority of residents. Also, the same question arose at the Ecomusée de la Haute-Beauce, namely, whether increased professionalization corresponds to community needs.

While it is difficult to draw general conclusions on the funding of "new" museums, institutionalization and professionalization tend to increase with more abundant government support (the Anacostia Neighborhood Museum and Ecomusée de la Haute-Beauce, for example). This situation also entailed a certain distancing and independence of the museum from the population.

Conversely, however, modest financial resources do not automatically guarantee closeness to the citizens if other measures are not operating concurrently. The experiences of the Ecomusée de la Haute-Beauce in its initial phase and of the Casa del Museo II show that local financial support is more likely if residents identify with and value the projects to be financed. Moreover, to be attractive to the community, projects had to be easily understood and adapted to the local living conditions. In some cases, this caused professional standards to be put aside.

Spatial decentralization of "new" museums is a strategy to ensure affinity with the population and to open up opportunities for identification and influence. While traditional museums occupy a single building in a regional center, "new" museums, in view of their special orientation, should be decentralized, that is, dispersed throughout the territory. Dividing the museum into a centrally located service center and local sub-centers can reach a broader stratum of the population and thereby satisfy the principle of public orientation and closeness to the citizens. At the same time, it can make its presence felt in identification markers spread throughout the territory covered by the museum.

In practice, decentralization seems primarily a characteristic of the ecomuseum. Other forms of the "new" museum–the neighborhood museum and the integral museum–do not exhibit decentralization as an objective, owing to the fact that they are already sub-centers, that is, decentralized facilities of a large national museum. With respect to their territorial reach, both the Anacostia Neighborhood Museum and the Mexican examples are de facto central establishments. They differ in this respect from traditional museums only in so far as they are in places where previously there were no museums. However, their location in a central museum building, and the limitation on their area of activity that this involves show strong parallels to the traditional museum.

On the other hand, ecomuseums, which originated in a centralized museology context but independent of central "parent institutions," push decentralization a step further. They seek to expand their radius of action throughout a region (Ecomusée de la Haute-Beauce) or a neighborhood (Ecomusée de la Fier-Monde) through so-called local "antennas," which form a network of roots in the community.

The Ecomusée de la Haute-Beauce has gone particularly far in this respect by establishing, from the beginning, a variety of antennas in the region. It funds three local interpretation centers as antennas (a fourth was in the planning stage), eight small open-air exhibits and five citizen groups associated with the ecomuseum. At first, the antennas did not so much express community sensitization as serve as a means for the museum to implement this process. Creating the antennas began the process of interchange between the museum and the population of Haute-Beauce.

What has become of the antennas? Whether and how they have been used by the citizens constitute indicators of sensitization and the social integration of the museum. Some of the open-air exhibitions dot the landscape like monuments, unused and run down. Apparently, planners overlooked the needs and interests of the population or museum intentions, and local concerns could not harmonize within a framework of a comprehensive sensitization process. The open-air exhibitions have remained foreign bodies. In sum, the museum should have adapted already existing parts of the local cultural and natural heritage for its use, rather than implant artificial elements.

Some of the local committees the museum set up have also begun to vegetate in more or less the same place. In contrast, the interpretation centers have succeeded. Local groups function independently and those open-air exhibitions that are integrated into a larger context are helpful interpretative aids.

The Ecomusée de la Maison du Fier-Monde also encountered community resistance in establishing antennas. At first, the museum explained the ecomuseum's antenna to a whole street, represented by a group of local residents. But this quite active initial phase, which produced a mural, has led to one where citizen involvement and contact have declined. Doubts as to the value of these antennas were also raised by the workers of the Ecomusée de la Maison du Fier-Monde. As a result, they have set new priorities.

On the whole, spatial decentralization may work in some cases but cannot be an end in itself. In my view, antennas should not be set up in the initial phase of a museum merely to give the impression, as quickly as possible, of outwardly satisfying a certain museum concept. In such a setting, antennas can only have the character of add-ons essentially free of content. Antennas appear to be unsuitable as initiators of community sensitization. "New" museums should begin by creating lasting contacts with citizen groups, a move which holds greater promise of sensitization and ensures antennas will be geared to local needs and interests. If antennas are to be more than reminders that a museum exists in the region or neighborhood, they must express the declared will and reflect the identity of the community.

These considerations lead to another aspect of "new" museums: participation. This is not to be confused with the so-called participatory museums that are coming into fashion, where museum visitors are offered the possibility of actively organizing their leisure time. With regard to citizen participation, "new" museums go somewhat further. Each target group of the "new" museum is treated as a supporter and principal actor. This requires a specific participatory structure that confers on the population the necessary competence to intervene actively in the museum. It varied considerably in the practices of the museums studied.

The first Casa del Museo produced a questionnaire to help gear its work to the wishes and needs of the population, there was no official participatory body. The citizens of the Zona Observatorio were basically excluded from decision-making. The second more informal and structureless Casa del Museo, too, had no mechanism that would have enabled the population to control "its" museum. Here, informally and in direct contact with interested citizens, the museum used self-government structures that already existed in the community to enable the residents of Santo Domingo, together with the museum staff, to have de facto control over Casa del Museo and determine what activities were to be carried out. Considering the particular conditions under which the Casa del Museo II operated, I believe that theirs was a perfectly acceptable way to confer competence on a "new" museum's target group.

The Anacostia Neighborhood Museum began with an informal founding committee. Every interested citizen could, in principle, take part and make proposals, express opinions on the planned projects, and discuss them with museum workers. Subsequently, this founding committee was turned into the museum's official advisory committee, composed of 15 to 20 representatives of socially relevant groups and interested citizens. It met at irregular intervals with the museum director to give advice on upcoming project proposals, which are then, as a rule, developed by the museum. Concerning the competence vested in the population in connection with these two advisory groups, it should be noted that they are not bodies in which the population has an established right to participate, but merely advisory groups that the museum can consult. The committee's advice and decisions are not binding on the Anacostia Neighborhood Museum.

Citizen participation has so far declined with the museum's growing institutionalization that it has practically reached zero. The museum advisory committee's insignificance need not necessarily mean such bodies are unsuited to represent community interests. Rather, in Anacostia's case, the situation is owing to the change in the way the museum views itself. Advisory committees can harmonize the museum and the local population, but this always presupposes good will and readiness to negotiate on the part of the museum, since the advisory group has no specific decision-making power.

However, in view of the concept of the "new" museum as a grassroots organization, it is not enough merely to consult the community. Rather, structures must be created to assure that the population has specific areas of competence.

The ecomuseums may serve as models, since their democratic structural framework of citizen involvement allows for far-reaching decision-making authority. The ecomuseums are based on citizens' organizations in which anyone can participate, although local people hold a predominant position. In accordance with established organizational bylaws, the members meet regularly. They submit proposals and subject them to democratic decision-making processes.

Likewise, members choose representatives to the museum's board of directors, which functions as a management body, communicating to the staff the expressed interests of the members.

Although staff make many decisions independently in the course of their daily work, they are bound by and accountable to the members and the board of directors. Both the Maison du Fier-Monde and the Ecomusée de la Haute-Beauce present this complex participatory structure. In addition, the latter organized an executive committee and a users' committee as well as five subject-related advisory committees.

The Ecomusée de la Haute-Beauce's executive committee consists of a small group of board members who, together with the museum staff, follow the instructions of the board and membership, supervising the daily operations of the museum. This committee was set up because the board of directors was too large to effectively run daily operations. Interested citizens from the ecomuseum's various localities serve on the users' committee. It selects a portion of the board of directors, who represent the specific geographic areas of the Haute-Beauce. Originally it served as a link between the museum and the Haute-Beauce population, and functioned as such in the early days of the ecomuseum. When its initial vigor evaporated, the activities of the users' committee gradually came to a standstill. To compensate, the Ecomusée de la Haute-Beauce formed five new, subject-related working groups. But results of this step are very much in question, owing to the fundamental problem of citizen passivity.

In principle, the population of the Haute-Beauce could fully control the museum and make it its own tool. Nevertheless, on the basis of the two ecomuseums studied here, having a democratic participatory structure with wide-ranging decision-making authority available to the population, is in no way a guarantee that citizens will actually assume the positions to which they are entitled and exhaust the possibilities. Why is that? What is the matter? What must happen for the population to exercise its decision-making power, as new museology intends?

I have discussed some of the points relating to specific living conditions in connection with the Ecomusée de la Haute-Beauce. However, I do not believe that grounds such as lack of time are sufficient to explain the population's reserve. The fact is people always find ways to engage in matters that directly affect their everyday lives and that they consider to be important. In my opinion, it must be concluded that the museums in question either have not succeeded in proving their worth to the population or do not understand the resident's everyday life.

Committed citizens who expect to benefit concretely from the "new" museum behave in a rather reserved and passive way toward the ecomuseums that I studied. They do not speak up and decide for themselves what should take place in the museum. Although some of these "new" museums have a democratic participatory structure, there is a serious problem with regard to relations between specialists and lay community members.

Specialists control the museum's everyday operations and decision-making processes.

Most projects are developed by professionals and presented for approval to the bodies representing the population, where discussion is frequently too short because of time pressures imposed by the specialists. Because community relations are neglected or handled superficially, many projects are out of step with the everyday reality of those concerned. Also, citizens taking part feel that too much is expected of them and they cannot keep up with the fast pace of museum activities. Thus, working groups and committees become simple implementation bodies whose volunteers merely receive orders. In this way, the rift between specialists and population is broadened rather than bridged.

The specialists have not fulfilled their promise to cooperate on an equal basis with representatives of the population (an exception is Casa del Museo II). In practice, cooperation between specialists and residents creates inequalities and hierarchies-either intended or unintended. What results is a pseudo-participation that serves to cover up the actual power structures in the museum's everyday work. It appears appropriate, therefore, to examine the museologist's role and authority in the "new" museum.

Cooperation based on equal rights presumes that participants enjoy comparable initial conditions. In the "new" museums I studied this presumption is not a given. Professionals differ from the population in having more education and knowledge and occupy the museum's executive positions. To curtail the museologist's excessive authority an appropriate structure can be devised that gives the population extensive opportunities for control. In practice, however, as shown above, this is not enough, since the population feels intimidated by the specialists and is not sufficiently informed. In the end, those involved in the on-going work process, that is, professional employees, make the decisions.

Only a change in the behavior and self-view of the museum professional can remedy this problem. This depends chiefly on an act of individual will. In this respect, new museology shows interesting parallels to "action anthropology," which primarily seeks new respectful relationships between an anthropologist and a given population, which place the anthropologist radically in the service of the population concerned (cf. Seithel, 1986). The congruence in approach between so called "action anthropology" and new museology will be clear from the following quotation (Seithel 1986, p. 336f): "It is not enough for the new cultural anthropology ... to produce knowledge within the boundaries set by the conventional scientific methods and information theories, which have ... little or no relevance for the problems of the people being studied. Rather than that, it goes beyond the traditional scientific framework ... and assumes, on behalf of the suppressed peoples and ethnic groups fighting for their physical and cultural survival, the responsibilities and tasks incumbent on it because of its intellectual knowledge and capabilities... The action anthropologist acts, intervenes, changes; he understands his values and knowledge as guidance for social and political practice. He wants to be a catalyst, supporter and participant in the processes of change, renewal and resistance." Seithel's remarks (1986) on the role of the action anthropologist, borrowed basically from the approaches of Sol Tax and Karl Schlesier, are, in my view, directly transferable, with small changes, to new museology and can impart to it important impulses, which will be shown below.

The museologist (or any other specialist, motivator, etc.) who wants to work interactively with a given population on behalf of the "new" museum must attempt, in the first place, to share his or her knowledge and skills with the population. In the second place, the museologist must become acquainted with the population's knowledge and skills through a learning process based on reciprocity and include these as a constituent element in the museum's work. This applies similarly to the values, interests and needs underlying the museum's work. This does not mean, in any sense, that an unrealistic demand for freedom from values should be placed on the museologist. The museologist cannot work independently of his or her own values and interests.

However, these should be made explicit to the population and its representatives so that his or her position can be made clear and subject to assessment. The museologist must also be aware of the community's constellation of values and interests, and must consistently gear his or her work to them.

The view the "new" museologist has of him or herself is determined essentially by their function as a catalyst. A main task is to point out alternatives and perspectives regarding an area of concern expressed by the population, to discuss with the population the pros and cons and their consequences. The decision-making power, in accordance with the principles of the "new" museum, must rest exclusively with the people.

These principles are not taken sufficiently into consideration in the practice of new museology. Hence, it is deceitful to blame material constraints and other pragmatic considerations, which may be an artificial pressure placed on a community that the museum professionals do not feel because their priorities lie elsewhere. Should the museologist consider the decision-making process too ponderous, citing practical necessities can accelerate the decision. However, professional authority should never bring about something for which the community is not ready. In such an event, the project would, most probably, encounter misunderstanding, ignorance and, at worst, out-and-out rejection. While the project may look good on the museologist's resumé, it will be totally useless to the population.

By respecting the population and entrusting it with full responsibility and freedom of decision, the "new" museologist can boost the community self-awareness and self-confidence. In conjunction with new or revived knowledge and skills, this can lead to a population gradually assuming its rightful place in the "new" museum. This means managing the museum themselves–actively using it, initiating projects and carrying them out independently.

The "new" museologist's role, if needed or desired, will then be merely advisory, and ideally, in time, dispensable.

The "new" museologist's function as a catalyst and adviser should be underscored by a decision not to occupy official museum positions such as director or chair. But this was certainly not the case in the museums studied here, in which all important positions were occupied by specialists. In these situations, the more developed the institution, the more the specialists tend to feel that they were indispensable and take the important positions.

In the Ecomusée de la Haute-Beauce, despite the existence of a democratic participatory structure, power–in the sense of decision making and freedom to act– ultimately resided in the hands of those who carry out the museum's daily work and occupy the corresponding positions. Hence the need to train nonprofessionals to occupy the important positions of permanent employees and thus determine the museum's work themselves.[5] Possibly citizens occupying these positions could have a specialist assigned (who would retain an advisory status) to carry out jointly the tasks at hand and thereby provide non-formal, practical professional education.[6]

In general, the "new" museum's promise of grass-roots democracy is a long way from being fulfilled. It is evident that mechanisms to stem institutionalization and prevent the museum from becoming autonomous, which opens the museum to the will of the community, enjoy only limited success and raise numerous problems themselves. Noble aims, principles and a responsive museum-structure are frequently not enough to generate broad grassroots involvement and establish the museum as an instrument of local self-determination in the service of the population. One of the main problems is motivating residents in the first place and stimulating their cooperation. Important points of departure center on the "new" museum's ability to make itself useful and relevant to the community's everyday world.

---

[5] But the mere fact that important positions are occupied by the citizens does not completely preclude the danger that power will be misused.
[6] Pay inequality could be solved by splitting the salaries.

4.4 Approach

The "new" museum's work ideally reflects an integrated approach that best fulfills its objectives and basic principles. This approach first establishes the subject matter of the "new" museum and then proposes a way to tackle it.[7]

While the object forms the main subject in traditional museums (thus, a materialized cross-section of reality), the "new" museum selects human interaction with the cultural and natural milieu as the focus of its various tasks. Thereby it attempts to do justice to the complex everyday reality of its various target groups. For museum practice to record and interpret this complex reality, an interdisciplinary and theme-oriented approach is required, one that links past, present and future.

The case studies have shown that the museums in question have partly satisfied this general requirement in their work, particularly their consideration of sociocultural aspects. Human society as the bearer of a given cultural heritage always stands at the center of the "new" museum's work. However, the human-ecological dimension of its subject matter, that is, the interaction between people and their natural environment, has been severely neglected in practice.

The only museum that explicitly includes the natural environment in its sphere of responsibility is the Ecomusée de la Haute-Beauce, which is located in a rural area. However, it should be noted that the museum devotes itself primarily to the pleasant aspects of nature, that is, to the beauties of the landscape. Ecological problems that directly affect and detract from the lives of the residents of the Haute-Beauce, such as, for example, acid rain and water pollution, have thus far received no attention as subjects of the museum's work.

It should be emphasized here that even urban museums (Casa del Museo I, Casa del Museo II, Anacostia Neighborhood Museum, Ecomusée

---

[7] The specific approach followed by the "new" museum is reflected in basically all areas of its work. However, because it is manifested most clearly in the museum's programs, the examples cited below are drawn mainly from this area.

de la Maison du Fier-Monde) devote themselves almost exclusively to sociocultural aspects of reality and ignore the ecological plight of their cities. Yet this is one of the areas in which museum work could improve the quality of life and represent a significant advance in the realization of the objectives of the "new" museum. The question "Just where is nature in the city?" is characteristic of a short-sighted view of nature that does not respond to the requirements of a post-industrial society threatened by ecological collapse. Air and water pollution, wasted energy, garbage disposal and contaminated, nutrient poor food are examples of current ecological problems "new" museums must tackle. This is especially true for ecomuseums, the very name of which implies such an orientation. Its prefix "eco-" must be reflected in its practice.

A multi-dimensional subject matter requires an interdisciplinary approach. However, the subject matter of the "new" museums studied here has thus far been oriented in practice primarily to the sociocultural aspects of community life. They have taken only preliminary steps in adopting an interdisciplinary approach. Like the Casa del Museo I, the Mexican Program for the Development of the Educational Function of Museums has an interdisciplinary team, but this is hardly reflected in its programs. In the case of the Anacostia Neighborhood Museum, historians staff the department that prepares programmatic content. Accordingly, with the exception of exhibits on African-American art, the museum focuses exclusively on social or cultural history. The same applies to the Ecomusée de la Maison du Fier-Monde. Of the museums examined here, the Ecomusée de la Haute-Beauce stands out by defining its subject matter in a multidimensional way and creating interdisciplinary displays and programs. Nevertheless, the subjects of its programs are predominantly one-dimensional.

It is difficult for a museum to adopt an interdisciplinary approach in practice. Even when ideal initial conditions exist through the presence of various departments, such as natural history and ethnology, structural constraints and "snobbery" often stand in the way of real interdisciplinary cooperation. The result is often a situation where elements of natural history and ethnology coexist but are unrelated. If they are to live up to their claims, "new" museums must avoid this kind of juxtaposition.

A further distinguishing element of the "new" museum is its theme-centered approach. In contrast to the object-centered work of traditional museums, "new" museums adopt themeoriented formulations, a shift which applies increasingly to modernized traditional museums as well.

All museums studied present this characteristic. While traditional museums concentrate on collecting, studying and conserving objects, for the purpose of aesthetic display in a glass case, only topics drawn from the reality of the population's life are decisive for "new" museums. Some examples include: "Day of Death" (Casa del Museo I), "The Mexican Revolution" (Casa del Museo II), "Evolution of a Community," "Black Churches" (Anacostia Neighborhood Museum), "Between the Factory and the Kitchen" (Ecomusée de la Maison du Fier-Monde) and "Appropriation of their Environment by the Citizens of the Haute-Beauce " (Ecomusée de la Haute-Beauce).

Objects serve to illustrate themes. They have no value in themselves for "new" museums, but simply help tell the story. Even the exhibits of the Ecomusée de la Haute-Beauce on baptismal clothing or tools, which may be object-oriented in nature when considered superficially, always intended to make a connection with the life and work of women, manual workers, and farmers. Objects appear only because of their thematic significance. The exhibition's title clearly illustrates this emphasis: "The Woman through Baptismal Clothing" and "The Language of the Tool."

The only museum among the case studies that deviates from exclusive theme-oriented practices is the Anacostia Neighborhood Museum, where about half of the exhibitions are extremely object-oriented art presentations that parallel the practices of traditional art museums in every way. Although the object-centered nature of a recent exhibit, "Contemporary Visual Expression," was somewhat modified by a video and educational material, the visual impression a visitor received was of a series of pictures on a wall, with tiny labels indicating only the artist's name and the title. Most visitors probably did not know how to decode works of art. I believe, therefore, that a "new" museum must place works of art in interpretative contexts so that the visitor can approach them as a learning experience. The Anacostia Neighborhood Museum could have shown how modem art reflected aspects of current social reality.

Regarding its obligation to link past, present and future, if "new" museums wish to be true to their claims and be useful to their public in understanding the present and shaping the future, they must be both relevant and concerned.

Illustrations of these approaches can certainly be found among "new" museums. For example, the workshops of the Casa del Museo II on themes such as "Home Construction," "Nutrition" and "Health Care," and the exhibition "The Rat" of the Anacostia Neighborhood

Museum, clearly derive from current problems their respective populations face. In other examples, such as "Evolution of a Community" (Anacostia Neighborhood Museum) and "Workers' Housing" (Ecomusée de la Maison du Fier-Monde), an effort was made to view historical themes from present-day perspectives. However, their effectiveness is questionable since current points of view were often added on to the end of the exhibits and remain relatively unconnected to the rest of it.

With the exception of these examples, a large part of the programs of the "new" museums that were studied, as well as of traditional museums, had an exclusively historical orientation and are, therefore, relatively worthless as tools for helping the population cope with the present and shape the future. In my opinion, "new" museums must make increased efforts in this regard.

History should not be confined to the past, but must be used in order to show the historical development of present-day reality. The core question for history should not be "How was it once?" but: How did it happen that we have this or that problem today? What choices or what decisions underlie it? Who made it? What possibilities do we have today to determine our future ourselves? What should this future look like? Only when "new" museums proceed on the basis of the present, do they stand a chance of influencing the future.

In this regard, cooperation with other local and regional organizations and institutions that are active in the social, economic and political spheres can provide support and help the museum go beyond its own traditional limits and achieve social relevance.

The Casa del Museo II, the Anacostia Neighborhood Museum, the Ecomusée de la Maison du Fier-Monde and the Ecomusée de la Haute-Beauce, all have sought out and successfully practiced cooperation with non-cultural organizations. (The Casa del Museo I had, by and large, shown itself to be self-sufficient.) The tasks that these museums carried out in cooperation with non-museum bodies such as schools and professional associations reflect close relationships to the present. However, as previously noted, the historical perspective sometimes fares badly. In their contacts with the outside world, "new" museums should generally work in a more focused and methodical fashion than they have up to the present. In addition to selective actions, longterm cooperative programs must be developed that permit the museums to introduce the heritage they preserve into the process of social change.

Regarding the specific, integral approach of the "new" museum, which constitutes the prerequisite for being able to record and influence a complex reality, a large number of gaps and problem areas can be identified. But it must be remembered that the formulation and interpretation of the individual museum task is as important as the approach taken.

4.5 Tasks

The basic tasks of the "new" museum do not differ from those of traditional museums: to collect, document, study, preserve and communicate a given heritage. However, "new" museums differ from conventional museums in that they ascribe utilitarian value to the tasks of preservation and connect the work to non-museum aims. Thus, there are crucial differences in comparison to traditional museums.[8] The special, socially oriented objectives of "new" museums entail broader shifts of emphasis and changes with respect to the interpretation of the individual tasks. The "new" museum is distinguished by the fact that it seeks to provide interested citizens with non-formal, museum-specific education and subjects itself to continual review (education and evaluation).

As the case studies show, the tasks of the "new" museum vary considerably in practice. All of the museum activities cited above are basically acts of preserving and activating a given heritage. The collection of objects, one of the key tasks of traditional museums, is viewed as the structural characteristic that distinguishes a museum from other similar institutions: archives, exhibition and cultural centers (cf. Definition of the Museum, ICOM 1974, p. 1). On the other hand, for the "new" museums studied here, amassing collections of objects is of secondary importance. As a rule, this is a thorn in the side of established museum curators, and earns for the "new" museum the reproach of critics who believe they are not "real" museums at all.

With one exception, the museums studied lack museum-housed collections. "New" museums target those groups whose cultural riches are not manifested so much in material objects and writing as in oral traditions, personal history and everyday experiences that are threatened with extinction. The concept of culture on which the "new" museum's work is based is more comprehensive. It includes areas such as the culture of everyday life, speech and collective memory. This expanded concept of culture, which goes far beyond the area of official culture as manifested materially, leads to a re-conceptualization of the cultural heritage to be preserved. It requires the museum to change its collection practices, and eschew the conventional museum focus on objects.

---

[8] However, I consider this to be perfectly legitimate against the background of the underlying, broadened cultural concept and the general claim of democratization of the "new" museum. It does not prevent, in any way, the classification of "new" museums as museums.

The Ecomusée de la Maison du Fier-Monde, like the Casa del Museo I and the Casa del Museo II, borrows objects from the residents, which are returned after being used. This was also the case, at first, with the Anacostia Neighborhood Museum, which enhanced its exhibitions with objects from the collections of the Smithsonian Institution and, more and more, from private collectors and galleries. Moreover, in its evolution into a traditional museum, the Anacostia Neighborhood Museum plans to acquire its own, museum-housed collection of objects. This surely reflects its desire to be recognized as an independent museum.

The only museum that has a museum-housed collection is the Ecomusée de la Haute Beauce. As discussed above, this was a representative collection of objects from the region's everyday culture, which was already in existence in the region and served as the pretext for establishing the museum.

However, the museum itself does not collect. Like the Ecomusée de la Maison du Fier-Monde in Montreal, the Ecomusée de la Haute-Beauce treats the natural environment and material and nonmaterial cultural expressions as the heritage to be preserved, because it helps establish local identity and the potential for change. Collecting takes place in the original contexts, outside the walls of the museum building. This requires identification of representative elements of the heritage considered most relevant by the community. These may include architecture, social institutions, everyday objects and, in the Haute-Beauce particularly, the landscape. These are the names of only the most significant examples.

In contrast to traditional museums, which ascribe to objects a value in themselves, "new" museums–particularly ecomuseums–view the material heritage as having an illustrative function relative to non-material traditions of thought, manifested in oral history. Collection emphasis in ecomuseums is placed on the population's true-life story. It is a reconstruction of the collective memory based on interviews with members of the community. Examples include "The Anacostia Story," an oral history project of the Anacostia Neighborhood Museum, the works of the Maison des Gens de St. Hilaire in the Haute-Beauce, and the series of interviews "Between the Factory and the Kitchen" of the Ecomusée de la Maison du Fier-Monde. The collective memory, community values and identity patterns they contain form an elementary component of the "new" museum's collection practice.

Establishment critics occasionally charge that this kind of collection policy opens the door to arbitrariness, and neglects important classes of objects. Yet objects in traditional museums also have no value in themselves but rather illustrate the world-view and values of the scholars doing the collecting. Thus, for example, established museums of cultural history systematically ignore the material heritage of the working-class, because it is considered not to belong to the official, bourgeois cultural material deemed worthy of preservation.

Thus, the distinction between "new" and traditional museums resides less in the esteem shown to objects than in who determines their value and from what viewpoint. In the "new" museum, the community decides what it identifies itself with and consequently, what is worth preserving. Collective memory guides this process of reconstructing community history.

Considering the systematic neglect of certain social groups by traditional museums, I think it is perfectly legitimate for "new" museums to devote themselves to those groups and have them determine what to collect based on their interests and needs for identification.

The risk that only positive identification markers of a culture would be selected was addressed previously. The collective memory of the Haute-Beauce, for example, appears to reveal considerable gaps in regard to the treatment of the region's Native American population. But the same can be said of much Canadian history that–with a few exceptions–is absent from the country's official, scholarly historiography. In my opinion, therefore, the objectivity of the reconstruction of history depends not so much on whether it is conducted by scholars or laymen as on the procedure employed and on the exhaustion of all available sources.

Collective memory is an invaluable witness of the thus far undiscovered history of the daily lives of a broad segment of the population. In this way, it expands the traditional spectrum of historical research. It constitutes one version of history, beside others; it is neither more nor less objective than the others. What distinguishes this history is the role played by the community in forming the collection.

Collection practices of "new" museums, therefore, extend strongly into the areas of research and documentation. For "new" museums, collecting means primarily gathering information about the living and working conditions of a given population, in which the investigation of data (research) and the recording of data (documentation) play prominent roles. The data holders that constitute the so-called "community collection" can basically be all the components of a sociocultural and natural environment (cf. above).

Collective memory here determines all aspects of the museum's collection focus, and helps place the "real" collections in a social context, whether they are housed in the museum or located outside it.

The specific collection practices of the museums studied always center on documenting interrelationships (this is true in particular of ecomuseums). What the storeroom is to the traditional museum, the documentation center is to the "new" museum. Both the Ecomusée de la Maison du Fier-Monde and the Ecomusée de la Haute-Beauce have such a documentation center or archive of the community collection. Here photographs and drawings of remembered images are kept along with publications and documents, that is, evidence of the overall material and immaterial heritage of a place or region and its context.

For the "new" museum with no or a limited collection, the documentation center makes up the core of its work. It is, in fact, the collection itself. In the case of the Ecomusée de la Haute Beauce, the archive or documentation center does not house, for example, the 60 baptismal dresses that the museum exhibited. Instead, it maintains inventory cards on each object, notes the memories of its owners and has publications and photographs that elucidate the functional context of the object. The baptismal dresses themselves remain in the possession of the original users, along with a duplicate of the inventory card.

For "new" museums, recording information about a given heritage and "knowing about" it are acts of conservation. This unorthodox view of conservation evokes loud protests from traditional curators, which I believe are unjustified. The protection of the object may perhaps not always be sufficiently assured, but one must ask whether this is always the case in traditional museums. Certainly not! Especially in small museums, comparable to the ones we are dealing with here, there are indeed storerooms with prevailing conditions of conservation that leave much to be desired. Objects there are not always protected from moisture, dryness, light and dust, or from being eaten by insects, etc. Ecomuseums, in fact, make a virtue of not having adequate or suitable storage facilities by attempting to sensitize the local population to be careful stewards of their objects, historical monuments and natural environment. In this way the heritage in question can be preserved in situ by the population itself.

Public Programs

Unlike traditional museums, the "new" museum always links the preservation of a given heritage to its communication, since it is not conserved for itself, but rather seen in association with its bearers. Communication is at the same time an act of conservation, for it expands the knowledge of a given heritage and thereby imparts value to it, opening up possibilities for its preservation.

"New" museums must emphasize communication because of their fundamental orientation toward the public and their self-view as agents of education and information. Compared with other tasks–including administration–that bring about learning by involving the population, the museums studied comply broadly with their educational function through varied programs of activities and events. Differently from traditional museums, whose only public oriented measure still frequently consists in putting up permanent exhibits and otherwise leaving the visitors to themselves, "new" museums attempt to perform active, focused communication work by all the means at their disposal. It should be stressed, however, that in recent years a change may be seen in modernized traditional museums, so that the lines dividing them from "new" museums are becoming partially blurred.

In their communication work, "new" museums emphasize exhibitions. Depending on the professional standards and the costs, the museums studied mount (or mounted) from one exhibit per year (Ecomusée de la Maison du Fier-Monde, Ecomusée de la Haute-Beauce, Anacostia Neighborhood Museum) to fourteen per year (Casa del Museo II, Anacostia Neighborhood Museum in the early phase, five to nine). However, because "new" museums do not as a rule have collections, exhibits are rarely permanent. Even the Ecomusée de la Haute-Beauce, which has its own collection, gives it relatively little space and concentrates its main attention on putting on special exhibits. Moreover, the fact that the permanent exhibit has changed twice in seven years suggests it is not static but rather an evolving display.

While traditional museums are chiefly concerned with increasing the number of visitors to achieve a quantitative improvement, "new" museums are more interested in qualitative considerations. Building ongoing relations with a community, in which exhibiting is only one approach, is an important precondition for achieving social relevancy. When the museum has nothing new to offer, the public's interest may be exhausted for the next five or ten years after a single museum visit. As a result, the museum is little more than entertainment. "New" museums wish to remedy this. In their temporary exhibitions, they show they learned from established museums that only by varying its offerings can a museum create a permanent relationship with a community. This variety allows for new impulses, and awakens new interests among visitors.

"New" museums also deploy complementary methods of communication that interpret exhibit content. These include elements that since the 1970s have also played an increasing role in the communication work of modernized, established museums: publications, lectures, sound and slide shows, films, musical and theatrical events, guided tours of the museum, tours outside the museum and, above all, educational events that give the visitor opportunities for active involvement (the "participatory" museum), material for school groups, curriculum material for teachers, orientation events for teachers, work with target groups (for example, children, youth, women, representatives of specific occupational groups, senior citizens, etc.), publicity work (recruitment), etc.; no limits are put on the imagination. In general education work is probably the area in which "new" museums correspond most closely to established museums.

Training

The above-mentioned activities and programs may give the appearance, as in traditional museums, of being a pure, unilateral item of consumption the museum offers to visitors who are there merely to receive it. This is indeed partly the case. But over and above that, the "new" museums try hard to involve interested citizens to become actors and producers in their activities and programs, as well as in other areas of museum work such as administration, collection, research, documentation and conservation. One of their particular concerns, therefore, which distinguishes them from traditional, strongly professionalized museums, is in the informal way they impart knowledge and skills toward making interested citizens able to act independently and assume more responsibility for aspects of the museum's work.

The educational activities of the museums studied are carried out on many different levels. The workers of the Casa del Museo II were satisfied with giving interested citizens some explanations in a rather informal way; the design and production unit of the Anacostia Neighborhood Museum at one time ran a program to train young people to be exhibit specialists. It had a very strong element of vocational training.

Until recently, the Ecomusée de la Maison du Fier-Monde did no training of volunteers, because its staff considered volunteerism to be exploitation. In my opinion, they misunderstood the nature of volunteer work. Contrarily to other social contexts, here no one is forced to become an unpaid volunteer. It is each person's decision whether, how often and how long to volunteer, therefore there can be no question of it being exploitation. Incidentally, training is well suited to enabling volunteer workers to develop their skills and learn to work independently.

As the experience of the Ecomusée de la Maison du Fier-Monde demonstrates, when citizens work over a longer period of time, the institution wants to pays them for it. So, the museum tries to create jobs, at least temporarily. In view of its present mode of financing through subsidies, the Maison du Fier-Monde's qualification of volunteers as specialists can definitely be useful as a strategy to enable the museum to take advantage of work-creation opportunities and other measures.

Later, the Maison du Fier-Monde revised its volunteer policy. In a large-scale project to study the industrial history and de-industrialization of the Centre-Sud neighborhood, the museum began training residents as lay historians to enable them to research their own history. The training itself introduced them, and the current work of promoters and coordinators is subject to continuous, systematic evaluation and change.

In this respect, the Mexican museum projects distinguished themselves from all other studied. It is clear that goal-directed museum work can be significantly optimized through critical evaluation of prior experience. When museums face a crisis, as is the case currently with the Ecomusée de la Haute-Beauce, a museum should examine its prior activities in a critical way. Such evaluations make it possible to reach systematic, relevant conclusions before rushing into new actions that may cover up and intensify the problems. Despite innumerable activities, some museums show no real progress toward problem-solving. Since there is no concrete evaluation data that could form the solid basis for goal-directed action, it appears workers concerned are more or less left to their intuition. Therefore, one wonders if the highly extolled dynamic of "new" museums is rather an appearance of movement that leads nowhere.

4.6 Critical assessment

What actually is this new museology? How is it faring in practice? How do promise and reality interact? What general conclusions can be drawn from this analysis of "new" museums? Some possible answers are summarized below.

Proceeding from an expanded concept of culture inspired by ethnological theory, the demand arose at a time of radical social change for a far-reaching democratization of culture. From this demand emerged the concept of the "new" museum. It is based on the assumption that culture can be both the subject and instrument of an emancipatory educational process directed toward democratic social change. The innovative approach of new museology to modem museum work supplements and expands that of traditional museums. In part, it also presents alternatives.

Although new museology originated in the examination of practical museum experiences, it is not in the strict sense a scientific theory derived from systematic, empirical research. Rather it is a relatively diffuse constellation of ideas consisting basically of instructions for programmatic action. Because new museology, as an action-oriented concept, does not form a conclusive whole, representatives attempted to identify and systematize its "new" elements and link them together in an analytical schema (cf. chapter 2). We are dealing, then, with a theoretical construct of an ideal "new" museum, which I developed from my analysis of the discourse of new museologists at a certain point in time and under specific conditions. Its validity depends on existing conditions.

New museology does not have a definitive character that excludes the possibility of change. The lack of a dogmatic schema should not prevent a wider dissemination of its nature and possibilities, to make new museology useful for those beyond the circle of its partisans.

For many of its representatives, new museology is a dynamic process of cf.king innovative forms of museum work. It is less directed at the development of definitions and theories than strongly action-oriented. The concrete actions are substantiated intuitively rather than rationally.

Attempts at analytical clarification and delimitation are occasionally characterized as "resistant to change" and "against new museology" (René Rivard, discussion of 11-18-86). New museologists worry that when one defines what new museology is, it will lose its dynamic and the scope for innovation. This is, in my view, incomprehensible and unjustified. Any attempt at definition can only be provisional and invite discussion and clarification. It is open to new experiences and knowledge. By refusing to be pinned down, new museologists risk maneuvering new museology into a dead end and depriving it of criticism and assessment, that is, in the end, preventing change.

The principal objective of this monograph has been to make new museology accessible to review through the systematic, empirical study of its programs so that problem areas can be identified. Although the problem areas of the individual museums differ, comparison reveals certain consistencies that allow general conclusions. The case studies have shown that those elements of the "new" museum that promise to contrast with traditional museums are, on the whole, still relatively underdeveloped. This constitutes one of its greatest problem areas.

The following elements can be characterized as problematic: the objectives of development and coping with everyday life; structural elements such as a low degree of institutionalization, funding from local resources, participation and non-hierarchical teamwork; and the work areas of collection, documentation, research, conservation, evaluation and education.

Other problem areas identified include the fundamental principle of public orientation, the structural element of decentralization and, with regard to approach, the definition of the museum's theme as complex reality, interdisciplinarity and cooperation with other organizations. Decentralization and outside cooperation differ significantly among the various museums.

On the other hand, those elements that vary little from the practice of modernized traditional museums can be characterized as relatively problem-free. These include the objective of building identity, the fundamental principle of territoriality, the theme-centered approach and the task of communication. Thus, one might say that at first glance the practice of "new" museums is not dissimilar to that of modernized traditional museums. However, this should not obscure the existence of basic conceptual differences.

In my view, the problems that arise when implementing the innovative elements of the "new" museum in no way suggest that the allegedly new is basically identical to the traditional, or that going beyond traditional practice is impossible. On the contrary, the "new" museum, like any other social innovation, must surmount enormous obstacles. Evidently, strategies for doing this have not (yet) taken hold. The model of the "new" museum as outlined above, is and generally remains, a goal. As in the case of action anthropology (cf. Seithel 1986, p. 308), goals and methods are fused together in a process of learning and action. Methods are simultaneously goals, and the formulation of goals is method and action. The elements that make up the "new" museum are, on the one hand, a precondition for the "new" museum and, on the other hand, its product.

As this study demonstrates, many of the problems occur in areas associated with social integration and relevance. What I believe has not been adequately addressed in practice is the need for critical, unqualified respect for each community, for its peculiarities, interests, needs and abilities, and for its accessibility and its rhythm. The solution is to create and maintain an ongoing process of interaction between the museum and the population.

Only committed involvement and critical distance can bring to reality the idea of the "new" museum as an educational instrument in the service of social development.

Bibliography[1]

ABEL, Herbert. *Vom Raritatenkabinett zum Bremer Übercf.museum* [From Collection of Rarities to the Bremen Übercf.museum]. Bremen, 1970.

ADOVETI, Stanislas S. Le musée dans les systemes éducatifs et culturels contemporains [The museum in contemporary educational and cultural systems]. ln: ICOM (ed.). *Le musée au service des hommes aujourd'hui et demain*. Actes de la 9ieme Conférence Générale de l'ICOM, Grenoble, 1971. Paris, 1972, pp.19-30.

AGENCE REGIONALE D'ETHNOLOGIE RHONE-ALPES/ECOMUCF. NORDDAUPHINE (ed.). *Actes des premieres rencontres nationales des écomusées, l'Isle d'Abeau* [Proceedings of the first national meetings of ecomuseums], 11/13-14, 1986. Grenoble, 1987.

AGRAWAL, Om Prakash. *Asia-Pacific Seminar on Conservation of Cultural Property*. New Delhi, 1972. Rome, 1974.

AITHNARD, M.K. Museums and Socio-Economic Development in Africa. ln: *Museum*, vol.28/1976(4), pp.188-195.

ALEMAN, Heine von and Peter ORTLIEB. Die Einzelfallstudie [The individual case study]. ln: KOOLWIJK, Jürgen van and Maria WIEKEN-MAYSER (ed.). *Techniken der empirischen Sozialforschung*. Munich, 1975, pp.157-177.

ALEXANDER, Elizabeth. Smithsonian Southeast. Anacostia's Own Museum. ln: *Washington Post*, 7/5, 1983, p.C9.

---

[1] The bibliography is reproduced in its entirety from the German edition of this monograph. Not all of the references listed below appear in the English-language edition, but they are included here to assist the reader who may wish to pursue the subject in greater depth.

ALINSKY, Saul. *Rules for Radicals.* New York, 1972.

AMERY, Jean. Wieviel Heimat braucht der Mensch? [How much homeland does man need?]. In: FREILING, Frank-Dieter (ed.). *Heimat. Begriffsempfindungen heute.* Königstein/Ts., 1981, pp.44-47.

AMES, Michael. *Museums, the Public and Anthropology. A Study in the Anthropology of Anthropology.* Vancouver/New Delhi, 1986.

AMES, Michael and Claudia HAAGEN. *A New Native Peoples History for Museums.* Lecture given at the "Annual Conference of the Alberta Museum Association", Lake Louise, 10-5-1986. Vancouver, 1986 (unpublished lecture manuscript).

ANDERSON, James N. Ecological Anthropology and Anthropological Ecology. In: HONIGMANN, J. (ed.). *Handbook of Social and Cultural Anthropology.* New York, 1973, pp.179-239.

AN EXPERIMENT IN MUSEUM EXTENSION. In: *The Pennsylvania Museum Bulletin,* vol.2611 931(142), pp.3-4.

ANACOSTIA NEIGHBORHOOD MUSEUM. *Doodles in Dimension.* Washington D.C., 1967.

ANACOSTIA NEIGHBORHOOD MUSEUM. *19 Washington Artists.* Washington D.C., 1968.

ANACOSTIA NEIGHBORHOOD MUSEUM. *Black Patriots of the American Revolution.* Washington D.C., 1970a.

ANACOSTIA NEIGHBORHOOD MUSEUM. *D.C. Art Association Second Annual Art Exhibition.* Washington D.C., 1970b.

ANACOSTI A NEIGHBORHOOD MUSEUM. *Lorton Reformatory: Beyond Time.* Washington D.C., 1970c.

ANACOSTIA NEIGHBORHOOD MUSEUM. *Moments.* Washington D.C., 1970d.

ANACOSTIA NEIGHBORHOOD MUSEUM. *The Speakers' Bureau*. Washington D.C., 1970e.

ANACOSTIA NEIGHBORHOOD MUSEUM. *The Rat: Man's Invited Affliction*. Washington D.C., 1970f.

ANACOSTIA NEIGHBORHOOD MUSEUM. *Toward Freedom*. Washington D.C., 1971

ANACOSTIA NEIGHBORHOOD MUSEUM. *Anacostia Neighborhood Museum -*

5th Anniversary. Washington D.C., 1972.

ANACOSTIA NEIGHBORHOOD MUSEUM. *The Barnett-Aden Collection*. Washington D.C., 1974a.

ANACOSTIA NEIGHBORHOOD MUSEUM. *Exhibition 1974-75*. Washington D.C., 1974b.

ANACOSTIA NEIGHBORHOOD MUSEUM. *Blacks in the Westward Movement*. Washington D.C., 1975.

ANACOSTIA NEIGHBORHOOD MUSEUM. *John Robinson. A Retrospective*. Washington D.C., 1976.

ANACOSTIA NEIGHBORHOOD MUSEUM. *The Anacostia Neighborhood Museum 1967/1977*. Washington D.C., 1977a.

ANACOSTIA NEIGHBORHOOD MUSEUM. *D.C. Art Association Exhibition '78*. Washington D.C., 1977b.

ANACOSTIA NEIGHBORHOOD MUSEUM. *Phil Ratner's Washington*. Washington D.C., 1978

ANACOSTIA NEIGHBORHOOD MUSEUM. *Out of Africa (leaflet)*. Washington D.C., 1979.

ANACOSTIA NEIGHBORHOOD MUSEUM. *A Visitor's Guide to "Anna J. Cooper: A Voice From the South".* Washington D.C., 1981.

ANACOSTIA NEIGHBORHOOD MUSEUM. *The Anacostia Neighborhood Museum - Fifteenth Anniversary (1967-1982).* Washington D.C., 1982a.

ANACOSTIA NEIGHBORHOOD MUSEUM. *"Here, Look at Mine!".* Washington D.C., 1982b.

ANACOSTIA NEIGHBORHOOD MUSEUM. *Calendar of Events. July - August 1983.* Washington D.C., 1983a.

ANACOSTIA NEIGHBORHOOD MUSEUM. *Through Their Eyes. The Art of Lou and Di Stoval.* Washington D.C., 1983b.

ANACOSTIA NEIGHBORHOOD MUSEUM. *Calendar of Events. February 1984.* Washington D.C., 1984a.

ANACOSTIA NEIGHBORHOOD MUSEUM. *Exhibits and Events.* Washington D.C., 1984b (unpublished manuscript).

ANACOSTIA NEIGHBORHOOD MUSEUM. *From the Suggestion Box, 10/21 12/21, 1984.* Washington D.C., 1984c, (unpublished manuscript).

ANACOSTIA NEIGHBORHOOD MUSEUM. *Calendar of Events. March-June 1985.* Washington D.C., 1985.

ANACOSTIA NEIGHBORHOOD MUSEUM. *The Anacostian.* Washington, no year(a).

ANACOSTIA NEIGHBORHOOD MUSEUM. *Exhibit Design and Production Apprenticeship Training Program, Curriculum.* Washington D.C., no year(b) (unpublished manuscript).

ANACOSTIA NEIGHBORHOOD MUSEUM/EDUCATION DEPARTMENT. *Frederick Douglass. A Fighter for Freedom (1817?-1895). A Resource Unit for Intermediate Students.* Washington D.C., 1978.

ANACOSTIA NEIGHBORHOOD MUSEUM/EDUCATION DEPARTMENT. *How and Why African People Came to North America*. Washington D.C., 1979.

ANACOSTIA NEIGHBORHOOD MUSEUM/EDUCATION DEPARTMENT. *"Here, Look at Mine!". Teacher's Resource Packet*. Washington D.C., 1983.

ANACOSTIA NEIGHBORHOOD MUSEUM/EDUCATION DEPARTMENT. *Black Women: Achievements Against the Odds. Teacher's Resource Booklet*. Washington D.C., 1984.

ANACOSTIA NEIGHBORHOOD MUSEUM/SITES. *The Frederick Douglass Years*. Washington D.C., 1970.

ANTÚÑEZ, Cristina; ORDONEZ, Coral; DENMAN, Kathy; and Miriam ARROYO DE KERRIOU. *Evaluación:"Influencia y alcance de la casa del museo en la Zona Observatorio, Ciudad de Mexico"* [Evaluation: The influence and reach of the Casa del Museo in the Zona Observatorio, Mexico City]. Mexico D.F., 1976 (unpublished study).

ANTÚÑEZ, Cristina and Miriam ARROYO DE KERRIOU. *Casa del Museo. Paper presented at the 12th General Conference of ICOM*, Mexico City, 10/25-1114, 1980. Mexico D.F., 1980 (unpublished lecture manuscript).

ARBEITSGEMEINSCHAFT BREMERGESCHICHTSGRUPPEN with the support of the Senator for Education, Science and Art. Entdeckte Geschichte. *Bremer Stadtteile/Betriebe und ihre Geschichte. Geschichtsgruppen stellen sich vor* [Discovered History. Bremen Neighborhoods and Businesses and their Histories. History Groups Present Themselves]. Bremen, 1986.

ARDEY, Robert. *The Territorial Imperative. A Personal Inquiry into the Animal Origins of Property and Nations*. New York, 1967.

ARMAND POMERLEAU. *Lebenserinnerungen aufgezeichnet von Monique POMERLEAU* [Life Experiences Recorded by Monique Pomerleau]. Ste. Clothilde, no year.

ARROYO DE KERRIOU, Miriam. *Untitled*. Mexico D.F., 1984(?) (unpublished manuscript).

ARROYO DE KERRIOU, Miriam. *El museo comunitario como contribución a la educación permanente y a la popular* [The Community Museum as a Contribution to Permanent and Popular Education]. Mexico D.F., 1986 (unpublished manuscript).

ARROYO DE KERRIOU, Miriam. *Personal communication of 1/26/87*. Mexico D.F., 1987a (unpublished manuscript).

ARROYO DE KERRIOU, Miriam. Untitled. *Lecture given within the framework of the Fourth International Workshop on New Museology"*, Zaragoza, 10/18-24, 1987. Mexico D.F., 1987b (photocopied lecture manuscript).

ARROYO QUAN, Miriam. *Informe de las actividades realizadas durante el Año 1984* [Report of the Activities Carried Out During the Year 1984]. Mexico D.F., 1985 (unpublished manuscript).

ASSOCIATION DES ECOMUCES DU QUEBEC. *Untitled leaflet*. Montreal, 1984.

ASSOCIATION OF AMERICAN MUSEUMS. *Museum Accreditation*. Washington D.C., 1973.

LES ATELIERS DE L'ECOMUSEE. [THE ECOMUSEUM WORKSHOPS]. In: *Muséambule*, vol.1/1987(1), pp.5-6.

AUER, Hermann et al. *Denkschrift Museen. Zur Lage der Museen in der Bundesrepublik Deutschland und Berlin (West)* [Memorandum on Museums. On the Place of the Museum in the German Federal Republic and West Berlin]. Boppard, 1974.

AUER, Hermann (ed.). *Das Museum in technischen und sozialen Wandel unserer Zeit. Bericht über ein internationales Symposium, veranstaltet von den ICOM-Nationalkomitees der Bundesrepublik Deutschland, Österreichs und der Schweiz, 13.-19. 5. 1973 am Bodencf.* [The Museum in the Technological and Social Changes of our Time. Report on an International Symposium Arranged by the ICOM National Committee of the German Federal Republic, Austria and Switzerland, 5/13-19, 1973, in Bodencf.]. Pullach (Munich), 1975.

AUER, Hermann (ed.). Das Museum und die Dritte Welt. Bericht über ein internationales Symposium, veranstaltet von den ICOM-Nationalkomitees der Bundesrepublik Deutschland, Österreichs und der Schweiz, 7.-10. 5. 1979 am Bodencf. [The Museum and the Third World. Report on an International Symposium Arranged by the ICOM National Committee of the German Federal Republic, Austria and Switzerland, 5/13-19, 1973, in Bodencf.]. Munich/ New York/London/Paris, 1981. AUSSTELLUNGSGRUPPE OTTENSEN/ALTONAER MUSEUM. Ottensen. Zur Geschichte eines Stadtteils [The History of a Neighborhood]. Hamburg, 1982.

AVALOS Y PEREZ, Aurea. Sugerencias sobre mobiliario museografico [Suggestions on Mobile Museography]. Mexico D.F., 1985 (photocopied manuscript).

BAGCHI, S.K. Science Museums and Social Relevance - an Indian Experiment. In: *Museum*, vol.38/1986a(2), pp.106-107.

BAGCHI, S.K. *Personal communication of 2/24,1986*. Calcutta, 1986b (unpublished manuscript).

BAGHLI, Ahmed. Museums and Development. In: uncited, pp.42-44. (The article is in *Proceedings No. 5.4 of the Reference Center of the Smithsonian Institution in Washington D.C.*)

BAGHLI, S.A. Les musées d'histoire et le développement des pays du Tiersmonde [History museums and the development of Third-World countries]. In: *Journal of World History*, vol.14/1972(1), pp.111-1 26.

BANERJEE, N.R. The Museums and the Education System. In: *Journal of Indian Museums*, vol.35/1979, pp.3-14.

BARAL, Gerhard. Sociakulturelle Zentren - mehr als nur ein Anspruch [Sociocultural centers - more than merely a claim]. In: *Kulturpolitische Mitteilungen*, Nr.23/1983(4), 12-13.

BARBE, Jean-Michel. Présence et avenir du passé, contribution à une problématique des nouvelles muséologies [The presence and future of the past, a contribution to a problem of the new museologies]. In: *Cahiers d'animation*, Nr.51/1985, pp.55-64.

BARGATZKY, Thomas. *Einführung in die Kulturökologie. Umwelt, Kultur und Gesellschaft* [Introduction to Cultural Ecology. Environment, Culture and Society]. Berlin, 1986.

BARON, Guy. *Réflexions sur l'aménagement du territoire* [Reflections on Establishing the Territory]. Courcelles, 1985 (unpublished manuscript).

BARON, Guy. Ecomusée de la Haute-Beauce [Ecomuseum of the Haute-Beauce]. Courcelles, 1986 (unpublished manuscript).

BARON, Guy. *Nouvelle Muséologie et écomuséologie en milieu amérindien* [New Museology and Ecomuseology in the Environment of the American Indian]. Courcelles, 1987 (unpublished manuscript).

BARY, Marie-Odile. Une théorie mise en pratique à l'écomusée de la Haute-Beauce [A theory put in practice in the Ecomuseum of the Haute-Beauce]. In: *M.N.E.S. Info*, Nr.2-3/1984, p.7.

BARRERA, Alfredo. Le musée d'histoire naturelle de la ville de Mexico: sa structure et ses fonctions [The Natural History Museum of Mexico City: its structure and its functions]. In: *Museum*, vol.24/1972 (4), pp.218-227.

BARRETTE, Christian et al. *Les jeunes et la crise: au jour le jour ...* [The Youth and the Crisis: One Day at a Time], Montreal, 1986.

BARRY, Michel. Interprétation et méthode [Interpretation and Method]. In: *Conseil des Monuments et Sites du Québec Bulletin* Nr.16/1982, pp.6-8.

BARTH, Frederik (ed.). *Ethnic Groups and Boundaries. The Social Organization of Culture Difference.* London, 1969.

BAUSINGER, Hermann. *Volkskultur in der technischen Welt* [Popular Culture in the Technological World]. Stuttgart, 1961.

BAUSINGER, Hermann. Heimat und Identität [Homeland and Identity]. In: KÖSTLIN, Konrad and Hermann BAUSINGER (ed.). *Heimat und Identitat.* Kiel, 1980, p.9-24.

BAUSINGER, Hermann. *Kulturelle Identität* [Cultural Identity]. Tübingen, 1982.

BAUSINGER, Hermann. Senseless Identity. In: JACOBSON-WIDDING, Anita (ed.). *Identity: Personal and Socio-Cultural.* Uppsala, 1983, pp.337-345.

BAUSINGER, Hermann. Auf dem Wege zu einem neuen, aktiven Heimatverstandnis [On the way to a new, active understanding of homeland]. In: LANDESZENTRALE FÜR POLITISCHE BILDUNG BADEN-WÜRTTEMBERG (ed.). *Heimat heute.* Stuttgart/Berlin/ Cologne/ Mainz, 1984, pp.11-27.

BAXI, Smita J. and Vinod P. DWIVEDI. *Modem Museums. Organisation and Practice in India.* New Delhi, 1973.

BECKMANN, Gudrun. Der Rumpelstilzchenkomplex [The Rumpelstilzchen complex]. In: KULTURPOLITISCHE GESELLSCHAFT (ed.). *Lernen zwischen Sinn und Sinnlichkeit. - Brauchen wir eine Kulturpadagogik?* Document Nr.24, Hagen, 1985, pp.56-57.

BEDEKAR, V.H. Museums and Rural Community: An Introduction. In: *Journal of Indian Museums,* vol.35/1979, pp.15-20.

BELLAIGUE-SCALBERT, Mathilde. Territorialité, Mémoire, et Développement. L'Ecomusée de la Communauté Le Creusot/Montceaules-Mines (France) [Territoriality, Memory and Development. The Ecomuseum of the

Community of Le Creusot/Montceaules-Mines, France]. In: ICOFOM (ed.). *Museum-Territory-Society. New Tendencies/New Practices.* Stockholm, 1983, pp.34-39.

BELLAIGUE-SCALBERT, Mathilde. Trifling and Essential: The Ethnographical Artefacts. In: ICOFOM (ed.). *Collecting Today for Tomorrow.* Stockholm, 1984, pp.75-78.

BELLAIGUE-SCALBERT, Mathilde. Actors in the Real World. In: *Museum*, vol.37/1985(4), pp.194-197.

BENNETT, John W. (ed.). *The New Ethnicity: Perspectives from Ethnography.* St. Paul, 1975.

BENNINGHOFF-LÜHL, Sibylle. Wirkungsaspekte der Museumsarbeit in einem Entwicklungsland am Beispiel der Rezeption des Sahel-Museums in Mali (Westafrika) [Operating aspects of museum work in a developing country on the example of the reception of the Sahel Museum in Mali, West Africa]. In: Baessler *Archiv*, N.F., vol.30/ 1982(2), pp.371-393.

BENOIST, Jean-Marie. Facetten der Identität [Facets of identity]. In: BENOIST, J.M. (ed.). *Identitat. Ein interdisziplinäres Seminar unter Leitung von Claude Lévi-Strauss.* Stuttgart, 1980, pp.11-21.

BENTLEY, G. Carter. *Ethnicity and Nationality: A Bibliographic Guide.* Washington D.C., 1981.

BENTLEY, G. Carter. Theoretical Perspectives on Ethnicity and Nationality. In: SAGE Race *Relations Abstracts*, vol.8/1983(2), pp.1-53. Bibliography, vol.8/1983(3), pp.1-26.

BERGER, John. Heimat. Wo ist das? [Home. Where is that?]. In: *Psychologie heute*, vol.1 0/1983(12), pp.20-25.

BERGER, John. *Sauerde.* Frankfurt a.M./Berlin/Vienna, 1984.

BERGER, Peter L. and Thomas LUCKMANN. *Die gesellschaftliche Konstruktion der Wirklichkeit* [The Social Construction of Reality]. Frankfurt a.M., 1980.

BERGMANN, Klaus and Rolf SCHÖRKEN (ed.). *Geschichte im Alltag - Alltag in der Geschichte* [History in Everyday Life - Everyday Life in History]. Düsseldorf, 1982.

BERLINER FESTSPIELE GmbH (ed.). *Keltische Woche Berlin 1980* [Celtic Week, Berlin 1980]. 2 vols., Berlin, 1980.

BERNAL, Ignacio. Le musée national d'anthropologie de Mexico [The National Museum of Anthropology of Mexico]. In: *Museum*, vol.19/1966(1), pp.1-14.

BOBERG, Jochen. Thesen zur Kulturpadagogik im Museum [Theories on Cultural Educational Work in the Museum]. In: SPICKERNAGEL, Ellen and Brigitte WALBE (ed.). Das *Museum. Lernort contra Musentempel*. GieBen, 1976, pp.76-81.

BINETTE, René and Lisette CLOUTIER. *Un écomusée dans Centre-Sud. La Maison du Fier Monde* [An ecomuseum in Centre-Sud. La Maison du Fier-Monde]. In: Intervention, March 1983.

BÖHNER, Kurt. Die museale Darbietung der Vorzeit einst und heute [Museum presentation of prehistoric times yesterday and today]. In: BRÜCKNER, Wolfgang and Bernward DENECKE (ed.). *Volkskunde im Museum*. Würzburg, 1976, pp.149-156.

BOLLNOW, Otto-Friedrich. Der Mensch braucht heimatliche Geborgenheit [Man needs the security of a homeland]. In: LANDESZENTRALE FÜR POLITISCHE BILDUNG BADEN WÜRTTEMBERG (ed.). *Heimat heute*. Stuttgart/Berlin/Cologne/Mainz, 1984, pp.28-33.

BOMANN, Wilhelm. Das vaterländische Museum in Celle [The fatherland museum in Celle]. In: *DIE MUSEEN ALS VOLKSBILDUNGSSTÄTTEN*. Berlin, 1904, pp.51-55.

BOSCH, Manfred. *Kulturarbeit. Versuche und Modelle demokratischer Kulturvermittlung* [Cultural Work. Experiments and Models of the Democratic Transmission of Culture]. Frankfurt a.M., 1977.

BOSE, Amalendu. Can Museums of Science Serve the Rural Community? In: *Journal of Indian Museums*, vol.35/1979, pp.101-104.

BOTTIN POP DES GROUPES POPULAIRES DE CENTRE-SUD [POP REGISTERS OF THE PEOPLE'S GROUPS OF CENTRE-SUD]. Montreal, 1983.

BOURDIEU, Pierre and Alain DARBEL. *L'amour de l'art* [The Love of Art]. Paris, 1969.

BRAUDEL, Fernand. *Der Alltag* [Everyday Life]. Munich, 1985.

BRAUNER, Hilmar. *Die Phänomenologie Edmund Husserls und ihre Bedeutung für soziolo gische Theorien* [The Phenomenology of Edmund Husserl and its Significance for Sociological Theory]. Meisenheim, 1978.

BREDOW, Wilfried von and Hans-Friedrich FOLTIN. Zwiespältige Zufluchten. *Zur Rennaissance des Heimatgefühls* [Shelters in Two Columns. The Renaissance of the Feeling of Homeland]. Berlin, 1981.

BRISBOIS, Gaston. *Kultur und Entwicklung* [Culture and Development]. Bonn, 1983.

BRÜCKNER, Wolfgang and Bernward Denecke (ed.). *Volkskunde im Museum* [Folklore in the Museum]. Würzburg, 1976.

BRYANT, Mavis (ed.). *Museums of Mexico and the United States: Policies and Problems. Paper from two conferences*, San Antonio, October 1976, Mexico City, December 1976. Austin, 1977.

BUCHWALD, Konrad. Heimat heute: Wege aus der Entfremdung [Homeland today: a way from alienation]. In: LANDESZENTRALE FÜR POLITISCHE BILDUNG BADEN\ VÜRTTEMBERG (ed.). *Heimat heute*. StuttgartíBerlin/CologneíMainz, 1984, pp.34-59.

BURGESS, M. Elaine. The Resurgence of Ethnicity: Myth or Reality? In: *Ethnic and Racial Studies*, vol.1/1978(3), pp.265-285.

CADENA, Felix. *Investigación participativa y movimientos populares en los 80* [Participative research and popular movements in the 1980's]. Paper given at the 3rd Latin American Seminar on Participative Research, Sao Paulo, 14.-17. 10. 1984. Mexico D.F., 1984a (unpublished manuscript).

CADENA, Felix. Popular Adult Education and Peasant Movements for Social Change. In: *Convergence*, vol.17/1984b(3), pp.31-36.

CALDWELL, Carey. *Native American Humanities and Archives Projects: Issues, Needs, and Future Directions.* Suquamish, 1980 (unpublished manuscript).

CALDWELL, Carey. *Suquamish Tribal Cultural Center Self Study Project.* Suquamish, 1984 (unpublished manuscript).

CAMARGO-MORO, Fernanda. Riches of the Psyche. In: *Museum*, vol.33/1981(3), pp.166-168.

CAMERON, Duncan F. The Museum: a Temple or the Forum. In: *Curator*, vol.14/1971(1), pp.11-24.

CAMUSAT, Pierre. *La participation: Utopie ou réalité?* [Participation: utopia or reality?]. In: Musées, vol.8/1985(1), pp.25-26.

CARLIER, Jean. Vous avez dit «pare»? Avant propos [Did you say "park"? Foreword]. In: DESJEUX, Catherine and Bernard DESJEUX. *Les pares Naturels Régionaux de France - Campagnes vivantes.* Nouette, 1984, pp.7-12.

CARVALHO DE MEDEIROS, Ione Maria. *The Community Didactic Museum.* No place, 1985 (unpublished manuscript).

CENTRE ST. PIERRE. *Portrait du Centre-Sud. Dossier démographique 1984* [Portrait of the Centre-Sud. Demographic File 1984]. Montreal, 1984.

CÉRÉ, Maude. De Théodule à Trefflé... l'écomusée de la Haute-Beauce [From Théodule to Trefflé ... the ecomuseum of the Haute-Beauce]. In: *Possibles*, vol.6/1982a(3/4), pp. 207-218.

CÉRÉ, Maude. Les trousses pédagogiques facilitent l'accès des enfants au musée [Educational kits facilitate children's access to the museum]. In: *Musées*, vol.5/1982b(l), pp.12-14.

CÉRÉ, Maude. Haute-Beauce créatrice [Haute-Beauce, the creator]. In: Vision Nr.32/1983, pp.28-29.

CÉRÉ, Maude. *La portée éducative des écomusées: le cas Haute-Beauce* [The Educational lmportance of Ecomuseums: the Case of the Haute-Beauce]. Montreal, 1985 (unpublished master's thesis).

CÉRÉ, Maude (with the cooperation of Pierre Rastoul). La Maison du Granit: du solide! [The Maison du Granit: solid!]. In: *Muséambule*, vol.11, 1987(1), pp.7-8.

CÉRÉ, Maude and Carole AUDET. *Les trousses éducatives* [Educational Kits]. Montreal, 1981.

CHAKRABORTI, R.M. Museums of Science for the Rural Community of India. In: *Journal of Indian Museums*, vol.35/1979, pp.105-112.

CLOUTIER, Lisette and René BINETTE. Une murale synonyme de fierté [A mural synonymous with pride]. In: *Vision*, Nr.32/1983, pp.8-1 O.

COLLETTA, Nat. Tradition for Change: Indigenous Socio-cultural Forms as a Basis for NonFormal Education and Development. In: KIDD, Ross and Nat COLLETTA (ed.). *Tradition for Development: Indigenous Structures and Folk Media in Non-Formal Education*. Berlin, 1980, pp.9-59.

COLLIN, Gérard. L'Ecomusée du Mont Lozère [The Ecomuseum of Mont Lozère]. In: ICOFOM (ed.). *Museum-Territory-Society. New Tendencies/ New Practices*. Stockholm, 1983a, pp.40-44.

COLLIN, Gérard. Quelques réflexions à propos des communications sur «Ecologie-Ecomusées» reçues à la date du 10 juin 1983 [Some reflections on the communications on «ecology ecomuseums» received on June 10,

1983]. In: ICOFOM (ed.). *Museum-Territory-Society. New Tendencies/New Practices*. Stockholm, 1983b, pp.45-47.

COLLIN, Gérard. *Musées Locaux et Defense du Patrimoine*. Mont Lozère, 1985 [Local museums and defense of the heritage. Mont Lozère, 1985]. Presented at the "2nd international workshop of local museums and new museology". Lisbon, 1113-9, 1985). No place, 1985 (unpublished manuscript).

LE COMITE CULTUREL DE LA GUADELOUPE. *Le centre historique de la Guadeloupe* [The historic center of La Guadeloupe]. La Guadeloupe, no year (unpublished manuscript).

COMITE NACIONAL MEXICANO DEL ICOM (ed.). *III. Coloquio Nacional de Museos. El Museo Mexicano: Funciones y Responsabilidades*, Morelia/Michoacan, 23.-26. 8. 1984 [3rd National Colloquium on Museums. The Mexican Museum: Functions and Responsibilities, Morelia/Michoacan, 8/23-26, 1984]. Mexico D.F., 1984.

COMMISSION D'ETUDE SUR LA FORMATION DES ADULTES. *Apprendre: une action volontaire et responsable* [Learning: a Voluntary and Responsible Action]. Montreal, 1982.

COMPTE RENDU DE LA REUNION DU 16 DECEMBRE 1980 [REPORT OF THE MEETING OF DECEMBER 16, 1980]. Montreal, 1980 (unpublished minutes).

LE CONSEIL D'ADMINISTRATION DE VOTRE MUSEE. [THE BOARD OF DIRECTORS OF YOUR MUSEUM]. In: *Muséambule*, vol.1/1987(1), p.1.

CRUS-RAMIREZ, Alfredo. The Heimatmuseum: a Perverted Forerunner. In: *Museum*, vol.37/1985(4), pp.242-244.

DANA, John. *The New Museum*. Woodstock, 1917.

DANA, John. *A Plan for a New Museum*. Woodstock, 1920.

DAUPHIN, Jean. MRC du Granit: Une économie au milieu de nulle part [MRC of Granit: An economy in the middle of nowhere]. In: *Commerce*, July 1984, pp.40-51.

DAUPHIN, Jean. Gardien d'une tradition [Guardian of a tradition]. In: *Commerce*, July 1984, pp.32-37.

DAVALLON, Jean. Penser l'exposition comme rituel de représentation [Thinking of the exhibit as a ritual of representation]. In: DAVALLON, Jean (ed.). *Claquemurer pour ainsi dire tout l'univers la mise en exposition*. Paris, 1986a, pp.269-279.

DAVALLON, Jean. Philosophie de l'écomusée et mise en exposition [The philosophy of the ecomuseum and setting up the exhibit]. In: DAVALLON, Jean. Claquemurer, *pour ainsi dire, tout l'univers. La mise en exposition*. Paris, 1986b, pp.106-126.

DECLARATORIA DE OAXTEPEC [DECLARATION OF OAXTEPEC]. Oaxtepec, 1984 (photocopied manuscript).

DECLARATION DE QUEBEC [DECLARATION OF QUEBEC]. In: *Musées*, vol.8/ 1985(1), p.13.

DECOUVRIR LES ECOMUCF.S. MUCF. DE BRETAGNE - ECOMUCF. LES BITINAIS [DISCOVERING ECOMUSEUMS. MUSEUM OF BRITTAINY - ECOMUCF. LES BITINAIS]. Rennes, 1984.

DEFINITION DE L'ECOMUCF., approuvée par l'Assemblée générale de la Fédération des parcs naturels de France, les 4 et 5 octobre 1978 [Definition of the ecomusuem approved by the General Meeting of the Federation of Natural Parks of France, October 4 and 5, 1978]. In: FEDERATION DES PARCS NATURELS DE FRANCE (ed.). *Les parcs naturels régionaux et le patrimoine ethnologique*. No place, 1979, pp.23-26.

DENNIS, Emily. Seminar on Neighborhood Museums. In: *Museum News*, vol.48/1970(5), pp.13-19.

DENNIS HARVEY, Emily. *A Museum for the People.* New York, 1971.

DEPARTMENT OF URBAN AND REGIONAL PLANNING/GEORGE WASHINGTON UNIVERSITY. *Old Anacostia: A Planning Study.* Washington D.C., 1973 (unpublished report).

DEPPE, H. Carola. Ra*um und Zeit im Museum - Möglichkeiten historisch-geographischer Inhalte am Beispiel des Westfälischen Freilichtmuseums Hagen* [Space and Time in the Museum - Possibilities of Historical and Geographical Content Using the Westfalia Freilichtsmuseum, Hagen, as an Example]. Göttingen, 1986 (unpublished dissertation).

DE SAMISKE SAMLINGER KAROSJAK. No place, no year.

DESEMEC. *Boletin Bimestral* [Bimonthly Bulletin]. Nr.1/May 1984, Nr.2/July-Aug. 1984, Nr.3/Sept.-Oct. 1984. Mexico D.F., 1984a.

DESEMEC. Scholar Museums and Community Museums. Mexico D.F., 1984b (video film). DESEMEC. Metodología [Methodology]. Mexico D.F., 1985a (photocopied manuscript).

DESEMEC. Curso de Capacitación para promotores de museos escolares y comunitarios [Training Course for Promoters of School and Community Museums] (Program). Mexico D.F., 1985b (photocopied manuscript).

DESEMEC. Programa para el desarrollo de la función educativa de los museos del INAH [Program for the Development of the Educational Function of the INAH Museums]. Mexico D.F., 1985c.

DESEMEC. Estadística general de museos nuevos y promotores que coordina el Departamento de Servicios Educativos, Museos Escolares y Comunitarios [General Statistics on New and Promotional Museums Coordinated by the Department of Educational Services and School and Community Museums]. Mexico D.F., 1985d (unpublished manuscript).

DESEMEC. El proceso de evaluación en el programa de museos escolares y comunitarios [The Evaluation Process in the School and Community Museums Program]. Mexico D.F., 1986a (photocopied manuscript).

DESEMEC. Programa del cuarto curso de capacitación para promotores de museos escolares y comunitarios [Program of the Fourth Training Course for Promoters of School and Community Museums]. Mexico D.F., 1986b (photocopied manuscript).

DESEMEC. Programa para el desarrollo de la función educativa de los museos del INAH [Program for the Development of the Educational Function of the INAH Museums]. Mexico D.F., no year (unpublished manuscript).

DESJARDINS, Paul. L'interprétation historique et naturelle. Un moyen de mettre en valeur notre patrimoine [Historical and natural interpretation. A means of giving value to our heritage]. In: *Conseil des Monuments et Sites du Québec Bulletin* Nr.16/1982, pp.26-28.

DESROSIERS, Guy and Gérard LAFLEUR. *La Maison du Fier-Monde* [The Maison du Fier Monde]. Montreal, 1981.

DESVALLEES, André. Les écomusées [Ecomuseums]. In: ICOFOM (ed.). *Museum-Territory-Society. New Tendencies/New Practices.* Stockholm. 1983, pp.15-16.

DESVALLEES, André. Muséologie (nouvelle) [(new) Museology]. In: *Encyclopedia Universalis.* Paris, 1980, pp.958-961.

DESVALLEES, André. *Point sur la «nouvelle muséologie». Communication devant la commission consultative de l'ICOM*, Paris, 1. 7. 1985. [A Point About the "New Museology". A Communication to the ICOM Consultative Commission, Paris, 7/1, 1985.] Paris, 1985a (unpublished manuscript).

DESVALLEES, André. Nouvelle muséologie [New museology]. In: *Encyclopedia Universalis.* Paris, 1985b, pp.771-774.

DESJEUX, Catherine and Bernard DESJEUX. *Les Parcs Naturels de France - Campagnes vivantes* [The Natural Parks of France - Living Countryside]. Nouette, 1984.

DEUTSCHE UNESCO-KOMMISSION (ed.). *Die soziale Dimension der Museumsarbeit* [The Social Dimension of Museum Work]. Pullach (Munich), 1976.

DEYMANN, Ursula and Udo LIEBELT (ed.). *Museumspadagogik. Welt der Arbeit im Museum* [Museum Education. The Working World in the Museum]. Marburg, 1983.

DIALLO, Aly. *Problemes d'élaboration des concepts en muséologie: Quelques exemples* [Problems of Developing Concepts in Museology: Some Examples]. Hamburg, 1986 (unpublished manuscript).

DIOP, A.S. Museological Activity in African Countries: Its Role and Purpose. In: *Museum*, vol.25/1973(4), pp.250-256.

DIOP, A.S. Musée et développement culturel et scientifique [The museum and cultural and scientific development]. In: *Bull. de l'IFAN*, Series B, vol.38/1976, pp.351-376.

DOCUMENT DE TRAVAIL [WORKING DOCUMENT]. Quebec/Montreal, 1984.

DÖRING, Carla E. *Das kulturgeschichtliche Museum. Geschichte einer Institution und Möglichkeiten des Selbstverstandnisses, dargestellt am Beispiel „Heimatmuseum"* [The Museum of Cultural History. History of an Institution and Possibilities of a Concept of Self, Using the "Heimatmuseum" as an Example]. Dissertation, Frankfurt a.M., 1977.

DÖSCHER, Susanne and Elke URBAN. *Der Stadtteil Vahrenheide - ein soziales Spannungs feld. Möglichkeiten und Grenzen einer Stadtteilidentität in einem nicht gewachsenen Stadtteil durch Aktionen von Bürgern* [The Vahrenheide Neighborhood - an Area of Social Conflict. Possibilities and Limits of

Neighborhood Identity in a Non-Mature Neighborhood through Citizen Action]. Hannover, 1983.

DOTER LE QUEBEC D'INSTITUTIONS MUSEOLOGIQUES DE PREMIERE IMPORTANCE Entrevue avec Clément Richard, ministre des Affaires Culturelles du Québec [Giving Quebec Museological Institutions of the First Magnitude. Interview with Clément Richard, Minister of Cultural Affairs of Quebec]. In: *Forces*, Nr.65/1983-84, pp.14-23.

DÜCKER, Elisabeth von. Vom Dorf zur Industriestadt: Ottensen - Museum und Bewohner entdecken die Geschichte ihres Stadtteils [From village to industrial city: Ottensen - museum and residents uncover the history of a neighborhood]. In: DEYMANN, Ursula and Udo LIEBELT (ed.). *Museumspädagogik. Welt der Arbeit im Museum*. Marburg, 1983, pp.42-54.

DÜCKER, Elisabeth von. Spurensicherung im Stadtteil. Das Stadtteilarchiv Ottensen [Securing the evidence in a neighborhood. The Ottensen neighborhood archives]. In: HEER, Hannes and Volker ULLRICH (ed.). *Geschichte entdecken. Erfahrungen und Projekte der neuen Geschichts bewegung*. Reinbek b. Hamburg, 1985, pp.364-367.

DUCLOS, Jean-Claude. MINOM Communiqué [MINOM Communique]. Grenoble, 1986 (photocopied manuscript).

DUCLOS, Jean-Claude et.al. *Elements pour un essai de définition de la nouvelle muséologie* [Elements for an Attempt to Define the New Museology]. Grenoble, 1986 (photocopied manuscript).

DUCLOS, Jean-Claude et.al. *Elaboration d'un texte de base sur la nouvelle muséologie. Analyse des contributions* [Development of a Basic Text on the New Museology. Analysis of Contributions]. Grenoble, 1987 (photocopied manuscript).

DUKE, Chris. Wichtige Fragen der Erwachsenenbildung und der Entwicklung [Important questions of adult education and development]. In: HINZEN,

Heribert and Wolfgang LEUMER (ed.). *Erwachsenenbildung in der Dritten Welt*. Braunschweig, 1982, pp.74-93.

DUNDES, Alan. Defining Identity through Folklore. In: JACOBSON-WIDDING, Anita (ed.). *Identity: Personal and Socio-Cultural*. Uppsala, 1983, pp.235-261.

DWIVEDI, V.P. and G.N. PANT (ed.). *Museums and Museology: New Horizons. Essays in Honour of Dr. Grace Morley, on her 80th Birthday*. New Delhi, 1980.

ECHEANCIER 1981-1982 [BOOK OF ACCOUNTS 1981-1982]. Montreal, 1981 (unpublished manuscript).

UN ECOMUSEE, CE N'EST PAS UN ECOMUSEE COMME LES AUTRES [AN ECOMUSEUM IS NOT A MUSEUM LIKE THE OTHERS]. In: *Histoire et Critique des Arts*, Nr.7-8/1978, pp.90-120.

ECOMUSEE. DE LA HAUTE-BEAUCE. *Reglements généraux* [Ecomusée de la Haute Beauce. General Regulations]. St. Evariste, 1983 (photocopied manuscript).

ECOMUSEE DE LA HAUTE-BEAUCE. *La Maison du Granit*. St.Evariste, 1984a.

ECOMUSEE DE LA HAUTE-BEAUCE. *Rapport du président* [Ecomusée de la HauteBeauce. Chairman's Report]. St. Evariste, 1984b (unpublished report).

ECOMUSEE DE LA HAUTE-BEAUCE. *Leaflet*. St. Evariste, no year.

L' ECOMUSEE. EN GENERAL. *Ecomusée de la communauté urbaine Le Creusot-Montceau les-Mines: Quelques traits d'une programmation, à l'état de premieres esquisses* [The Ecomuseum in General. Ecomuseum of the Urban Community of Creusot-Montceau-les-Mines: Some Programming Outlines in the First-Draft Stage]. Le Creusot/Paris, 1973 (unpublished manuscript).

EDITORIAL. In: *Museum*, vol.25/1973(3), p.127.

EDWARDS, Yorke. Museums Must Decide: Hands-on or Hands-off? In: Muse, vol.5/1987(1), pp.18-23.

EGNER, Dieter. Arbeitskreis 2. Möglichkeiten zu einem kulturellen Selbstverständnis [Working Group 2. Possibilities for a cultural concept of self]. In: KULTURPOLITISCHE GESELL SCHAFT (ed.) *Region und Regionalismus*. Hagen/Erlangen, 1982, pp.63-66.

EHALT, Hubert (ed.). *Geschichte von unten. Fragestellungen, Methoden und Projekte einer Geschichte des Alltags* [History from Below. Questions, Methods and Projects of a History of Everyday Life]. Vienna/Cologne/Graz, 1984a.

EHALT, Hubert. Geschichte von unten [History from Below]. In: EHALT, Hubert (ed.). *Geschichte von unten. Fragestellungen, Methoden und Projekte einer Geschichte des Alltags*. Vienna/Cologne/Graz, 1984b, pp.11-39.

EHMER, Hermann K. „Lernen zwischen Sinn und Sinnlichkeit" - Brauchen wir eine Kulturpädagogik? ["Learning between sense and sensuality" - Do we need cultural education?] In: KULTURPOLITISCHE GESELLSCHAFT (ed.). *„Lernen zwischen Sinn und Sinnlich keit" - Brauchen wir eine Kulturpädagogik?* Document Nr.24, Hagen, 1985, pp.5-14.

EIDMANN, Heinrich. *Heimatmuseum, Schule und Volksbildung* [Heimatmuseum, school and people's education]. Die Volkskultur, Heft 11, Leipzig, 1909.

EIRA. Mari Teigmo. *Sami Museums in Norway and the Nordic Countries. Lecture given within the framework of the "3rd International Workshop on New Museology - Nordic Traditions and Perspectives"*, Totn, 9/14-9, 1986. No place, 1986 (photocopied lecture manuscript).

ELWERT, Georg. *Der entwicklungssoziologische Mythos vom Traditionalismus* [The Social Development Mythos of Traditionalism]. Bielefeld, 1982.

ENGSTRÖM, Kjell. The Ecomuseum Concept is taking Root in Sweden. In: *Museum*, vol.37 /1985(4), pp.206-210.

ENTWICKLUNG UND ZUSAMMENARBEIT. 1979(6); 1979(7-8); 1980(7-8); 1981(7-8); 1983(7); 1986(8-9).

ERBE, Michael. *Zur neueren französischen Sozialgeschichtsforschung* [The New French Social-History Research]. Darmstadt, 1979.

ERIKSON, Erik H. Identität und Lebenszyklus [Identity and Life Cycle]. Frankfurt a.M., 1973.

ERIKSON, Erik H. Dimensionen einer neuen Identität [Dimensions of a New Identity]. Frankfurt a.M., 1975.

ERKLÄRUNG VON MEXIKO-CITY ÜBER KULTURPOLITIK [MEXICO CITY DECLARATION ON CULTURAL POLICY]. In: *Unesco Service, Special Issue*, September 1982, pp.1-6.

THE ESROM DECLARATION. Esrom, 1987.

ESSOMBA, Joseph-Marie. *Study of the Development of Museums for Improved Integration of the Cultural Heritage into the Education System in French-Speaking African Countries*. Lecture given at the UNESCO "Sub-Regional Seminar on the Use of Cultural Heritage in Education", Freetown, 9/29-3/10, 1980. No year, 1980 (unpublished lecture manuscript).

ETHIER, Suzanne. Ecomusée, musée territoire de la Haute-Beauce [Ecomuseum, territorial museum of the Haute-Beauce]. In: *Réseau*, vol.13/1981(4), pp.8-10.

ETHNOLOGIE FRANÇAISE, *nouvelle série*, vol.17/1987(1) «Hommage de la Société d'Ethnologie Française à Georges Henri Riviere» [«Homage of the French Society of Ethnology to Georges Henri Riviere].

EVANS, Richard J. Die "History Workshop"-Bewegung in England [The History Workshop Movement in England]. In: HEER, Hannes and Volker ULLRICH (ed.). *Geschichte entdecken. Erfahrungen und Projekte der neuen Geschichtsbewegung*. Reinbek b. Hamburg, 1985, pp.37-45.

EVRARD, Marcel. L'Ecomusée de la Communauté Urbaine Le CreusotMontceau-les-Mines [The Ecomuseum of the Urban Community of Le Creusot-Montceau-les-Mines]. In: *CRACAP/ Informations*, Nr.2/3, 1976, pp.9-14.

EVRARD, Marcel. Le Creusot-Montceau-les-Mines: la vie d'un écomusée, bilan d'une décennie [Le Creusot-Montceau-les-Mines: the life of an ecomuseum, summing up a decade]. In: *Museum*, vol.32/1980(4), pp.226-234.

EVRARD, Marcel. L'Ecomusée, une expérience en patrimoine industriel [The ecomuseum, an experiment in industrial heritage]. In: *Musées*, vol.8/1985(1), pp.32-34.

EVRARD, Marcel and Mathilde SCALBERT-BELLAIGUE. L'Ecomusée de la Communauté Le Creusot-Montceau-les-Mines [The ecomuseum of the community of Le Creusot-Montceaules-Mines]. In: *Les Cahiers de l'animation*, Nr.27/1 980, pp.35-44.

LE FAUBOURG A M'LASSE. *L'histoire de l'institutionalisation de l'éducation dans le milieu défavorisé du Centre-Sud* [The History of the Institutionalization of Education in the Disadvantaged Environment of the Centre-Sud]. Université du Québec à Montréal, Cahier No.3. Montreal, 1983.

FELTON, Zora. *A Walk Through 'Old' Anacostia*. Washington D.C., no year.

FERNANDEZ, Miguel Angel. Historia de los Museos de Mexico [History of the Museums of Mexico]. In: *Obras Maestras de la Pintura. Museos de Mexico*. Barcelona, 1983.

FISCHER, Gero. Autobiographische Texte als historische Quelle [Autobiographical texts as historical sources]. In: EHALT, Hubert (ed.). *Geschichte von unten. Fragestellungen, Methoden und Projekte einer Geschichte des Alltags*. Vienna/Cologne/Graz, 1984, pp.81-94.

FITZGERALD, Thomas K. (ed.). *Social and Cultural Identity. Problems of Persistence and Change*. Athens, 1974.

FLOU, Bjame. *Suggestions for a Continuation of the Research Project on Museal Activities at Local Level in Tanzania*. Århus, 1975 (unpublished manuscript).

FLOU, Bjarne. *Can Ordinary Tanzanian Peasants really do Research? They do it Already*. Århus, 1976a (unpublished manuscript).

FLOU, Bjame. *The Significance of Local-Levei Museums in the Transformation of Tanzanian Culture - the Strategy of "Folk-Research"*. Århus, 1976b (unpublished manuscript).

FOHRBECK, Karla. *Kultur und Entwicklung. Ergebnis eines Expertengesprächs* in Bonn, 23.- 24. 11. 1982 [Culture and Development. Results of a Colloquium of Experts in Bonn, 11/23-24, 1982]. Bonn, 1982.

FREIRE, Paolo. *Pädagogik der Unterdrückten* [Education of the Oppressed]. Stuttgart, 1971.

FREIRE, Paolo. *Erziehung als Praxis der Freiheit* [Education as the Practice of Freedom]. Stuttgart, 1974.

FREIRE, Paolo. *Der Lehrer ist Politiker und Künstler. Neue Texte zu befreiender Bildungsarbeit* [The Teacher is a Politician and an Artist. New Texts on Liberating Educational Work]. Reinbek b. Hamburg, 1981.

FREIRE, Paolo. Brief an Erwachsenenbilder [Letter to adult educators]. In: HINZEN, Heribert and Wolfgang LEUMER (ed.). *Erwachsenenbildung in der Dritten Welt*. Braunschweig, 1982, pp.44-49.

FRIEDRICHS, Jürgen. *Methoden empirischer Sozialforschung* [Methods of Empirical Social Research]. Reinbek b. Hamburg, 1973.

GABUS, Jean. *L'objet témoin. Les références d'une civilisation par l'objet* [The Object as Testimony. The References of a Civilization through the Object]. Neuchâtel, 1975.

GAGNON, Carolle. *Critique de la muséologie traditionnelle et de la nouvelle muséologie: sont-elles conciliables?* [Critique of Traditional Museology and

New Museology: Are They Reconcilable?]. Québec, 1984 (unpublished manuscript).

GAITHER, Edmund Barry. *Anacostia Review: Minority Report.* Boston, 1979 (unpublished manuscript).

GANSLMAYR, Herbert. *Die Neuplanung der völkerkundlichen Abteilung des Übercf. Museums* [Modem Planning of the Folklore Section of the Übercf. Museum]. In: Veröffent lichungen aus dem Übercf.-Museum, Series B, vol.3/1973, pp.43-65.

GANSLMAYR, Herbert. Has Appropriate Technology in Museums of Science and Technology only the Function of the Dinosaurian in the Museums of Natural History? In: *Workshop on the Establishment of Science Museums in Asian Countries: Training and Exchange*, Bangalore, 1980, pp.153-156.

GANSLMAYR, Herbert. *Le rôle des musées dans les régions sahéliennes* [The role of Museums in the Sahel Region]. Bremen, 1981 (unpublished manuscript).

GANSLMAYR, Herbert. *Untitled* [Documentation on the Cooperation of the Übercf. Museum with the Musée National du Mali]. Bremen, 1983 (unpublished report).

GANSLMAYR, Herbert. *Museen: Investition für Entwicklung* [Investment for Development]. Lecture given at the Conference of the Museum Working Group of the German Society for Folk Art, Offenbach, October 1984. Bremen, 1984 (unpublished lecture manuscript).

GANSLMAYR, Herbert. *Museums and Crafts.* Lecture given at the Conference of the World Craft Council "The Role of Crafts in the Development Process", Djakarta, 8/20-25, 1985.

Bremen, 1985 (unpublished lecture manuscript).

GANSLMAYR, Herbert. *Keynote Paper for the Seminar "Integrating Museums into the Life of the Community",* Seoul, January 1986. Bremen, 1986 (unpublished lecture manuscript).

GANSLMAYR, Herbert and Jeffrey JORDAN. *Preliminary Proposal for a Museum-Culture House at New Wadi Halfa, Sudan.* No year, 1983 (unpublished manuscript).

GARIÉPY, Céline. *L'écomusée de la Haute-Beauce et le développement communautaire* [The Ecomusée de la Haute-Beauce and Community Development]. Quebec, 1986 (unpublished dissertation).

GAUDIBERT, Pierre. *Du culturel au sacré* [From the Cultural to the Sacred]. Paris, 1981.

GEH' ÜBER DIE DÖRFER! [GO THROUGH THE VILLAGES!]. In: *Der Spiegel* vol.38/1984(40), pp.252-261.

GERNDT, Helge. Zwischen Weihehalle und Klippschule: Das Kulturhistorische Museum als Herausforderung (Kulturkommentar) [Between ceremonial hall and second-rate school: the museum of cultural history as a challenge (a cultural comment)]. In: BRÜCKNER, Wolfgang and Bernward DENECKE (ed.). *Volkskunde im Museum.* Würzburg, 1976, pp.245-249.

GHOSE, Saroj. Science, Museums, Rural Community, and the Missing Link. In: *Journal of Indian Museums*, vol.35/1979, pp.117-122.

GHOSE, Saroj. Science Museums beyond their Four Walls. In: *Museum*, vol.3811986(2), pp.100-106.

GJESTRUM, John Age. 1900-tallet - snart forrige århundre Okomucf.t - et bindeledd mellom fortid, nåtid og framtid. In: *Totn Årbok* 1985. Gjovik, 1986, pp.6-15.

GLASER, Grete Mostny. Introduction. In: *Museum*, vol.25/1973(3), (The Role of Museums in Today's Latin America), p.128.

GLASER, Hermann. Beitrag zu einer sozialdemokratischen Kulturtheorie [Contribution to a social democratic theory of culture]. In: FRIEDRICH, Bruno (ed.). *Kulturelle Demokratie.* Bonn, 979, pp.32-40.

GLASER, Horst-Albert. Heimat unterm bösen Blick. Anmerkungen zur neueren Heimatliteratur [Homeland under the evil eye. Notes on the recent literature of homeland]. In: *Die politische Meinung*, vol.29/Sept.-Oct. 1984, pp.67- 77.

GLAZER, Nathanael and Daniel P. MOYNIHAN. (ed.). *Ethnicity, Theory and Experience*. Cambridge, 1975.

GOLDMANN, Margarethe. Regionale Kultur-Beispiele einer neuen kulturpolitischen Praxis [Regional culture: exarnples of a new practice of cultural policy]. In: KULTURPOLITISCHE GESELLSCHAFT (ed.). *Region und Regionalismus*. Hagen/Erlangen, 1982, pp.41-56.

GOLDMANN, Margarete and Michael ZIMMERMANN. „Kohle war nicht alles". Das „Hochlarmarker Lesebuch" [„Coal wasn't everything." „The Hoch Larrnark reader"]. In: HEER, Hannes and Volker ULLRICH (ed.). Geschichte entdecken. Erfahrungen und Projekte der neuen Geschichtsbewegung. Reinbek b. Hamburg, 1985, pp.345-351.

GONZALES, Antonio and Richard JOSEPH (with the cooperation of Richard Morin). *Desindustrialisation et devenir du quartier Centre-Sud*. Rapport de stage. Montreal, 1984 (unpublished report).

GORENSTEIN, Shirley. The Role of the Museum in Mexico. In: *Curator*, vol.14/1971(1), pp.56-61.

GOSH, Sarnbhu Nath. Science Museums and Rural Development. In: NATIONAL COUNCIL OF SCIENCE MUSEUMS (ed.). *lndo-FRG Workshop on Science Museums for Rural Development*, Purulia, 12/2-7, 1983. Calcutta, 1983, pp.19-20.

GOUVERNEMENT DU QUEBEC. *La politique québécoise du développernent culturel* [The Quebec Cultural Development Policy]. 2 vols., Quebec, 1978.

GRAHAM-BELL, Margaret. Preservation Paramount to Museum Mission. In: *Muse*, vol.5/1987(1), p.5.

GRASSKAMP, Walter. *Museumsgründer und Museumsstürmer. Zur Sozialgeschichte des Kunstrnuseums* [Museum Founders and Museum Assaulters. A Social History of the Art Museurn]. Munich, 1981.

GREVERUS,Ina-Maria. *Der territoriale Mensch. Ein literaturanthropologischer Versuch zurn Heimatphänomen* [The Territorial Man. A Search for the Phenomenon of Homeland in the Literature of Anthropology]. Frankfurt a.M., 1972.

GREVERUS, Ina-Maria. *Kultur und Alltagswelt* [Culture and Everyday Life]. Munich, 1978.

GREVERUS, Ina-Maria. *Auf der Suche nach Heimat* [ln Search of Homeland]. Munich, 1979a.

GREVERUS, Ina-Maria. Kulturökologische Aufgaben im Analyse- und Planungsbereich Gemeinde [Data from cultural ecology in the area of community analysis and planning]. In: WIEGELMANN, G. (ed.). *Gemeinde im Wandel.* Münster, 1979b, pp.87-99.

GREVERUS, Ina-Maria. ÖKO PRO REGION. In: GREVERUS, Ina-Maria and Erika HAINDL (ed.). *ÖKOlogie, PROvinz, REGIONalismus.* Frankfurt a.M., 1984a, pp.15-44.

GREVERUS, Ina-Maria. Pladoyer für eine multikulturelle Gesellschaft [Plea for a multicultural society]. In: GREVERUS, Ina-Maria and Erika HAINDL (ed*.). ÖKOlogie, PROvinz, REGIONalismus.* Frankfurt a.M., 1984b, pp.309-316.

GREVERUS, Ina-Maria and Erika HAINDL (ed.). *ÖKOlogie, PROvinz, REGIONalismus* [ECOlogy, PROvince, REGIONalism]. Frankfurt a.M., 1984.

GRIESSHAMMER, Birke. *Das Heimatmuseum als Lernort - ein Beitrag zur Museumspädagogik* [The Heimatmuseum as a place of learning: a contribution to museum education]. In: Blatter für Lehrerfortbildung, 29/1977, pp.180-185.

GRIFFING, Robert. *Asia and Pacific Regional Seminar on The Museum as a Cultural Centre in the Development of the Community*, Tokyo, 9/4-30, 1960. Paris, 1962.

GROUPE DE RECHERCHE EN PATRIMOINE (ed.). *Journée d'étude sur les écomusées. Document de travail* [Study day on ecomuseums. Working document]. Université du Québec à Montréal, 5/26, 1983. Montreal, 1983.

GÜNTER, Roland and Rolf-Joachim RUTZEN. *Kultur tagtäglich* [Culture every day]. Reinbek b. Hamburg, 1982.

LES HABITATIONS COMMUNAUTAIRES CENTRE-SUD (ed.). *Untitled*. Montreal, 1980 (unpublished manuscript).

HALBWACHS, Maurice. *La mémoire collective* [The Collective Memory]. Paris, 1950.

HALL, Edward T. Die Sprache des Raumes [The Language of Space]. Düsseldorf, 1976.

HALLER VON HALLERSTEIN, Nina and Manfred TEUFEL. *Kleine Gemeinde zwischen Marginalität und Anpassung am Beispiel Südwestirlands* [A small community between marginality and adaptation based on the example of southwest Ireland]. In: WIEGELMANN, Günther (ed.). Gemeinde im Wandel. Münster, 1979, pp.209-213.

HAMACHER, Ulrich. *Möglichkeiten und Grenzen „Alternativer Geschichtsarbeit". Das Projekt Stadtteilgeschicihte Bremen-Nord* [Possibilities and Limits of "Alternative History Writing". The Bremen-Nord Neighborhood History Project]. Bremen, 1987 (unpublished dissertation).

HANGEN, Hedwig. Heimatmuseum im Umbruch. Ein Praxisbericht aus der Museumsarbeit im ländlichen Raum [The Heimatmuseum in change. A report of experience in museum work in the countryside]. In: *Europäische Ethnologie in der beruflichen Praxis. Berichte aus Museum und Hochschule*, vol.12/1983, pp.35-41.

HANGEN, Hedwig. *Museumsfachstelle MOBiLe* [The MOBiLe museum technical site]. In: Ostfriesland 1985(1), pp.27-29.

HANGEN, Hedwig u.a. *Der museumspädagogische Modellversuch MOBiLe (Museen Ostfrieslands als Bildungsstätten und Lernorte)* [The MOBiLe (Ostfriesland Museums as Places of Learning) Model Experiment on Museum Education]. Aurich, 1983 (photocopied report).

HANNERZ, Ulf. Tools of Identity and Imagination. In: JACOBSON-WIDDING, Anita (ed.). *Identity: Personal and Socio-Cultural.* Uppsala, 1983, pp.347-360.

HANNIBAL, Emmett R. *The Social and Educational Context of the Community Arts Movement.* No place, 1975.

HARTFIEL, Günter. *Wörterbuch der Soziologie* [Dictionary of Sociology]. Stuttgart, 1976.

HASSAN, M.M. The Exhibition a Developing Country needs. In: *Museums and Monuments,* vol.15/1973 (Museums, Imagination and Education), pp.113-122.

HAUMANN, Heiko (ed.). *Arbeiteralltag in Stadt und Land. Neue Wege der Geschichtsschrei bung* [The Everyday Life of Workers in City and Country. New Ways of Writing History]. Berlin, 1982.

HAUMANN, Heiko. *Alltagsgeschichte, Regionalgeschichte, Gesellschaftsgeschichte. Zu einigen Neuerscheinungen* [Everyday history, regional history, social history. Some recent publications]. In: Das Argument, Nr.151, vol.2711985, pp.405-418.

HEER, Hannes and Volker ULLRICH (ed.). *Geschichte entdecken. Erfahrungen und Projekte der neuen Geschichtsbewegung* [History Uncovered. Experiences and Projects of the New History Movement]. Reinbek b. Hamburg, 1985a.

HEER, Hannes and Volker ULLRICH. Die „neue Geschichtsbewegung" in *der Bundesrepublik. Antriebskräfte, Selbstverständnis, Perspektiven* [The "new history movement" in the German Federal Republic. Powers, Conception, Prospects]. In: HEER, Hannes and Volker ULLRICH (ed.). Geschichte entdecken. Erfahrungen und Projekte der neuen Geschichtsbewegung. Reinbek b. Hamburg, 1985b, pp.9-36.

HEIGL, Otto et al. *Von James Baldwin zum Free Southern Theater. Positionen schwarzameri kanischer Dramatik im soziokulturellen Kontext der USA* [From James Baldwin to the Free Southern Theater. Positions of Black American Drama in the Sociocultural Context of the USA]. Bremen, 1979.

HELD, Jutta. Konzeptionen historischer Museen [Concepts of historical museums]. In: KUHN, Annette and Gerhard SCHNEIDER (ed.). Geschichte lernen im *Museum*. Düsseldorf, 1978, pp.11-31.

HENSE, Heidi. *Das Museum als gesellschaftlicher Lernort. Aspekte einer pädagogischen Neubestimmung* [The Museum as a Social Place of Learning. Aspects of a New Educational Concept]. Frankfurt a.M., 1985.

HERREMAN, Yani; Sergio GONZALES DE LA MORA and Guillermo SCHMIDHUBER. Mexico: Museums 1972-80. In: *Museum*, vol.32/1980 (3), pp.88-102.

HIGGS, John W.Y. The Role of Agricultural Museums in the Advanced and Developing Countries. In: Acta Museorum Agriculturae, vol.11/1976(1-2), pp.53-60.

HIGGS, John W.Y. and J. DRAKE. L'amélioration des ressources alimentaires dans le monde: un rôle pour les musées [The improvement of the world's food resources: a role for museums]. In: *Museum*, vol.24/1972(3), pp.138-144.

HINTEN, Wassilia von. *L'ecomusée. Ein museologisches Konzept zur Identität von und in Räumen* [The ecomuseum. A museological concept of identity of and in spaces]. In: Zeitschrift für Volkskunde, vol.78/1982, pp.70-76.

HOCHLARMARKER LESEBUCH KOHLE WAR NICHT ALLES. 100 JAHRE RUHRGEBIETSGESCHICHTE [HOCH LARMARK READER COAL WASN'T EVERYTHING. 100 YEARS OF HISTORY OF THE RUHR]. Oberhausen, 1981.

HOFER, Tamás. Gegenstände im dörflichen und städtischen Milieu. Zu einigen Grundfragen der mikroanalytischen Sachforschung [Objects in the rural and urban milieu. Some basic questions in microanalytic factual research]. In: WIEGELMANN, Günther (ed.). *Gemeinde im Wandel*. Münster, 1979, pp.113-135.

HOFFMANN, Hilmar. Kultur für alle. Perspektiven und Modelle [Cuture for All. Prospects and Models]. Frankfurt a.M., 1981.

HOLLENSTEIN, Erich. Stichwort Kulturpädagogik 1. Anmerkungen zu einem widerspenstigen Begriff [Note on cultural education 1. Notes on an unmanageable concept]. In: *Materialien zum Thema „Kulturpädagogik", Kulturpolitische Mitteilungen, special issue* Nr.5. Hagen, 1984, pp.5-8.

HONEGGER, Claudia (ed.). M. Bloch, F. Braudel, L. Febvre et al. Schrift und Materie der Geschichte. Vorschläge zur systematischen Aneignung historischer Prozesse [Writing and Subject Matter of History. Suggestions on the Systematic Acquisition of the Historical Process]. Frankfurt a.M., 1977.

HOPF, Christel. Soziologie und qualitative Sozialforschung [Sociology and qualitative social research]. In: HOPF, Christel and Elmar WEINGARTEN (ed.). *Qualitative Sozialforschung*. Stuttgart, 1979, pp.11-37.

HORKHEIMER, Max and Theodor W. ADORNO. Dialektik der Aufklärung [The Dialectic of Enlightenment]. Frankfurt a.M., 1984 (pocket book edition).

HOVANEC, Denis. L'écomusée et l'école régionale [The ecomuseum and the regional school]. In: *Muséambule*, vol.1/1987(1), p.10.

HOROWITZ, Donald L. Ethnic Identity. In: GLAZER, Nathanael and Daniel P. MOYNIHAN(ed.). *Ethnicity, Theory and Experience*. Cambridge, 1975, pp.111-140.

HUBENDICK, B. Museums and Environment. In: ICOM (ed.). *Le musée au service des hommes aujourd'hui et demain. Le rôle éducatif et culturel de musée*. Actes de la 9ième Conférence Générale de l'ICOM, Grenoble, 1971. Paris 1972, pp.39-48.

HUBERT, François. Ecomuseums in France: Contradictions and Distortions. In: *Museum*, vol.37/1985(4), pp.186-190.

HÜBNER, Irene. *Kulturzentren. Gesellschaftliche Ursachen, empirische Befunde, Perspektiven soziokultureller Zentren* [Cultural Center. Social Causes, Empirical Findings, Prospects of Socio cultural Centers]. Weinheim/Basel, 1981.

HÜBNER, Irene. *Kulturelle Opposition* [Cultural Opposition]. Munich, 1983.

HUDSON, Kenneth. *Museums for the 1980s. A Survey of World Trends*. Paris/ London, 1977.

HUTCHINSON, Louise D. *Report to the Board of Directors of the Anacostia Neighborhood Museum. Anacostia Studies: Past - Present - Future*. Washington D.C., 1975 (unpublished report).

HUTCHINSON, Louise. *The Anacostia Story (1608-1930)*. Washington D.C., 1977.

HUTCHINSON, Louise. *Out of Africa. From West African Kingdoms to Colonization*. Washington D.C., 1979.

HUTCHINSON, Louise. Arma Cooper. A *Voice From the South*. Washington D.C., 1982 (second printing).

ICOFOM (INTERNATIONAL COMMITTEE FOR MUSEOLOGY, ed.). *Museological*

Working Papers No.1. Stockholm, 1980.

ICOFOM (ed.). *Symposium Museum - Territory - Society. New Tendencies/New Practices*, London, July 1983. Stockholm, 1983.

ICOFOM (ed.). *Symposium "Museology and Museums*, Helsinki/Espoo, 9/6-16, 1987. Stockholm, 1987.

ICOM (INTERNATIONAL COUNCIL OF MUSEUMS, ed.). *Le musée au service des hommes aujourd'hui et demain. Le rôle éducatif et culturel de musée* [The museum in the service of the people of today and tomorrow. The educational and cultural role of the museum]. Actes de la 9ième Conférence Générale de l'ICOM, Grenoble, 1971. Paris, 1972.

ICOM. *The Role of Museums in Adult Education for Development.* Symposium in Malacca/ Kuala Lumpur, 12/14-18, 1972. Kuala Lumpur, 1973.

ICOM. ICOM Statutes, adopted by the Eleventh General Assembly of ICOM, Copenhagen, 7/14, 1974. Paris, 1974.

ICOM. *Assistant Secretary General's Report on the Seminar "Territory - Heritage - Community - Ecomuseums: Man and His Environment"*, Oaxtepec, Mexico-City, 10/15-18, 1984. Paris, 1984 (photocopied manuscript).

ICOM ASIA. *Problems and Possibilities of Museums in Asia and Oceania. First Asian Regional Assembly*, Teheran, 11/13-18, 1976. Teheran, 1976.

ICOM ASIA. *The Second Asian Regional Assembly*, Bangkok/Chingmai, 12/10-14, 1979. Bangkok, 1980.

INAH/DEPARTAMENTO DE MUSEOS ESCOLARES. *Tollocan.* Toluca Edo. Mexico D.F., 1978a.

INAH/DEPARTAMENTO DE MUSEOS ESCOLARES. *Xalisco.* Guadalajara. Jalisco. Mexico D.F., 1978b.

INAH/DEP ARTAMENTO DE MUSEOS ESCOLARES. *La Leona.* Monterrey N.L. Mexico D.F., 1979a.

INAH/DEPARTAMENTO DE MUSEOS ESCOLARES. *Piltzintli*. Cuautla-Morelos. Mexico D.F., 1979b.

ISAACS, Harold R. Basic Group ldentity: The ldols of the Tribe. In: GLAZER, Nathanael and Daniel P. MOYNIHAN (ed.). Ethnicity, Theory and Experience. Cambridge, 1975, pp.29-52.

ISAR, Yudhishthir Raj. Patrimoine industriei et société contemporaine. Colloque international tenu à l'Ecomusée de la communauté urbaine Le Creusot-Montceau-les-Mines [Industrial heritage and contemporary society. International colloquium held at the Ecomuseum of the Urban Community of Le Creusot-Montceau-les-Mines]. In: *Museum*, vol.29/1977(4). pp.240-242.

JACOBSON-WIDDING, Anita (ed.). *Identity: Personal and Socio-Cultural*. Uppsala, 1983a.

JACOBSON-WIDDING, Anita. Preface and Acknowledgements: Introduction. In: JACOB SON-WIDDING, Anita (ed.). Identity: Personal and Socio-Cultural. Uppsala, 1983b, pp.9-11; pp.13-32.

JEANSON, Francis. *L'action culturelle dans la cité* [Cultural Action in the City]. Paris, 1973.

JELINEK, Jan and Vera SLANA (ed.). *Sociological and Ecological Aspects in Modem Museum Activities*. Brno, 1979.

JOOSS, Rainer. Heimat Geschichte [Homeland history]. In: LANDESZENTRALE FÜR POLITISCHE BILDUNG BADEN-WÜRTTEMBERG (ed.). *Heimat heute*. Stuttgart/Berlin/ Cologne/Mainz, 1984, pp.60-72.

JOURNAL OF INDIAN MUSEUMS, vol.35/1979 (Special Issue on Museums and Rural Community).

KAL, Wilhelmina H. Museum and anthropology. In: KLOOS, Peter und Henri CLAESSEN (ed.). *Current Issues in Anthropology: the Netherlands*. Rotterdam, 1981, pp.156-167.

KASSAM, Yusuf. Wir sind alphabetisiert! Mit Teilnehmern im Dialog [We are literate! With participants in the dialog]. In: HINZEN, Heribert and Wolfgang LEUMER (ed.). *Erwachsenen bildung in der Dritten Welt.* Braunschweig, 1982, S.103-110.

KIDD, Ross. *The Popular Performing Arts, Non-Formal Education and Social Change in the Third World: A Bibliography and Review Essay.* The Hague, 1982.

KIDD, Ross and Nat COLLETTA (ed.). *Tradition for Development. Indigenous Structures and Folk Media in Non-Formal Education.* Berlin, 1980.

KINARD, John. *The Making of a Museum.* Washington D.C., 1968 (unpublished manuscript).

KINARD, John. Intermediaries Between the Museum and the Community. In: ICOM (ed.). *Le musée au service des hommes aujourd'hui et demain. Le rôle éducatif et culturel de musée. Actes de la 9ième Conférence Générale de l'ICOM,* Grenoble, 1971. Paris 1972a, pp.150-156.

KINARD, John. More Than Another Idea. *In: ANACOSTIA NEIGHBORHOOD MUSEUM. Anacostia Neighborhood Museum - 5th Anniversary.* Washington D.C., 1972b, pp.1-2.

KINARD, John. Mittler zwischen dem Museum und der Gemeinschaft [Intermediaries between the museum and the community]. In: *Neue Museumskunde,* vol.16/1973(1), pp.11-14.

KINARD, John. *Interview for the program "Contrechamp"/Radio Canada, 10/10, 1984,* St. Evariste, Quebec (unpublished transcription).

KINARD, John. *Preparatory Statement for the Anacostia Museum Executive Committee Review.* Washington D.C., 1984 (unpublished manuscript).

KINARD, John. The Neighborhood Museum as a Catalyst for Social Change. In: *Museum,* vol.37/1985(4), pp.217-223.

KINARD, John. *The Neighborhood Museum and the Inner City*. Washington D.C., no year (unpublished manuscript).

KINARD, John and Esther NIGHBERT. The Smithsonian's Anacostia Neighborhood Museum. In: *The Curator*, vol.11/1968(3), pp.190-205.

KINARD, John and Esther NIGHBERT. The Anacostia Neighborhood Museum. In: *Museum*, vol.2411972(2), pp.102-109.

KINNANE, Derk. Ein Museum für Geschichte und soziale Probleme [A museum for history and social problems]. In: UNESCO-Dienst Nr.8/1983, pp.9-13.

KINTER, Jürgen; Manfred KOCK and Dieter TRIELE. *Spuren suchen. Leitfaden zur Erkundung der eigenen Geschichte* [Looking for Tracks. Guiding Themes on Looking for Ones Own History]. Hamburg, 1985.

KLAUSEWITZ, Wolfgang (ed.). *Museumspadagogik. Mucf.n als Bildungsstätten* [Museum Education. Museums as Educational Institutions]. Frankfurt a.M., 1975.

KOHNERT, Dirk. *Neuer Wein in alten Schlauchen. Der soziokulturelle Ansatz in der Entwicklungstheorie* [New Wine in Old Bottles. The Sociocultural Approach in Development Theory]. Bielefeld, 1983.

KONARE, Alpha Oumar. *Réflexions sur des possibilités de développement des activités muséologiques dans les conditions socio-économiques actuelles du Mali* [Reflections on the Possibilities of Developing Museological Activities in the Current Socioeconomic Conditions of Mali]. Bamako, 1973 (unpublished manuscript).

KONARE, Alpha Oumar. The Prospects of a Development of Museum Activities in Mali. In: *ICOM Education*, Nr.7/1975-76, pp.8-13.

KONARE, Alpha Oumar. Birth of a Museum at Bamako, Mali. In: *Museum*, vol.33/1981(1), pp.4-8.

KONARE, Alpha Oumar. Ecomuseums for the Sahel: a Programme. In: *Museum*, vol.37/ 1985(4), pp.230-236.

KONATE; Moussa. *Les musées régionaux de Gao et de Sikasso* - Mali [The Regional Museums of Gao and Sikasso, Mali]. Lecture given at the Symposium on Local Museums in West Africa, Bamako, 5-20/23, 1985. Bamako, 1985 (unpublished manuscript).

KONRAD, Helmut. Neue Wege in Forschung und Vermittlung von Geschichte [New Ways of Researching and Transmitting History]. In: EHALT, Hubert (ed.). *Geschichte von unten. Fragestellungen, Methoden und Projekte einer Geschichte des Alltags*. Vienna/Cologne/Graz, 1984, pp.41-58.

KOPPAR, D.H. Museums of Art and Crafts (Including Cultural Anthropology) for Rural Community in India. In: *Journal of Indian Museums*, vol.35/1979, pp.30-37.

KORFF, Gottfried. Didaktik des Alltags. Hinweise zur Geschichte der Bildungskonzeption kulturhistorischer Mucf.n [Everyday didactics. Comments on the educational concept of museums of cultural history]. In: KUHN, Annette and Gerhard SCHNEIDER (ed.). Geschichte lernen im Museum. Düsseldorf, 1978, pp.32-48.

KORFF, Gottfried. Die ‚Ecomusées' in Frankreich - eine neue Art, die Alltagsgeschichte einzuholen [The ‚ecomusées' in France - a new way of grasping the history of everyday life] . In: MUSEUM DER STADT FRANKFURT AM MAIN (ed.). Die Zukunft beginnt in der Vergangenheit. Museumsgeschichte und Geschichtsmuseum. Frankfurt a.M., 1982, pp.78-88.

KRACHT, Haja. Mit den Grünen: Heimat bewahren und verwirklichen [With the Greens: to preserve and make real the homeland]. In: Kommune, vol.2/1984a(3), pp.31-41.

KRACHT, Haja. Zankapfel Heimat [Homeland: a bane of contention]. In: Kommune, vol.2/1984b(8), pp.57-60.

KRAMER, Dieter. Kulturgeschichtliche Mucf.n und Sammlungen im Hessischen Museums Entwicklungsplan [Cultural history museums and collections in the development plan of the Hess Museum]. In: BRÜCKNER, Wolfgang and Bernward DENECKE (ed.). *Volkskunde im Museum*. Würzburg, 1976, pp.177-217.

KRAMER, Dieter. Gedanken zur kulturpolitischen Bedeutung kleiner Mucf.n [Thoughts on the significance of small museums in cultural policy]. In: SCHARFE, Martin (ed.). *Museen in der Provinz*. Tübingen, 1982, pp.9-19.

KRAMER, Joan. The Anacostia Tree. In: *The Sunday Star and the Washington Daily News*, 5/13, 1973, no page number.

KRAPPMANN, L. *Soziologische Dimensionen der ldentitiät* [Sociological Dimensions of ldentity]. Stuttgart, 4 1975.

KUHN, Andrea and Jörg RICHARD (ed.). *Kulturarbeit und Sozialarbeit* [Cultural Work and Social Work]. Volume of materials for the working session on "Cultural Work and Social Work", Berlin, 2/28-3/2, 1980, organized and financed by the Senator for Science and Research in cooperation with the College for Social Work and Social Teaching in Berlin. Berlin, 1980.

KUHN, Annette and Gerhard SCHNEIDER (ed.) *Geschichte lernen im Museum* [Teaching History in the Museum]. Düsseldorf, 1978.

KULTURBEHÖRDE DER FREIEN UND HANSESTADT HAMBURG (ed.). *Leben im Stadtteil* [Living in the Neighborhood]. Hamburg, 1980.

KULTURBEHÖRDE DER FREIEN UND HANSESTADT HAMBURG (ed.) *Stadtteilkultur in Hamburg* [Neighborhood Culture in Hamburg]. Hamburg, 1982.

KULTURBEHÖRDE DER FREIEN UND HANSESTADT HAMBURG (ed.). *Kulturaktion Hamburg 1983. Lebendige Stadtteilgeschichte* [Cultural Action in Hamburg, 1983. Living Neighborhood History]. Hamburg, 1984.

KULTURKOOPERATIVE RUHR (ed.). *Kultur konkret. Projekte und Perspektiven alternativer Kulturarbeit* [Culture Concretely. Projects and Prospects of Alternative Cultural Work]. Unna/Hagen, 1984.

KULTURPÄDAGOGIK IN DER DISKUSSION [CULTURAL EDUCATION IN DISCUSSION). In: *Materialien zum Thema „Kulturpädagogik", Kulturpolitische Mitteilungen, Special lssue* Nr.5, Hagen, 1984, pp.3-5.

KULTURPOLITISCHE GESELLSCHAFT (ed.). *Stadtteilkultur. Zur Arbeit von Bürger hausem, Freizeitstätten und Kommunikationszentren* [Neighborhood Culture. The Work of Citizens' Houses, Leisure Places and Communication Centers]. Documents of Sessions of the Working Groups of Neighborhood Cultural Centers. Hagen, 1981.

KULTURPOLITISCHE GESELLSCHAFT (ed.). *Region und Regionalismus* [Region and Regionalism]. Hagen/Erlangen, 1982.

KULTURPOLITISCHE GESELLSCHAFT (ed.). *Lernen zwischen Sinn und Sinnlichkeit. Brauchen wir eine Kulturpädagogik?* [Learning Between Sense and Sensuality. Do We Need Cultural Education?]. Document Nr.24, Hagen, 1985.

KUNTZ, Andreas. D*as Museum als Volksbildungsstätte. Museumskonzeptionen in der Volksbildungsbewegung in Deutschland zwischen 1871 und 1918* [The Museum as an lnstitution of Popular Education. Concepts of the Museum in the Popular Education Movement in Germany Between 1871 and 1918]. Dissertation, Marburg, 2 1980.

LACOUTURE, Felipe. Ecomusée, typologie et caractéristiques [Ecomuseum, typology and characteristics]. In: ICOFOM (ed.). *Museum-Territory-Society. New Tendencies/New Practices*, Addenda 2. Stockholm, 1983, pp.2-5.

LACOUTURE, Felipe. *Museo, Política y Desarrollo en Vision Retrospectica y Presente: México y América Latina* [Museum, Politics and Development in Retrospective and in the Present: Mexico and Latin America]. Lecture given at the Fourth International Workshop of New Museology, Zaragoza, 10/18-24, 1987. Mexico D.F., 1987 (photocopied lecture manuscript).

LACOUTURE, Felipe. *Ecomuséologie: Amérique Latine, Mexique* [Ecomuseology: Latin America, Mexico]. Mexico City, o.J (unpublished manuscript).

LAFLEUR, Gérard. La Maison du «Fier-Monde» [The Maison du Fier-Monde]. In: *Musées*, vol.5/1982(1), pp.25-26.

LANDESZENTRALE FÜR POLITISCHE BILDUNG BADEN-WÜRTTEMBERG (ed.). *Heimat heute* [Homeland Today]. Stuttgart/Berlin/Cologne/Mainz, 1984.

LARRABEE, E. *Museum and Education*. Washington D.C., 1968.

LARRAURI, lker. The School Museum Programme in Mexico. In: *Museum*, vol.27/1975(2), pp.61-70.

LARRAURI, lker. Basic Policy of INAH Museums. In: BRYANT, Mavis (ed.). *Museums of Mexico and the United States: Policies and Problems*. Austin, 1977, pp.3-18.

LATAPI, Pablo and Felix CADENA. La educación no formal en Mexico. Un análisis de sus metodologías [Non-formal education in Mexico. An analysis of its methodoligies]. In: *Revista - Educación de Adultos*, vol.2/1984(4), pp.6-33.

LAURENT, Jean-Pierre. Des choses ou des gens: La réalité muséale en France [Things or people: the museum reality in France]. In: M.N.E.S. *Info bulletin*, Nr.1/1984, pp.1-3.

LECAT, J. Ph. Ecomusées - Musées de France [Ecomuseums: museums of France]. In: *Musées et Collections Publiques de France*, Nr.153/1981 (4), pp.134-135.

LEHALLE, Evelyne. Edito. In: M.N.E.S. *Info bulletin* Nr.0/no year (1984?), p.1.

LEIPOLD, Georg. Arbeitskreis 3. Formen und Inhalte kulturpolitischer Arbeit [Working Group 3. Forms and content of work on cultural policy]. In: KULTURPOLITISCHE GESELLSCHAFT (ed.). *Region und Regionalismus*. Hagen/Erlangen, 1982, pp.67-68.

LEMIEUX, Johanne. La Maison du Fier-Monde [The Maison du Fier-Monde]. In: *Bulletin de l'association des écomusées au Québec*, vol.3/1987(1), S.13-16.

LENGEN, Hajo van. Heimatmucf.n im regionalen Verbund und ihre ErschlieBung als Bildungsstätten im ländlichen Raum: Das Beispiel Ostfriesland [Heimatmuseums in the regional context and their development as institutions of education in rural areas: the example of Ostfriesland]. In: SCHARFE, Martin (ed.). *Museen in der Provinz*. Tübingen, 1982, pp.71-81.

LENZ, Siegfried. *Heimatmuseum*. Munich, 1983.

LEVESQUE, Carole. Le musée éclaté [The museum in pieces]. In: *Gazette*, vol.8/1975(3), pp.18-21.

LEVITA, David J. de. *Der Begriff der Identität* [The Concept of Identity]. Frankfurt a.M., 1971.

LICHTWARK, Alfred. Museen als Bildungsstätten [Museums as educational institutions]. In: *DIE MUSEEN ALS VOLKSBILDUNGSSTÄTTEN*. Berlin, 1904, pp.6-12.

LIEBKIND, Karmela. Dimensions of Identity in Multiple Group Allegiance. In: JACOBSON WIDDING, Anita (ed.). *Identity: Personal and Socio-Cultural*. Uppsala, 1983, pp.187-203.

DES LIENS SE TISSENT AVEC EAST-BROUGHTON [BONDS ARE WOVEN WITH EAST-BROUGHTON]. In: *Muséambule*, vol.1/1987(1), p.2.

LINDQUIST, Sven. *Gräv där du står. Hur man utforskar ett jobb*. Stockholm, 1978.

LINDQUIST, Sven. Grabe, wo du stehst. Die „BarfuB-Historiker" in Schweden [Dig where you are. The „barefoot historian" in Sweden]. In: *Demokratie- und Arbeitergeschichte*, ed. by the Franz-Mehring-Gesellschaft, Yearbook 3. Stuttgart, 1983, pp.9-13.

LINDQUIST, Sven. Creuse là ou tu es [Dig where you are]. In: *Objets pour la philosophie* Nr.11/1985, pp.73-83.

LOCAS, Claude. L'écomusée de la Haute-Beauce, école de liberté [The Ecomusée de la Haute Beauce, school of liberty]. In: *DIRECTION DE LA TECHNOLOGIE EDUCATIVE* (ed.). Trois expériences d'utilisation pédagogique des musées. Quebec, 1982, pp.85-115.

LUCKMANN, Benita. The Small Life-Worlds of Modern Man. In: LUCKMANN, Thomas (ed.). *Phenomenology and Sociology*. No place (New York?), 1978, pp.275-290.

LUCKMANN, Thomas. Remarks on Personal Identity: Inner, Social and Historical Time. In: JACOBSON-WIDDING, Anita (ed.). *Identity: Personal and Socio-Cultural*. Uppsala, 1983, pp.67-91.

LYND, Helen M. *On Shame and the Search for Identity*. New York, 1958.

MACKENSEN, Götz. *Science Education - a Heritage for Developing Countries? Lecture at the 12th ICOM General Conference*, Mexico City, November 1980. Bremen, 1980 (unpublished manuscript).

MACKENSEN, Götz. Ethnography and Science Museums in Developing Countries. In: Towards the Year 2000 - Perspectives of Science and Technology. *Proceedings of a 1980 Conference organized by ASTC and CIMUSET*. Washington D.C., 1981, pp.72-73.

MACKENSEN, Götz. *Indo-FRG-workshop on "museums for development" in Purulia*, West Bengal, India, from 11/30/1983 to 12/9/1983. Bremen, 1983 (unpublished manuscript).

MACKENSEN, Götz. *Museumsarbeit und appropriate technology - Entwurf eines Forschungs konzeptes fur den Bereich Südpazifik* [Museum Work and Appropriate Technology: Outline of a Research Concept for the South Pacific Region]. Bremen, no year(a) (unpublished manuscript).

MACKENSEN, Götz. *Überlegungen zur Frage der "angepaBten" Technologie* [Documentation on the Question of "Adapted" Technology]. Bremen, no year(b) (unpublished manuscript).

MADIGAN, Richard A. MUSE. The New Museum in Brooklyn's inner city where "Please, touch" is the motto. In: *The Museologist*, Nr.107/1968, pp.15-17.

LA MAISON DU FIER-MONDE. *Reglement de régie interne* [Internal Regulation]. Montreal, 1982a (unpublished manuscript).

LA MAISON DU FIER-MONDE. *Questionnaire*. Montreal, 1982b (unpublished manuscript).

LA MAISON DU FIER-MONDE. *Les débuts de la Maison du Fier-Monde* [The Beginnings of the Maison du Fier-Monde]. Montreal, 1982c (unpublished report).

LA MAISON DU FIER-MONDE. *Rapport final du projet. La Maison du Fier-Monde prend forme* [Final Report of the Project. The Maison du Fier-Monde takes shape]. Montreal, 1982d (unpublished report).

LA MAISON DU FIER-MONDE. *Visite dans Centre-Sud* [Visit to Centre-Sud]. Montreal, 1982e.

LA MAISON DU FIER-MONDE. *Rapport d'activités 11. 1.-28. 5. 1982* [Activities Report, 1/11 to 5/28/1982]. Montreal, 1982f (unpublished report).

LA MAISON DU FIER-MONDE. *Compte rendu de l'assemblée générale de l'Ecomusée de la Maison du Fier-Monde, tenue à Montréal, le 7 décembre 1982* [Report of the General Meeting of the Ecomusée de la Maison du Fier-Monde held at Montreal, December 7, 1982]. Montreal, 1982g (unpublished minutes).

LA MAISON DU FIER-MONDE. *Il était une fois le logement ouvrier* [Workers' housing] [text to the slide presentation]. Montreal, 1983a (unpublished manuscript).

LA MAISON DU FIER-MONDE. *Plan triennal d'orientation pour la Maison du Fier-Monde* [Triennial orientation plan for the Maison du Fier-Monde]. Montreal, 1983b (unpublished manuscript).

LA MAISON DU FIER-MONDE. *Projet de création d'emploi du MAC* (3. 1. 1983) [Project for the creation of MAC employment (1/3/83)]. Montreal, 1983c (unpublished manuscript).

LA MAISON DU FIER-MONDE. *Bilan du projet de création d'emploi du MAC (25. 2. 1983)* [Evaluation of the project for the creation of MAC employment (2/25/83]. Montreal, 1983d (unpublished manuscript).

LA MAISON DU FIER-MONDE. *Centre de Documentation. Rapport du travail effectué du 3. 1.-20. 5. 1983* [Documentation Center. Report of the Work Carried Out from 1/3/83 to 5/20/83]. Montreal, 1983e (unpublished report).

LA MAISON DU FIER-MONDE. *Bilan des visites guidées, du 25. 6.-4. 9. 1983* [Evaluation of guided tours from 6/25/83 to 9/4/83]. Montreal, 1983f (unpublished report).

LA MAISON DU FIER-MONDE. *Historique de l'Ecomusée de la Maison du Fier-Monde* [History of the Ecomusée de la Maison du Fier-Monde]. Montreal, 1984a (unpublished manuscript).

LA MAISON DU FIER-MONDE. *Entre l'usine et la cuisine* [Between the factory and the Kitchen]. Montreal, 1984b.

LA MAISON DU FIER-MONDE. *Bilan du projet de l'école Plessis* [Report of the Plessis School Project]. Montreal, 1984c (unpublished report).

LA MAISON DU FIER-MONDE. *L'an 1 de la Maison du Fier-Monde. Rapport final du projet Canada au travail* [Year One of the Maison du Fier-Monde. Final Report of the Canada au travail Project]. Montreal, 1984d (unpublished report).

LA MAISON DU FIER-MONDE. *Rues et pignons* [Streets and Gables]. Montreal. 1985a.

LA MAISON DU FIER-MONDE. *Assemblée générale, tenue à Montréal le 15 avril 1985* [General Meeting Held at Montreal on April 15, 1985]. Montreal, 1985b (unpublished minutes).

LA MAISON DU FIER-MONDE. *Rapport final d'activités du projet Canada au travail (novembre 1985)* [Final Report of the Activities of the Canada au travail Project]. Montreal, 1985c (unpublished report).

LA MAISON DU FIER-MONDE. *Rapport annuel 1984-85* [Annual Report 1985-85]. Montreal, 1985d (unpublished report).

LA MAISON DU FIER-MONDE. *Plan d'action 1985-86* [Action Plan 1985-86]. Montreal, 1985e (unpublished manuscript).

LA MAISON DU FIER-MONDE. *Communiqué, novembre 1985* [Communique, November 1985]. Montreal, 1985f (photocopied manuscript).

LA MAISON DU FIER-MONDE. *L'histoire d'un quarlier populaire: Le Centre-Sud de Montréal. Projet au fond des services aux collectivités du Ministere de l'enseignement supérieur de la Science et de la Technologie* [History of a People's Neighborhood: the Centre-Sud of Montreal. Background Project of the Community Services of the Ministry of Higher Education, Science and Technology]. Montreal, 1986a (photocopied manuscript).

LA MAISON DU FIER-MONDE. *Le quartier Centre-Sud... C'est toute une histoire* [The Centre-Sud Neighborhood... This is a Whole History] (leaflet III). Montreal, 1986b.

LA MAISON DU FIER-MONDE. *7 ans d'histoire ...* [Seven Years of History ...]. Montreal, 1987.

LA MAISON DU FIER-MONDE. *Leaflet 1. Montreal,* no year(a). LA MAISON DU FIER-MONDE. Leaflet II. Montreal, no year(b).

LA MAISON DU FIER-MONDE. *Le faubourg à m'lasse d'hier à demain* [The Faubourg à M'lasse from Yesterday to Tomorrow]. Montreal, no year(c) (unpublished manuscript).

LA MAISON DU FIER-MONDE/LES HABITATIONS COMMUNAUTAIRE CENTRESUD. *Agenda 1983: Centre-Sud, Montréal - d'hier à aujourd'hui* [Agenda 1983: Centre-Sud, Montreal - From Yesterday to Today]. Montreal, 1982.

MAKAMBILA, P. *Musées et Ethnographie en Afrique* [Museums and Ethnography in Africa]. In: Veröffentlichungen aus dem Übercf.-Museum, series B, vol.3/1973, pp.82-88.

MARCIL, Claude and Danielle THIBAULT. *Le printemps indien* [The Indian Spring]. Quebec, 1985.

MARSH, Caryl. A Neighborhood Museum that Works. In: *Museum News*, vol.47/1968(2), pp.11-16.

MAUGER, Louise. Le langage de l'outil [The language of the tool]. In: *Muséambule*, vol.1 / 1987(1), p.11.

MAURE, Marc-Alain. Thoughts on a New Function of the Museum. In: *ICOM Education*, Nr.8, 1977/78, pp.33-34.

MAURE, Marc-Alain. *Identité, écologie, participation : Nouveaux musées, nouvelle muséologie* [Identity, ecology, participation: new museums, new museology]. In: *Musées*, vol.8/1985a(1), pp.17-21.

MAURE, Marc-Alain. *Ecomusée et musée de plein air: l'exemple norvégien* [Ecomuseum and open-air museum: the Norwegian example]. In: Musées, vol.8/print. 1985b, pp.27-28.

MAURER, Friedemann. *Lebensgeschichte und Lernen* [Everyday history and learning]. In: MAURER, Friedemann (ed.). Lebensgeschichte und Identität. Frankfurt a.M., 1981, pp.105-132.

MAYNTZ, Renate; HOLM, Kurt and Peter HÜBNER. *Einführung in die Methoden der empirischen Soziologie* [Introduction to the Methods of Empirical Sociology]. Opladen, 1974.

MAYRAND, Pierre. *Le metier d'inventeur de musées* [The trade of inventor of museums]. In: Musées, vol.3/1980(4), pp.13-15.

MAYRAND, Pierre. Ecomusée rural/Ecomusée urbain [Rural ecomuseum/ urban ecomuseum]. In: Association du Patrimoine (ed.). *Compte rendu des Ateliers* 1.-4. 4. 1982. Quebec, 1982, pp.48-56.

MAYRAND, Pierre. Les défis de l'écomusée, un cas, celui de la Haute-Beauce [The challenges of the ecomuseum, one case, that of the Haute-Beauce]. In: ICOFOM (ed.). *Museum - Territory - Society. New Tendencies/New Practices. Addenda.* Stockholm, 1983, pp.23-27.

MAYRAND, Pierre. Ecomusées - Muséologie Nouvelle. Un Colloque International au Québec [Ecomuseums - new museology. An international colloquium at Quebec]. In: *Continuité*, Nr.23/ 1984a, p.28.

MAYRAND, Pierre. A new concept of museology in Quebec. In: *Muse*, vol.2/1984b(1), pp.33, 36-37.

MAYRAND, Pierre. La déclaration de Québec [The declaration of Quebec]. In: *Musées*, vol.8/1985a(1), p.12.

MAYRAND, Pierre. The new museology proclaimed. In: *Museum*, vol.37/1985b(4), pp.200- 201.

MAYRAND, Pierre. Décentraliser: pour quoi faire? [Decentralize: Why do it?]. In: *Muséam bule*, vol.1/1987(1), pp.1-2.

MAYRAND, Pierre. *Sens et enjeux de la muséologie populaire* [Meaning and stakes of people's museology]. No place, no year (unpublished manuscript).

MELEISEA, Malama. *Culture is not something you can eat: Some Thoughts on Cultural Preservation and Development in Oceania.* No place, no year (unpublished manuscript).

MENDEZ, Raul Andres. La educación permanente [Permanent education]. In: *Boletin Bimestral*, vol.1/1984(3), pp.9-11.

MENSCH, Peter van. *Museology and the Object as Data Carrier.* Leiden, 1984 (unpublished manuscript).

MEY, Wolfgang E. *Documentation of Ethnographic Material Culture in Bangla Desh from the Point of View of European Collections. Some Critical Considerations Concerning the Role of National Museums as opposed to Regional Museums.* Lecture give at the First Meeting of the Asian Subcommittee of ICME, Bangkok, 12/7-8, 1979. Berlin, 1979 (unpublished lecture manuscript).

MEY, Wolfgang E. *On Ideological Bondage of National Museums.* Lecture given at the ICAES Symposium "Current Trends in Museum Anthropology", Montreal, 1983. Berlin, 1983 (unpublished lecture manuscript).

MEYER, Gerd. Stadtteilarbeit - Kooperation im Stadtteil [Neighborhood work: cooperation in the neighborhood]. In: *Kulturpolitische Mitteilungen*, Nr.22/1983(3), pp.2-4.

MEYER, Rolf and Elke MEYER-HOOS. Heimatmuseum Wustrow [The Wustrow Heimat museum]. In: HEER, Hannes and Volker ULRICH (ed.). *Geschichte entdecken. Erfahrungen und Projekte der neuen Geschichtsbewegung.* Reinbek b. Hamburg, 1985, pp.381-385.

MIGUEL I SERRA, Dominique. A propos de la «Déclaration du Québec» [Regarding the «Declaration of Quebec»]. In: *Musées*, vol.8/1985(1), pp.14-16.

MINISTERE DES AFFAIRES CULTURELLES DU QUEBEC. *Musée et Muséologie au Québec. Nouvelles Perspectives* [Museum and Museology in Quebec. New Perspectives]. Quebec, 1979a.

MINISTERE DES AFFAIRES CULTURELLES DU QUEBEC. *Nouvelle perspectives de la muséologie et des musées au Québec* [New Perspectives of Museology and Museums in Quebec]. Quebec, 1979b (photocopied manuscript).

MINISTERE DES SPORTS, DES ARTS ET DE LA CULTURE. *Pour une nouvelle politique muséale au Mali* [For a Museum Policy in Mali]. Bamako, 1976 (unpublished manuscript).

MINISTERE DES SPORTS, DES ARTS ET DE LA CULTURE. *Projet: Création du Musée du Sahel à Gao* [Draft: Creation of the Museum of the Sahel at Goa]. Bamako, 1980 (unpublished manuscript).

MINOM. *Assemblée générale constitutive* (Teil 3), Lissabon, 9. 11. 1985 [General Founding Meeting (Part 3), Lisbon, 11/9/85]. Lisbon, 1985a (unpublished minutes).

MINOM. *Statuts* [Bylaws]. Lisbon, 1985b (unpublished manuscript).

MINOM. *Actes du 2ième atelier international, musées locaux/nouvelle muséologie, Lissabon, November 1985* [Proceedings of the Second International Workshop on Local Museums and New Museology]. Lisbon, 1986.

MISSION STATEMENT FOR THE ANACOSTIA NEIGHBORHOOD MUSEUM. Washington D.C., 1981 (unpublished manuscript).

MITSCHERLICH, Alexander. *Die Unwirtlichkeit unserer Städte. Anstiftung zum Unfrieden* [The Inhospitableness of Our Cities. Incitement to Strife]. Frankfurt a.M., 1974, chapter: Konfession zur Nahwelt. Was macht eine Wohnung zur Heimat?, pp.123-139.

MORIN, Edgar. *La méthode* [The Method], vol.1 «La Nature de la Nature». Paris, 1977.

MORIN, Edgar. *La méthode* [The Method], vol.2 «La Vie de la Vie». Paris, 1980.

MORLEY, Grace. Asian Contribution to Rural Communities. In: *Journal of Indian Museums*, vol.3511979, pp.23-26.

MOTA, Manuela da. Musées = Territoire = Société [Museums = Territory = Society]. In: ICOFOM (ed.). *Museum - Territory - Society. New Tendencies/ New practices*, Addenda 2, Stockholm, 1983. pp.14-18.

MUSE. *Journal of the Canadian Museums Association*, vol.5/1987(1).

MUSEAMBULE. *Informations à nos annonceurs et commanditaires* [Information for Our Announcers and Associates]. St. Evariste, 1986 (photocopied manuscript).

LE MUSEE DU QUEBEC EN DEVENIR. CONCEPT MUSEOLOGIE [THE MUSEUM OF QUEBEC IN THE FUTURE. A CONCEPT OF MUSEOLOGY]. Quebec, 1979.

MUSEE ET CENTRE REGIONAL D'INTERPRETATION DE LA HAUTE-BEAUCE. *Règlement No.1* [Regulation No. 1]. No place, 1979 (unpublished manuscript).

MUSEE ET CENTRE REGIONAL D'INTERPRETATION DE LA HAUTE-BEAUCE. *Musée de la Haute-Beauce* [Museum of the Haute-Beauce]. St. Evariste, 1982a (photocopied manuscript).

MUSEE ET CENTRE REGIONAL D'INTERPRETATION DE LA HAUTE-BEAUCE. *Collectif de treize village* [Community of Thirteen Villages]. St. Evariste, 1982b (unpublished manuscript).

MUSEE ET CENTRE REGIONAL D'INTERPRETATION DE LA HAUTE-BEAUCE. *Procès verbal de l'assemblée spéciale du musée et centre d'interprétation de la Haute-Beauce inc* [Minutes of the General Meeting of the Museum and Interpretation Center of the Haute-Beauce]. Lac Drolet, 1983a (unpublished minutes).

MUSEE ET CENTRE REGIONAL D'INTERPRETATION DE LA HAUTE-BEAUCE. *Projet de refonte des statuts et règlements du Musée et centre régional d'interprétation de la Haute-Beauce* [Draft Revision of Bylaws and Regulations of the Museum and Regional Interpretation Center of the Haute-Beauce]. St. Evariste, 1983b (unpublished manuscript).

MUSEE ET CENTRE REGIONAL D'INTERPRETATION DE LA HAUTE-BEAUCE. *L'écomusée de la Haute-Beauce, musée territoire* [The Ecomuseum of the Haute-Beauce, a Territorial Museum]. La Guadeloupe, no year.

DIE MUSEEN ALS VOLKSBILDUNGSSTÄTTEN. *Ergebnisse der 12. Konferenz der Centralstelle für Arbeiter-Wohlfahrtseinrichtungen* [Results of the 12th Conference for Worker and Social Services]. Reports of the Centralstelle für Arbeiter-Wohlfahrtseinrichtungen, Nr.25, Berlin, 1904.

MUSEEN SIND IM AUFWIND [MUSEUMS ARE IN AN UPDRAFT]. In: *Braunschweiger Zeitung*, 9/8/86, p.3.

MUSEES, vol.8/1985(1).

MUSEES, vol.18/1965(3) *Museums in Africa*.

MUSEUM, vol.25/1973(1/2) *Museum and Environment*.

MUSEUM, vol.25/1973(3) *The Role of Museums in Today's Latin America*.

MUSEUM, vol.31/1979(3) *Museum and Education*.

MUSEUM AIDS CITIZENS TO UNDERSTAND PROBLEMS. In: *U.S. Conference of Mayors Bulletin*, vol.2/1970(2), pp.10-11.

MUSEUMS AND ENVIRONMENT. In: *ICOM News*, vol.25/1972(3), pp.173-176.

MUSEUMS: THEIR NEW AUDIENCES. *A Report to the Department of Housing and Urban Development by a Special Committee of the American Association of Museums*. Washington D.C., 1972.

MUSEUMSVERBUND OSTFRIESLAND in cooperation with the Museumsfachstelle der Ostfriesischen Landschaft (ed.). *Kiek mal rin. Mucf.n und Sammlungen in Ostfriesland* [Kiek mal rin. Museums and Collections in Ostfriesland] (leaflet). Aurich, 1987.

MUTAL, Sylvio. *The Role of Museums in Contemporary Society in Latin America*. Lima, 1985 (unpublished manuscript).

MWANSA, Dickson. *Volkstheater als Medium: Anregungen aus Sambia* [People's Theater as Medium: Ideas from Sambia]. In: HINZEN, Heribert and

Wolfgang LEUMER (ed.).Erwachsenenbildung in der Dritten Welt. Braunschweig, 1982, pp.118-124.

NABAIS, António. Le musée municipal de Seixal: um écomusée de développement. In: *Museum*, vol 36/1984(2), S. 71-74.

NABAIS, António. The development of eco museums in portugal. In: *Museum*, vol 37/1985(4), S. 211-216.

NATIONAL COUNCIL OF SCIENCE MUSEUMS (Hg.). *Info-FRG Workshop on Science Museums for Rural Development*, Purulia 2.-7.-12. 1983. Calcutta, 1983

NATIONAL COUNCIL OF SCIENCE MUSEUMS (Hg). *Symposium held in October 1969 at the Swedisch Museum of Natural History in Stickholm*. Oslo/Bergen/Tromso, 1973.

NDIAYE, Pape Touname. *Etude pour un projet d'écomusée à Ziguinchor. Plan d'étude*. Ziguinchor (unveröff. Manuskript)

NEWSOM, Barbara Y. und Adele Z. SILVER (Hg.). The Art Museum as Educator. Berkley/Los Angeles/London, 1978.

NICHOLSON, E.M. Das Museum und die heutige Welt-Probleme der Umwelt. In: *Neue Museumskunde*, vol. 18/1975, S. 224-228.

NICOLAS, Alain. Du musée institutionnel au «nouveau» musée. In : M.N.E.S. *Info bullettin*, Nr. 2-3/1984, S. 1-2.

NICOLAS, Alain. (Hg., «sous la direction de»). *Nouvelles Muséologie*. Marseille, 1985.

NIEDERSÄCHSISCHER HEIMATBUND E.V. *Brauchen wir noch mehr Museen? Funktion, Struktur und Förderung musealer Einrichtingen in Niedersachen. Protokoll des 69. Seminars für Landersforshung, Raumplanung und Umweltschutz, Hannover, 20.-23.2. 1986*. Hannover, 1986 (vervielf. Bericht).

NIETHAMMER, Lutz (Hg.). *Lebenserfahrung und kollektives Gedächtnis. Die Praxis der "Oral History"*. Frankfurt a.M., 1980.

NIGAM, M.L. Integrating Museum into the Life of the Community. Vortrag gehalten auf dem *Subregional Seminar on Integrating Museums into the Life of the Community*, Seoul, 28.1.-1.2.1986. O.O., 1986 (unveröff. Vortragsmanuskript).

NOLL, Adolf; Helmut BLUMBACH und Margarete GOLDMANN. *Wie man keine Netze baut*. Gelsenkirchen, 1984.

NORTH AMERICAN INDIAN MUSEUMS ASSOCIATION. *Directory of North American Indian Museums & Cultural Centers* 1981. Niagara Falls, 1981.

NORTON OLIVER, Ruth. *Museums and Environment*. Washington D.C./ New York, 1971.

NOTES DE PARCOURS SUR LES FONCTIONS. *Le projet de Musée de Voisinage*. Montréal, 1981 (unveröff. Manuskript).

NOTTEGHEM, Patrice. Des Ecomusées dans le cadre des Parcs Naturels Régionaux. In : *CRACAP/ Informations*, NR. 2-3/1976, s: 5-8.

NYERERE, Julius Kambarage. Erwachsenenbildung und Entwicklung. In: HINZE, Heribert und Wolfang LEUMER (Hg.). *Erwachsenenbildung in der Dritten Welt*. Braunschweig, 1982, S. 33-43.

OELSCHLAGEL, Dieter. Gemeinwesenarbeit, Kulturarbeit, Heimat – sieben Thiesen. In: *Kulturpolitische Mitteilungen*, Nr. 23/1983(4), S. 10-11.

OHE, Werner von der u.a. *Die Bedetung sozio-kultureller Faktoren in der Entwicklungstheorie und-praxis. Forchungsberichte des Bundesministeriums fur wirtshaftliche Zusammenarbeit*. Köln, 1982.

OLOFSSON, Ulla Keding (Hg.). *Museums and children*. Paris, 1979.

OMOLEWA, Michael. Methodology of Adult Education and Ancillaries to it: Supporting Institutions: Library, Museums, Exhibitions, Fairs, Shows and

Festivals. In: BOWN, Lalage und S.H. Olu TOMORI (Hg.). *A Handbook of Adult Education for West Africa*. London, 1979, S 159-180.

ORDOÑEZ GARCIA, Coral. The Casa del Museo, Mexico City – An Experiment in Bringing the Museum to the People. In: *Museums*, vol. 27/1975(2), S. 71-77-

PANKOKE, Eckart. Dimensionen der Lebenswelt. Zur Kulturellen Indentität sozialer Räume. In: *Kultur und sozialer Räume. Rahmenbedingungen der Kulturpolitik*. Loccum, 1980, S. 68-83

PARCS CANADA. *Parc Canada, c'est quoi?* [What is a Canadian Park?]. Ottawa, 1981.

PAUL, Gerhard and Bernhard SCHOSSIG (ed.). *Die andere Geschichte* [The Other History]. Cologne, 1986a.

PAUL, Gerhard and Bernhard SCHOSSIG. *Geschichte und Heimat* [History and Homeland]. In:

PAUL, Gerhard and Bernhard SCHOSSIG (ed.). *Die andere Geschichte*. Cologne, 1986b, pp.15-32.

PEEL, J.D.Y. Was heißt „fremde" Glaubenssysteme verstehen? [What does it mean to understand a "foreign" system of beliefs?] In: KIPPENBERG, H.G. and B. LUCHESI, Luchesi (ed.). *Magie. Die sozialwissenschaftliche Kontroverse über das Verstehen fremden Denkens*. Frankfurt a.M., 1978, pp.150-173.

PELTIER SAN PEDRO, Rodolfo. INAH's Local and School Museums Program. In: BRYANT, Mavis (ed.). *Museums of Mexico and the United States: Policies and Problems*. Austin, 1977, pp.19-28.

PEÑA, Rosa Esther. *Breve análisis de la función educativa de los museos mexicanos*. [Brief analysis of the educational function of Mexican museums]. In: Comite Nacional Mexicano del INAH (ed.). III. Coloquio Nacional... Mexico D.F., 1984, no page numbers.

PEÑA, Rosa Esther and Marco A. ORTEGA ALMAZAN. *Los talleres básicos en la promoción de museos escolares y comunitarios* [Basic Workshops on the Promotion of School and Community Museums]. Mexico D.F., 1986 (photocopied manuscript).

PEREA G., José Luís. *Elementos sobre la investigación participativa en el museo comunitario* [Elements of Participative Research in the Community Museum]. Mexico D.F., 1986 (photocopied manuscript).

PESSOA, Miguel and Lino RODRIGO. *A Exposiçao "Em Defesa da Memêria de Todos e os Fundamentos para a Criação de um Ecomuseu" em Cond*eixa [The Exhibit "In Defense of Everyone's Memory and the Basis for Creating an Ecomusuem" in Condeixa]. Figueira da Foz, 1985.

PEUKERT, Detlev. Arbeiteralltag - Mode oder Methode? [The Worker's Everyday Life - Mode or Method?]. In: HAUMANN, Heiko (ed.). *Arbeiteralltag in Stadt und Land. Neue Wege der Geschichtsschreibung.* Berlin, 1982, pp.8-39.

PFEIL, Ethnologie und Völkerkundemuseum. *Ein Beitrag zur museumsethnologischen Diskussion* [A Contribution to the Discussion of Museum Ethnology]. Diss., Hohenschäftlarn, 1978.

PRAKASH, B. Science and Technology, Rural Development and the Science Centres. In: NATIONAL COUNCIL OF SCIENCE MUSEUMS (ed.). *Indo-FRG Workshop on Science Museums for Rural Development*, Purulia, 12/2-7, 1983. Calcutta, 1983, pp.24-27.

THE PROBLEMS OF MUSEUMS IN COUNTRIES UNDERGOING RAPID CHANGE. *Symposium organized by the International Council of Museums*, Neuchâtel, 6/17-25, 1962. Bern/Paris, 1964.

PROJET DE MUSSE DE VOISINAGE DE CENTRE-SUD OU DE MAISON DU FIER MONDE [PROJECT FOR THE MUSEUM OF THE CENTRE-SUD NEIGHBORHOOD OR THE MAISON DU FIER-MONDE]. Montreal, 1980 (unpublished manuscript).

PROJETS ET TACHES 1982 [PROJECTS AND TASKS 1982]. Montreal, 1982 (unpublished manuscript).

QUELQUES NOTES (CONTESTABLES) SUR LA RECHERCHE EN VUE D'UN MUCF. DE VOISINAGE DANS CENTRE-SUD [SOME (CONTESTABLE) NOTES ON RESEARCH WITH A VIEW TOWARD A NEIGHBORHOOD MUSEUM IN CENTRESUD]. Montreal, no year (1980) (unpublished manuscript).

QUERRIEN, Max. Taking the Measure of the Phenomenon. In: *Museum*, vol.37/1985(4), pp.198-199.

RAMAMOORTHY, S. Work of Science Museums for Rural Community. In: *Journal of Indian Museums*, vol.35/1979, pp.113-116.

RAMOS GALICIA, Yolanda. The Museums and the Community. In: BRYANT, Mavis (ed.). *Museums of Mexico and the United States: Policies and Problems*. Austin, 1977, pp.29-40.

RASKE, Peter. Was verstehen wir unter Jugendkunstschulen und kulturpädagogischen Einrichtungen für Kinder und Jugendliche? [What do we mean by youth art schools and cultural educational establishments for children and youth?]. In: KULTURPOLITISCHE GESELL SCHAFT (ed.). *Lernen zwischen Sinn und Sinnlichkeit. Brauchen wir eine Kulturpädagogik? Document Nr.24*. Hagen, 1985, pp.17-18.

RATZEL, Friedrich. *Anthropogeographie* [Anthropogeography]. vol.I, Stuttgart, (1909. REA, Paul Marshall. The Museum and the Community. Lancaster, 1932.

RECOMMENDATIONS PRESENTED TO THE UNESCO BY THE ROUND TABLE OF SANTIAGO (CHILE). In: Museum, vol.25/1973(3), p.200 (Appendix 3).

REJHOLEC, Jutta. *Zur Umstrukturierung kolonialer Kulturinstitutionen - Probleme und Perspektiven im Senegal* [Restructuring of Colonial Cultural Institutions - Problems and Prospects in Senegal]. Diss., Bremen, 1984.

RENAUD, Paule. *L'écomusée et son application au* Québec [The Ecomuseum and its Application to Quebec]. Montreal, 1985 (unpublished master's thesis).

REPORT OF THE ADVISORY PANEL ON THE ANACOSTIA NEIGHBORHOOD MUSEUM TO THE SECRETARY OF THE SMITHSONIAN INSTITUTION. Washington D.C., 1979 (unpublished report).

RESOLUTIONS ADOPTED BY THE ROUND TABLE OF SANTIAGO (CHILE). In: *Museum*, vol.25/1973(3), pp.198-200 (Appendix 2).

RICHARD, Jörg. Stichwort Kulturpädagogik 3. Kultur vom Subjekt aus - Einspruch gegen die „Kultur-als..."-Pädagogik [Summary of Cultural Education 3. Cultural from the subject - claim against „culture as..."]. In: *Materialien zum Thema „Kulturpädagogik", Kulturpolitische Mitteilungen*, special issue Nr.5. Hagen, 1984, pp.10-13.

RIGAUD, Jacques. *La culture pour vivre* [Culture for Living]. Paris, 1975.

RIPLEY, Dillon S. Museums in North America. In: *Journal of World History*, vol.14/1972(1), pp.176-186.

RISTAU, Malte (ed.). Identität durch Geschichte [Identity through History]. *Document Nr.12 of the Kulturpolitische Gesellschaft*. Marburg, 1985.

RIVARD, René. *Le musée écologique* [The Ecological Museum]. Paris, 1979.

RIVARD, René. *Le Musée-Territoire* [The Territorial Museum]. Paper given at the Canadian Museums Association's Annual Conference, Ottawa, May 1981. No place, 1981 (unpublished manuscript).

RIVARD, René. Les centres d'interprétation: historique et perspectives de développement [Interpretation centers: history and prospects for development]. In: *Conseil des Monuments et Sites du Québec Bulletin* Nr.16/1982, pp.9-15.

RIVARD, René. L'interprétation: définitions, types et méthodes [Interpretation: definitions, types and methods]. In: LA SOCIETE DES MUCES

QUEBECOIS (ed.). *Techniques d'inter prétation historique.* Montreal, 1983a, pp.4-19.

RIVARD, René. *The Future of Museology.* Québec, 1983b (unpublished manuscript).

RIVARD, René. *Que le musée s'ouvre... ou vers une nouvelle muséologie : les écomusées et les musées 'ouverts'* [Let the Museum Open Up... or Toward a New Museology: Ecomuseums and «Open» Museums]. Quebec, 1984a (photocopied manuscript).

RIVARD, René. *Vers une muséologie nouvelle ...* [Toward a New Museology]. Lecture give at the Congres annuel de l'AMC-SMQ, Québec, 5/25, 1984. No place, 1984b (unpublished manuscript).

RIVARD, René. *Redéfinir la Muséologie* [Redefining museology]. In: Continuité, Nr.23/1984c, pp.19-22.

RIVARD, René. *Avataq Museum and Cultural Centre. Feasibility Study.* Quebec, 1985a (unpublished study).

RIVARD, René. Ecomuseums in Quebec. In: *Museum*, vol.37/1985b (4), pp.202-205.

RIVERA FERREIRO, M. Lucia. *La planeación del trabajo promocional* [Planning Promotional Work]. Mexico D.F., 1986 (photocopied manuscript).

RIVIERE, Georges-Henri. Un musée de l'espace et du temps [A museum of space and time]. In: *Cevennes*, Nr.1/1972a, pp.25-29.

RIVIERE, Georges-Henri. Le musée de plein air des Landes de Gascogne. Expérience française d'un musée de l'environnement [The open-air museum of the Landes de Gascogne. A French experience of an environmental museum]. In: *Ethnologie française*, vol.1/ 1 972b, pp.87-95.

RIVIERE, Georges-Henri. The museum as a monitoring instrument: Role of museums of art and of human and social sciences. In: *Museum*, vol.25/1973(1-2), pp.38-40.

RIVIERE, Georges-Henri. *Muséologie générale contemporaine, Leçon 1: Le musée à travers les ages* [Contemporary General Museology, Lesson 1: the Museum Through the Ages]. Paris, 1/12/74 (unpublished manuscript).

RIVIERE, Georges-Henri. Weltweite Tendenzen des heutigen Museums [Worldwide Tendencies of Today's Museum]. In: AUER, Hermann (ed.). *Das Museum in technischen und sozialen Wandel unserer Zeit.* Report of an international symposium organized by the ICOM National Committee for the German Federal

RIVIERE, Georges-Henri. L' Ecomusée. In: *CRACAP/Informations*, Nr. 2-3/1976, S. 15.

RIVIERE, Georges-Henri. *Dossier Ecomusée.* Paris, 25. 10. 1977 (unveröff. Manuskript).

RIVIERE, Georges-Henri. *Apperçu historique.* Paris, 1979 (unveröff. Manuskript).

RIVIERE, Georges-Henri. *Dossier Ecomusée.* Paris 26. 3. 1980 (unveröff. Manuskript).

RIVIERE, Georges-Henri. The ecomuseum - an evolutive definition. In: *Museum*, vol.37 / 1985 (4), S. 182-183.

ROBBINS, Michael W. The Neighborhood and the Museum. In: *Curator*, vol.14 / 1971 (1), S. 63-68.

ROBBINS, Richard H. Identity, Culture, and Behavior. In: HONIGMAN, J. (Hg.). *Handbook of Social and Cultural Anthropology.* New York, 1973, S. 1199-1222.

RODRIGUEZ, Joseph. *The "New" Museum Project, Teil I und II.* Washington D.C., 1984 (unveröff. Studie).

ROHMEDER, Jürgen. *Methoden und Medien der Museumsarbeit. Pädagogische Betreuung der Einzelbesucher im Museum.* Köln, 1977.

RÖHRBEIN, Waldemar. *Museen und Sammlungen in Niedersachsen und Bremen.* Hannover, 1986.

THE ROLE OF MUSEUMS IN CHANGING ASIAN SOCIETIES WITH SPECIAL REFERENCE TO ITS ROLE IN PRESERVING AND STRENGTHENING TRADITIONAL, RURAL ANO TRIBAL CULTURES. *Regional Symposium organized by the Department of national Museums of Sri Lanka in honour of the Centenary of the Colombo Museum,* Colombo, 10. -20. 12. 1977. New Delhi, 1978.

ROLLER, Hans-Ulrich. Aspekte des Leitthemas. ln: BRÜCKNER, Wolfgang und Bernward DENECKE (Hg.). *Volkskunde im Museum.* Würzburg, 1976, S. 19-57.

ROSENBUSH METHNER, Ellen. *Handbook of Outreach Programs for Museum Educators.* Tulsa, 1978.

ROSNAY, Joel de. *Le macroscope. Vers une vision globale,* Paris, 1975.

ROTH, Martin. *Heimatmuseum 1918-1945. Eine deutsche Institution im Wandel der politischen Systeme.* Diss., Tübingen, 1987a.

ROTH, Martin. Heimatmuseum und Nationalpolitische Erziehung. In: GERNDT, Helge (Hg.). *Volkskunde und Nationalsozialismus. Referate und Oiskussionen einer Tagung der Deutschen Gesellschaft für Volkskunde,* München, 23. 25. 10. 1986, München, 1987b, S. 185-199.

ROY, Johanne. L' écomusée, une formule remplie de promesses. ln: *Le Soleil,* 26. 6, 1985, S. B11.

ROY, Michel. Animation muséologique en milieu urbain. ln: *Bulletin de l' Association des écomusées du Québec,* vol.3 / 1987 (1), S. 4-8.

SAMUEL, Raphael. *People's History and Socialist Theory.* London, 1981.

SAMUEL, Raphael. Oral History in Großbritannien. In: NIETHAMMER, Lutz (Hg,). *Lebenserfahrung und kollektives Gedächtnis. Die Praxis der „Oral History".* Frankfurt a.M., 1985, 5, 75-99.

SCHARFE, Martin (Hg.). *Museen in der Provinz. Strukturen, Probleme, Tendenzen, Chancen.* Tübingen, 1982.

SCHILLING, Heinz. Region - kulturelles Selbstverständnis. 5 Fragen und 3 Thesen. In: KULTURPOLITICHE GESELLSCHAFT (Hg.). *Region und Regionalismus.* Hagen/Erlangen, 1982, S. 25-36.

SCHMIDT, Aurel. *Der Fremde bin ich selber.* Basel, 1982,

SCHMITZ, H. Walter. *Zum Problem der Objektivität in der völkerkundlichen Feldforschung.* In: *Zeitschrift für Ethnolgie,* vol.101/1976(1), S. 1-40.

SCHNEIDER, Klaus. *Ethnologische Museen in Afrika - Anspruch und Wirklichkeit einer Institution Köln,* 1982 (unveröff. Magisterarbeit).

SCHÖTTLER, Peter. Von den „Annales" zum „Forum Histoire", In: HEER, Hannes und Volker ULLRICH (Hg.). *Geschichte entdecken. Erfahrungen und Projekte der neuen Geschichtsbewegung.* Reinbek b. Hamburg, 1985, S. 58-71.

SCHWEIZER, Birgit und Gilles PIOT. *Unterrodach. Flößerdorf im 19. Jahrhundert. Begleitheft zur Ausstellung.* o. o., o. J.

SCHWENCKE, Olaf (Hg.). *Museum - Verklärung oder Aufklärung. Kulturpolitisches Kolloquium zum Selbstverständnis der Museen. Dokumentation einer Tagung der Evangelischen Akademie Loccum, 6.-8. 9. 1985.* Loccum, 1986.

SEIDENSTICKER, W. *Museums in Africa.* o. o., 1980 (unveröff. Manuskript).

SEITHEL, Friderike. *Action Anthropology. Eine Darstellung ihrer Entwicklung und Grundzüge anhand nordamerikanischer Projekte.* Mainz, 1986.

SILVESTER, J.W.H. The Fragmented Museum Project at Le Creusot. In: *Museums Journal,* vol. 75/ 1975 (2), S. 83 -84.

SILVESTER, J.W.H. An Education Function Built into a New Technical Museum. In: *Museums Journal,* vol.77 / 1977 (3), S. 134.

SMITHSONIAN INSTITUTION. *Official Guide to the Smithsonian*. Washington D.C., 1981 (rev. ed.).

SMITHSONIAN INSTITUTION. *The Smithsonian Experience*. Washington D.C., 1984a (5th printing).

SMITHSONIAN INSTITUTION. *Smithsonian Institution Visitor Count Statistics, 1981-1984*. Washington D.C., 1984b (unveröff. Manuskript).

SMITHSONIAN INSTITUTION. *Anacostia Neighborhood Museum Exhibit Design and Production Laboratory*. Washington D. C., o. J. b (unveröff. Bericht).

SMITHSONIAN INSTITUTION. *Proposal for the Anacostia Neighborhood Museum Exhibits Design and Production Laboratory*. Washington D. C., o. J. b (unveröff. Bericht).

SÖRENSON, Ulf und Ann-Charlotte BACKLUND. *Järn bryter bygd. Ekomuseum Bergslagen berättar i landskapet*. Skinnskatteberg, 1986.

SOLA, Tomislav. Ohne Titel. In: ICOFOM (Hg.). *Museum - Territory - Society. New Tendencies/New Practices, Addenda 2*. Stockholm, 1983, S. 19-36.

SOLA, Tomislav. The concept and Nature of Museology. In: *Museum*, vol.39 /1987 (1), S. 45-49.

LA SOCIETE DES MUSEES QUEBECOIS. *La part des musées*. Montréal, 1982 (unveröff. Bericht).

LA SOCIETE DES MUSEES QUEBECOIS. *Les musées. Etat de la situation, la rançon du progrès*. Montréal, 1984 (unveröff. Bericht).

SOUCY-ROY, Carmen. *Le quartier Ste. Marie 1850-1900*. Montréal, 1977 (unveröff. Manuskript).

SOZIALB KULTURARBEIT UND RULTURELLE SOZIALARBEIT. KONZEPTE, SELBSTVERSTÄNDNIS UND PRAXIS. XVI. *Loccumer Kulturpolitisches Kolloquium. Loccum*, 24.-26. 2. 1984. Loccum, 1984.

SPICKERNAGEL, Ellen und Brigitte WALBE (Hg.). *Das Museum. Lernort contra Musentempel.* GieBen, 1976.

SPRANGER, Eduard. *Der Bildungswert der Heimatkunde.* Berlin, 1923.

STEEN, Jürgen. Didaktische Aspekte einer Theorie des Historischen MUseums. In: KUHN, Annette und Gerhard SCNNEIDER (H g.). *Geschichte lernen im Museum.* Düsseldorf, 1978, S. 49-81.

STEINMEIER, Romy. *Das Heimatmuseum Gestern und Heute. Exempla- rische Darstellung des Modellversuchs „MOBiLE" in Ostfriesland.* Hamburg, 1986 (unverôff. Magisterarbeit).

STEVENSON, Sheila. The Territory as Muséums: New Muséum Directions in Québec. In: *Curator,* vol.25/1982(1) , S.5-16.

STEVENSON, Sheila. *What happened at the "premier atelier international 1984, écomusées/nouvelle muséologie du 7 au 13 octobre, 1984"?* Halifax, 1984 (unverôff. Manuskript).

STEVENSON, Sheila. Balancing the Scales: Old Views and a New Muse. In: *Muse,* vol.5/1987(1), S.30-33.

STILLER, Wolfgang und Dieter THIELE (Hg.). *Stadtteil-Bilderbo- gen. Hamburger Quartiere und ihre Geschichte.* Hamburg, 1985.

STRANSKY, Zbynek. Muséum - Territory - Society. In: ICOFOM (Hg.). *Muséum - Territory - Society. New Tendencies/NewPractices.* Stockholm, 1983, S.27-33.

STRAUSS, Anselm. *Mirrors and Masks. The Search for Identity.* Glencoe, 1959.

STUBENVOLL, Willi. Alltagskultur im Muséum. Ein Beispiel. In: KÔSTLIN, Konrad und Hermann BAU8XNGER (Hg.). *Heimat und Identitàt.* Kiel, 1980, S.135-146.

SUD, P.D. Muséums and Rural Communities. In: *Journal of Indian MUseums,* vol.35/1979, S.38-45.

SYGU8CH, Frank u.a. *Das Problem der sozialen Konstruktion historisch dokumentierter Wirklichkeit. Auswahlbibliographie.* Linden, o.J. (1985?).

TABORSKY, Edwina. *Monograph „Régional Structures".* Ottawa, 1978 (unveröff. Bericht).

TABORSKY, Edwina. *The Sociostructural Rôles of Industrialism, Literacy and Muséums.* Diss., Toronto, 1982.

TABORSKY, Edwina. Syntax and Society. In: *Canadian Review of Sociology and Anthropology,* vol.22/1985(1), S.80-92.

TALALLA, Ida R. *Dezentralization of Muséums. A Muséums Collaborative Project.* New York, 1974 (unveröff. Manuskript).

TEDLOCK, Dennis. Die analogische Tradition und die Anfänge einer dialogischen Anthropologie. In: *Trickster,* Nr.12-13/1985, S.62-74.

TERRADAS, Jaume A. Ecologie, environnement, éducation. Le rôle des musées. In: ICOFOM (Hg.). *Muséum - Territory - Society. New Tendencies/New Practices.* Stockholm, 1983, S.8-14.

TERUGGI, Mario E. The Round Table of Santiago (Chile). in: *Muséum,* vol.25/1973(3), S.129-133.

THOMAS, Larry Erskine. *Center for Anacostia Studies. Final Report.* Washington D.C., 1972 (unveröff. Bericht).

THURN, Hans-Peter. *Grundrisse einer Anthropologie des Alltags- lebens.* Stuttgart, 1980.

TORRE, Marta de la und Luis MONREAL. *Muséums: An Investment for Development.* Paris, 1982.

TOÜCET, Pablo. Le musée de Niamey et son environnement, in: *Muséum,* vol.24/1972(4), S.204-207.

TOÜCET, Pablo. An Economie Rôle for Muséums in the Developing Countries. In: *Muséums and Monuments*, Nr.15/1973 (Muséums, Imagination and Education), S.31-42.

TRICKSTER-REDAKTION. Ethnologische Erfahrung und Imagination. In: *Trickster*, Nr.12-13/1985, S.12-18.

TROTTIER, Louise. *Nouvelles perspectives dans la muséologie au Québec*. Québec, 1984 (unveröff. Manuskript).

TRUDEL, Jean. *Le réseau des musées de la Beauce*. Etude de faisabilité et de planification. Montréal, 1984.

UBICACION DEL DEPARTAMENTO DE SERVICIOS EDUCATIVOS, MD8EOS ESCOLARES Y COMUNITARIOS, DENTRO DES INSTITUTO NACIONAL DE ANTROPOLOGIA B HISTORIA. In: *Boletin Bimestral* (DESEMEC), vol.1/1984(1), S.6-8.

ÜCHE-OKEKE, Ego. *The Muséum as an Educational Resource Centre. The Rôle of the Living Museum/Gallery System in the Nigérian Educational Progress*. Nsukka, 1981 (unveröff. Manuskript).

ULLRICH, Volker. Alltagsgeschichte. über einen neuen Ge- schichtstrend in der Bundesrepublik. In: *Neue politische Literatur*, vol.29/1984, S.50-71.

UNESCO. Folk Media and Mass Media: *Their Integrated Use in Community Programmes and Family Planning*. London, 1972.

UNESCO. World Conférence on Cultural Policies, Mexico City, 26. 7.-6. 8. 1982, *Final Report*. Paris, 1982.

VARINE, Hugues de. A 'Fragmented' Muséum: the Muséum of Man and Industry, Le Creusot-Montceau-les-Mines. In: *Muséum*, vol.25/ 1973(4), S.242-249.

VARINE, Hugues de. *La Culture des Autres*. Paris, 1976a.

VARINE, Hugues de (Varine-Bohan). Le musée moderne : conditions et problèmes d'une rénovation. In : *Muséum*, vol.28/l976b (3), S.126-139.

VARINE, Hugues de. A Grass-Roots Révolution: Community Initiative in Culture. In: *Culture*, vol.5/1978a(1), S.62-86.

VARINE, Hugues de. L'écomusée. In: *Gazette*, vol.ll/1978b(2), S.28-40.

VARINE, Hugues de. Le musée peut tuer ou faire vivre. In: *Techniques et Architecture*, Nr.326/1979, S.82-83.

VARINE, Hugues de. Le patrimoine industriel et les travailleurs. In: *Les Cahiers de l'Animation*, Nr.27/1980, S.25-33.

VARINE, Hugues de. *Persônliche Mitteilung an René Rivard* von 9. 1. 1983. O.O., 1983a (unverôff. Manuskript).

VARINE, Hugues de. La problématique de l'écomusée. In: GROUPE DE RECHERCHE EN PATRIMOINE (Hg.). *Journée d'étude sur les écomusées. Document de travail. Université du Québec à Montréal, 26.5.* 1983. Montréal, 1983b, o.S. (vervielf. Manuskript)

VARINE, Hugues de. *Musées pluridisciplinaires et interdisciplinaires : Ecomusées*. Paris, 1983c (unverôff. Manuskript).

VARINE, Hugues de. La Historia de los Museos. In: *Boletin Bimestral* (DESEMEC), vol.1/1984(3), S.4-8.

VARINE, Hugues de. Notes en forme d'avant-propos. In: NICOLAS, Alain (Hg.). *Nouvelles muséologies*. Marseille, 1985, S.3-4.

VARINE, Hugues de. *Rapport de voyage au Québec (13.-17. 5. 1987)*. Paris, 1987a (unverôff. Bericht).

VARINE, Hugues de. *Politiques muséales et stratégies de développement local et national. De l'exhibitionnisme à la communication sociale*. Vortragsrésumé in Abwesenheit des Verfassers vorgelegt beim «4ième atelier international de nouvelle muséologie», Zaragoza, 18.-24. 10. 1987. Paris, 1987b (vervielf. Vortragsmanuskript).

VARINE, Hugues de. *The Muséum in the Forth Dimension*. O.O., o.J. (unveröff. Manuskript).

VATSYAYAN, Kapila Malik. *Some Aspects of Cultural Policies in India*. Paris, 1972.

VEILLARD, Jean Yves. Problèmes du Musée d'histoire à partir de l'expérience du Musée de Bretagne, Rennes. In: *Muséum*, vol.24/ 1972(4), S.193-203.

VEILLARD, Jean-Yves. Observations et reflexions. In: ICOTOM (Hg.). *Muséum - Territory - Society. New Tendencies/New Practices*, Addenda 2. Stockholm, 1983a, S.9-10.

VEILLARD, Jean-Yves. 'Le Musée de Bretagne, Musée d'Histoire, Musée de Combat. In: ICOTOM (Kg.). *Muséum - Territory - Society. New Tendencies/ Nev Practices*. Stockholm, 1983b, S.54-60.

VEILLARD, Jean-Yves. "The valueless object". In: *Muséum*, vol.37/1985(4), S.191-193.

VÔLGER, Gisela. Fast eine Volksbewegung - Das Musée National du Niger in Niamey. In: *Museumskunde*, vol.43/1978(2), S.83-86.

VOLKERKÜNDEMÜSEEN HORGEN - AUFÔABE» UNO 2IELE. *Sonderband der Zeitschrift für Ethnologie*, vol.101/1976 (2).

VOSÔEN, Rüdiger u.a. Bilanz und Zukunft der Volkerkundeitiuseen. In: *Zeitschrift für Ethnologie*, vol.101/1976(2), S.198-205.

VUILLEUMIER, Jean-Pierre. Muséum Programming and Development Policy. In: *Muséum*, vol.35/1983a(2), S.94-97.

VUILLEUMIER, Jean-Pierre. *Das\Musée du Sahel in Gao (Mali-West- afrika)*. Killwangen, 1983b (unyeröff. Manuskript).

WEIL, Stephen. Questioning Some Premises. In: *Muséum News*, vol.64/1986(5), S.20-27.

WEHLER, Hans-Ulrich. *Geschichte als Historische Sozialwissenschaft*. Frankfurt a.M., 31980.

WEHLER, Hans-Ulrich. Geschichte - von unten gesehen. Wie bel der Suche nach dem Authentischen Engagement mit Methodik verwechselt wird. In: *Die Zeit*, 3. 5. 1985, S.69.

WEHLING, Hans-Georg. Vorwort. In: LANDE8ZENTRALE FÜR POLITISCHE BILDüNG BADEN-WÜRTTEMBERG (Hg.). *Heimat heute. Stuttgart/Berlin/Kôln/Mainz*, 1984, S.7-9.

WEIS, Hélène. *Présentation des projets de l'Association des Amis de Goerges-Henri Rivière*. Vortrag gehalten im Rahmen des «2ième atelier international de nouvelle muséologie - traditions et perspectives nordiques», Totn, 14.-19. Sept. 1986. Paris, 1986.

WESCHENFELDER, K. und W. ZACHARIAS. *Handbuch der Museumspâdagogik. Orientierungen und Methoden für die Praxis*. Düsseldorf, 1981.

WICH-HEITER, Gerhard. Das FlôBermuseum Unterrodach. In: *Volkskunst*, vol.9/1986(2), S.5-10.

WOLZOGEN, Wolf von. Kultur von unten - Anmerkungen zum Stadtteilmuseum. In: MUSEUM DER STADT FRANKFURT AM MAIN (Hg.). *Die Zukunft beginnt in der Vergangenheit: Museumsgeschichte und Geschichtsmuseum*. Frankfurt a. M., 1982, S.51-77.

WOODS, James und William H. MC WHINNEÏ. *A Curator for the Future/ Cultural Democracy*. Paper read at the Annual Meeting of the Association of American Muséums, Mexico City, 21. 6. 1972. 0.0., 1972 (unverôff. Manuskript).

ZACHARIAS, Wolfgang. Stichwort Kulturpàdagogik 2. Ein neuer Anlauf? In: *Materialien zum Thema „Kulturpàdagogik", Kulturpolitische Mitteilungen*, Beiheft Nr.5. Hagen, 1984a, S.8-10.

ZACHARIAS, Wolfgang. Soziokulturelle Animation als Wiedergewin- nung sinnlich-gegenstàndlicher Erfahrung. In: *Materialien zum Thema „Kulturpàdagogik", Kulturpolitische Mitteilungen, Beiheft* Nr.5. Hagen, 1984b, S.20-23.

ZANG, Gert. *Die unaufhaltsame Annàherung an das Einzelne. Reflexionen über den theoretischen und praktischen Nutzen der Régional- und Alltagsgeschichte.* Konstanz, 1985.

ZIMMERMANN, Harm-Peer. Heimatutopie und politischer Regionali- smus. In: *Nordfriesland,* Nr.65/1983(3), S.16-20.

ZU VIELE MÜSEEN AUF DEM LANDE. Fachleute warnen vor inflationàrer Gründungswelle. In: *Bremer Nachrichten,* 12. 12. 1985. S.7

ZWEIG, Stefan. *Die unsichtbare Sammlung.* St.Augustin, 1972.

www.ingramcontent.com/pod-product-compliance
Lightning Source LLC
Chambersburg PA
CBHW031607210526
45464CB00004B/1470